Singing
the Soul
Back Home

Singing the Soul Back Home

Shamanic wisdom for every day

Caitlín Matthews

CONNECTIONS
BOOK PUBLISHING

Dedication

For John Cutrer, a great soul.

A CONNECTIONS EDITION
First published in Great Britain and the USA in 1995 by
Element Books Limited.

This edition published in Great Britain in 2002 by
Connections Book Publishing Limited
St Chad's House, 148 King's Cross Road, London WC1X 9DH

This edition published in the U.S.A. in 2002 by
Connections Book Publishing Limited.
Distributed in the U.S.A. by Red Wheel/Weiser,
368 Congress Street, Boston, MA 02210

British Library Cataloguing-in-Publication data available on request.
ISBN 1-85906-103-6

1   3   5   7   9   10   8   6   4   2

Typeset in Truesdell and Artifact using Quark XPress
on Apple Macintosh

Printed in Italy by Amadeus Industria Poligrafica Europea, Rome

Contents

• CHAPTER 1 •

The Shamanic Universe

• CHAPTER 2 •

The Shamanic Journey

• CHAPTER 3 •

Spirit Helpers

Preface to the New Edition

I am delighted to see the publication of this revised edition of *Singing the Soul Back Home*. Since its first release in 1995, I have received many wonderful letters from readers worldwide who have used the book to help sustain their own shamanic training, and I take this opportunity to thank all who have written and shared their experiences with me.

This edition has been revised with a light hand, stressing helpful formats for shamanic practice, updating important contact lists and bibliography, but the primary change is found in the rephrasing of the 'permissions'. Throughout the first edition, I scattered various 'permissions' through the text to help encourage the reader to tear down preconceived barriers about key concepts. Opinion about these seems to have been divided between experienced shamanic practitioners who felt they were unnecessary, and readers with little or no personal shamanic experience who found them helpful. My inclusion of these permissions arose from my experience with clients in my shamanic practice. Whatever presenting symptoms of imbalance clients brought, it seemed to me that nearly all arrived with great gifts that society and upbringing had attempted to dismantle or disparage. Both then and now, I find that people need encouragement to use their gifts with confidence and that permissions do help break down the constraints that have restricted freer living. We live in a society where we defer to 'experts', forgetting that our personal life experience qualifies us in many fields. So, since this book addresses the shamanic student rather than the professional who is securely confident and experienced in shamanic work, I have merely rephrased these permissions to begin 'Permit yourself to ...' without more apology!

May you find what you seek within this book, so that you can recognize and explore the landscape of your own soul.

CAITLÍN MATTHEWS
Oxford, Midsummer 2002

Foreword
Re-membering

When I was a little girl, my mother made me a huge multi-coloured blanket out of squares of wool. This blanket quickly became my friend. It kept me warm on cold days and nights, and played with me in all my games. Most especially, it was my cave.

I would lie on the floor and put it over and round me, tucking in the edges, so that no chinks of light could penetrate. To an outside observer, I was just a child playing at being an unmoving rock. However, within were the stars, the mighty forests, the deep seas.

In the darkness of my cave, I met many beings who came to play with me. They told me stories and informed me about the universe. I talked to them all the time, even in public places, to the mortification of my parents. Their embarrassment eventually became so great that I was forced into ever more solitary places in order to pursue my ongoing dialogue. Who was I talking to? was my parents' preoccupation. Instinctively, I knew that this question could not be answered to their satisfaction, since my parents did not share that world of mine.

What were these beings like? Some were animals, some were people and others were not like anything I then had a name for. These abstract and sometimes geometrical shapes burned behind my eyes in dancing colour. I called them 'the Shapers'. Platonists would recognize them as intelligences of the Platonic realms, perhaps; kabbalists would recognize them as the 'flashing colours' of kabbalistic vision.

The animals and humans spoke of a world I was preparing for, but the abstract beings hinted at wider worlds which were outside my young experience. The animals showed me how to rejoice in my body, to enjoy speed, tracking, dancing, how to endure, be patient and accepting. The humans, whom I now know were the deep ancestors, talked to me about lives before birth and about human relationships: they helped me understand why I had such a young body and such a mature understanding. I am very grateful to them for this, for it was a terrible burden I could not share with a soul, this responsibility for the knowledge of mortality and reincarnation. Adults thought me broody and miserable, and I think that this was a fair assessment of my childhood, with no living being with whom to share my experiences. But they did not see the moments of ecstasy which were as private as sexuality and perhaps not unconnected with the vital impulse. And the beings also taught me singing and encouraged me to use my voice to express the wonders of human life, as well as how to sing alchemically sorrow into joy again.

My lasting reservoir of wonder and delight was brought to me by the Shapers. Their form of communication was instantaneous and subtle, speaking directly to my soul. They showed me shape and pattern, interaction and connection, quantity and quality, rhythm and notation – the great philosophical principles of my childhood. These teachings, which were non-verbal, have been very useful to me in my daily life, as well as guiding me into the uncharted worlds of creative shamanism. I also see now that the rather dull, culturally restrictive upbringing I had was the ideal soil for the shamanic communication I was receiving. With no books and few toys, I was driven as surely to the spiritual teachings of my blanket-cave as any shamanic apprentice, forced by his teacher to watch ice melt for days at a time, is driven to hear and understand the voices of the spirits.

I now know that the images I saw before my eyes accord with what scientists call phosphenes – neurally induced light patterns which are common to all human beings and cultures. These geometrically shaped images can be experienced whenever we close our eyes and feature significantly in the ancient sacred art of many cultures. Their prismatic brilliance and intricacy may have a scientific explanation, but all I know was that the patterns that they made were my teachers. Some hallucinogens produce similar effects, but I received these impressions quite naturally.[1] They are commonly experienced by people when they first start shamanic work, as was the case with my friend, an Estonian artist. By drawing the patterns observed in her first shamanic journeys, she began to make sense of her experiences and to receive teachings by the spirits. I believe that it is by tracing similar patterns in our lives that we can re-member the creative worlds we enjoyed in childhood and reconnect with the cosmic web whose filaments thread our universe.

Our childhood play is a time of primal learning where we discover the universe. Play is about becoming and acting out, about discernment and understanding. In play, we discover our soul-food, our ability to recreate ourselves. Without this consolation and soul-food, we become sealed off and separated from sources of joy, which is often what happens when we grow up. Anything which subsequently reconnects us with the source of creative play is accordingly held precious by us.

I discovered my own reconnection sometime later, when I began to research the ancient Celtic world. I came across descriptions of Gaelic poets in the Western Highlands of Scotland who, up until the seventeenth century and beyond, still practised the ancient Celtic shamanic method of incubating a poem. Poet-masters gave their pupils a subject for composition and then the pupils would retire to the 'houses of darkness', where they lay unseeing, without communication, often with a large stone on their stomachs to keep them wakeful. In this darkness, they would track their composition down the pathways of metaphor and poetic pattern.[2] I grew more and more excited as I read this, for I knew that this was closely akin to the method of shamanic communication I had myself developed (or been taught) as a child, when I lay curled up under my woollen blanket tracking my spirits.

When I grew up I trained to be an actress and began to encounter the spirits in different ways, through the techniques of body and voice; I began to look forward to an acting career. But the spirits had other plans for me. They arranged a series of consecutive ordeals for me which I endured, first quite stoically, then with increasing passivity, as I began to relinquish most of my power until I was dangerously ill and had no creative outlet left. Having spent most of my adolescence fighting to keep the creative doors open, I was utterly cast down. This crisis, which is sometimes grandiloquently termed 'the shamanic illness', is something that comes to many of us. It does not have to be a dramatic life-threatening illness which brings us to this threshold; sometimes it may entail being brought low by the circumstances of life in order to see clearly into the heart of multi-dimensional reality, so that we may focus more perfectly on the spirits' gift and learn to trust it alone. My illness lasted eight years, during which time I had been pronounced incurable by three specialists. My will to live was seriously diminished by these prognostications, and I began to enter that half-world which is neither living nor dying.[3]

I now see that I could only remember my place in the universe by being temporarily railroaded to one side of it. In this half-state I drew near once again to my former companions of subtle reality, somehow realizing that they could assist me where medical practitioners could not. They woke me up to the fact that I had become inured to my illness and that I needed to ask for their help very urgently. Instead of dismissing my old companions as childish figments of my imagination, I actually began to turn to them as teachers who had healing wisdom. They told me to cease taking chemically based medication and to turn to the helping powers of homeopathic medicines. I regained full health in six months.

My recovery was also brought about by a series of simple but necessary gifts: the supportive gift of love, the restorative gift of self-respect and the recreative gift of reweaving the worlds. By rekindling the fires of my creative soul, my companions ensured my active return to the universe. This re-membering of myself was a major soul-restoration which changed my life. I made a promise then that I would offer my life to the rekindling of the creative soul-life in others by whatever means I could, to help 'sing the soul back home'. One of these ways has been by exploring, writing and teaching about the spiritual pathways of Britain and Ireland, to help people reconnect with their land and the rich traditions that imbue it with creative fire. This has been a necessary re-membering for the fragmented soul-life of these islands. Another part of my work has been the reanimation of the ancestral and spiritual presences of our heritage, especially a reappreciation of the Divine Feminine among those who have been orphaned of female spirit – whether men or women. As a 'midwife of the soul' I rekindle the creative fire of the soul's hearth so that the fragmented soul can be welcomed home.

I remain a walker between the worlds within my own native tradition in Britain, having learned from the land spirits, from ancestors and non-human spirits, as well as from the deep presences within my culture and Celtic ancestry. I have also trained in non-cultural, or core, shamanism. I am at home wherever and however people inter-relate with the free passage of Spirit is welcomed, for wherever spiritual hospitality is offered, there Spirit makes its home.

Now that you know what kind of person is talking to you in these pages, I will retire and let you read on. This book offers the fruits of my experience and teaching in simple and practical ways, so that you may be reconnected with the cosmic web of the universe and walk between the worlds. It aims to put you into deep communion with the power and Spirit of the cosmic web, which is always available. As you practise these teachings, you will learn to trust this process and become animated by it; by becoming animated by it, you will be shown by your spirits how to sing your soul back home.

CAITLÍN MATTHEWS
Oxford: July 1994

13

Introduction
Approaching the Threshold

My intentions in writing this book have been to communicate clearly methods of shamanic practice which can be implemented in everyday life: these have been taught to me by my spirits and teachers; they are not mined out of cultural contexts of which I have no understanding. There are no terrestrial or cultural boundaries in the otherworlds: the knowledge that you find there is universal in application.

Shamanism is the practice of reconnecting, healing or bringing balance to all beings who live within the cosmic web of life. It is one of the ways in which our ancestors connected with the universe. But it is not only for far-off times and peoples: it is practised, under different names, within all the continents of our planet. Shamanism is the servant of all spiritual traditions and is thus the heritage of all people.

Many people ask why shamanism should be so popular at this time, especially when so many parts of the world have become exiled from their traditional background. Surely shamanism is not of relevance to our modern society, they cry, while others complain that the spiritual culture of traditional peoples should not be appropriated by civilized Westerners. This raises two important issues: that of usefulness and that of cultural appropriation.

While there are many different people, groups and institutes teaching shamanism, each with their own cultural, ethnic, methodological, anthropological ways of doing so, there is only one criterion for shamanism: that it should bring balance to any situation, wherever and whenever it occurs. It must work effectively or no-one would either practise it or seek its help. What is taught in these pages does not derive from different cultures, it derives from the confluence of personal experience with the revelations of spiritual teachers who accompany the soul-path of each person. Shamanism must always work in the context of our daily lives: we cannot transplant techniques from other cultures and expect them to work within our own. That is why this book deals with the here and now.

The need for shamanism in Western culture seems to be instigated by the spirits of the otherworlds, who want to help bring wisdom, healing and inspiration to the whole world through the most direct means of the shamanic journey. They see our plight and our disconnection from spiritual sources of help; they see that, for all our modern technology and sophistication, we are losing our way. The spirits and teachers are calling people to help them preserve the web of life with better respect.

This book will not enable you to become a shaman, although it will help you live 'shamanically'. It will show you how you can use shamanism creatively, how to be a 'walker between the worlds' – someone skilled in moving between the worlds of physical and subtle reality, someone who can learn from, connect with and co-operate with the spirits who are also inhabitants of the universe.

Why should you wish to do such a thing? Shamanism reveals to us the unspoken subtext, the patterns which interweave our lives; it shows us connections which no other earthly means can. By learning to walk between the worlds we learn to read and recognize the subtle messages encoded in or received by our soul. We learn how to do this by becoming aware, not just of physical reality – the mundane world which is apprehensible by our senses – but also of the subtle reality of the spiritual world which encompasses it.

This requires a great leap of understanding for many people, since we have grown up in a society which neglects or ignores subtle reality in all its aspects: our society is impatient of artists, visionaries, mystics and all people who cross-reference their lives and actions with an unseen reality. Not everyone finds shamanism to their taste, perhaps because it deals with subtle reality or because its parameters are too wide. Some people will be far happier exploring the unseen worlds through a form of meditation or with the backing of a spiritual group that teaches a code of ethics or provides a well-worn map of reality. If, however, you are willing to make the ultimate leap of faith and explore the landscape of your own soul so that you can sing it alive, you may discover the way between the worlds very much to your taste.

Walking between the worlds brings us to a non-dual perception of the universe which enables our soul and our integrity to be aligned with all that is, seen or unseen. This in turn will bring a spiritual dimension to our daily lives as well as a practical dimension to our spiritual lives. Rather than isolating us in a personal spiritual enclave, it will bring us into greater contact with what is happening around us.

This book is not intended to blast open otherworldly gates so that you are sucked inside; it is to help you find the existing doors and pathways that already track your life, to explore the resonances already resounding upon the cosmic web so that you are enabled to sing the soul back into your life. To this end, the first three parts of this book unfold quite slowly, so that you will gradually gather together the relevant instructions and begin to focus upon your own direction before you strike off into the otherworlds. I have concentrated upon the daily applications of this work and have purposely chosen examples and parallels from Western culture in order to help the reader identify with concepts proposed in this book.

It is not my intention to alienate any reader from her spiritual tradition. The practice of shamanism is compatible with the practice of any spirituality: it may provoke a more profound appreciation of your religion's mystical application or bring you to a wider understanding of certain religious strictures. Shamanism speaks of spirits, but every religion, even the most apparently monotheistic, contains spiritual beings – angels, faeries, ancestors, great teachers – all of whom communicate with and assist us in our lives. You may encounter difficulties with shamanism, however, if you adhere to a strongly dualistic faith in which everything is seen as either good or evil.

This book has many 'permissions': this is not because I am a bountiful being who holds authority for all things, but because the encouragement to be resourceful and creative is so rarely given in our everyday lives. In our society printed words have all the weight of holy writ. In shamanism, how-ever, oral tradition and personal experience have a greater authority than what is written. The permissions which appear in these pages are to be taken as oral encouragements. Thus:

Permit yourself to explore creatively what you experience from this book and to be recreated!

How to Use This Book

Before you read the main text, please read this first. It will save you a lot of time and frustration.

1. Read this book through at least once and understand the shamanic concepts and principles before attempting any of the practices.
2. There is a glossary of specialist words and expressions used in this book on p.256. Some terms used are particular to this book, so please check there.
3. Since shamanism is and always has been practised by both women and men, female and male pronouns have been used in variation.
4. Reading and practising this book will not qualify you to work as a shaman: this is specialist work. If you wish to use shamanism to help others then seek out a teacher in physical reality. See Resources on p.263.
5. Try skills the way they are set out here. If you can't work these after a series of good and sequential attempts, then adapt them intelligently and creatively, with recourse to your own spiritual allies and helpers – your real teachers.
6. When you have established a firm bond with your shamanic allies, trust their help and advice. If they give you different instructions or information to that given here, ask them how to implement and practise these. You retain your free will in this work. Steps on how to confirm and recognize your allies are given on p.110.
7. Shamanism is not a solitary practice but a social one: the more you practise it for the help of the universe, the better. Although shamanism may have ther-apeutic effect, it is not a substitute for therapy of any kind.
8. Do not mix these practices with others you have learned in other non-shamanic disciplines. Do not treat them as psychological exercises.

9. Keep your sense of proportion in balance by regularly, preferably daily, visiting the natural world.
10. Keep your sense of self-importance in line with humour and common sense.

Important Note

The practices in this book can be very powerful. Please do not attempt any of them if you are suffering from mental instability or are taking consciousness-changing drugs or potent medications where driving is contra-indicated. The use of these practices outside a strong personal ethical framework and a broad personal experience of shamanism is inappropriate and sometimes dangerous.

All writers and teachers have a responsibility to their readers and students – to guide them safely and surely, to present effective skills and methods which can be reproduced, to ensure that the teachings are transmitted clearly and respectfully. In any book where the writer cannot personally supervise the reader's training there is the danger that the reader's interest in dynamic shamanic techniques may outrun ethical foundation work. Shamanic training is usually undertaken in the context of a traditional society where the apprentice is rooted in ethical, familial and tribal understandings. This is not so in modern society where people may learn techniques at workshops and yet lack any ethical framework.

Be aware that this work has a real effect. Do nothing if your intentions are vague or unfocused.

Permit yourself to take responsibility for your own experiences!

Note to the Reader

Shamanism is a way of restoring balance that requires both honour and respect. The practices in this book are part of a wider way of living, not just techniques. Your application of these practices can generate both temporary and permanent changes of consciousness, so it is advised that you use them within the context of the ideas and ethics outlined in the main text. As with all transformative traditions that show us respectful ways of living, the responsibility for end results and effects rests upon the user's intentions.

Key

This book unfolds in a sequenced way which is keyed into your growing comprehension of the subject: this means that certain instructions relating to practical shamanic journeying appear before you are ready to undertake the practices. This key will help you go to the appropriate part of the book.

No previous experience of shamanism? – Read the whole book first.
Grounding procedures – Chapter 4/2 and Chapter 6/1
Journey procedures in general – Chapter 2
The sequence of a journey – Chapter 2/1 and Chapter 2/2
How to source – Chapter 2/1
How to journey – Chapter 2/2
Finding a guardian animal – Chapter 4/1
Finding a Middleworld teacher – Chapter 4/1
Finding an Underworld teacher – Chapter 5/1
Finding an Upperworld teacher – Chapter 6/1
Framing your question – Chapter 2/3
Acknowledging the seven directions – Chapter 4/2
Help with journey problems – Chapter 2/3 and Chapter 7/1
Interpreting your journey – Chapter 7/1
Improving journey skills – Chapter 7/1
Recognizing power-loss – Chapter 8/1
Recognizing soul-loss – Chapter 8/1

20

The Shamanic Universe

He who desires the Soul, who plays with the Soul, who makes love with the Soul, who attains ecstasy in the Soul, becomes his own master and wanders at will through the worlds. But they who know otherwise are dependent. They dwell in perishable worlds and cannot wander at will.

— *Chandogya Upanishad*

1: SHAMANS AND SHAMANISM

I searched in the darkness, I was silent in the great silence of the dark. That is how I became a angaqoq, through visions and dreams and meetings with flying spirits ... The ancient ones dedicated their lives to the work of keeping the world in balance; they dedicated it to great things, immeasurable enormous things.

— Najagneq, Eskimo shaman

Shamanism has existed since the beginning of time. A shaman is a person – man or woman – who can enter alternate states of consciousness at will to travel in spirit between this world and the otherworlds in order to find healing, knowledge, guidance and help for others. A shaman works with power and energy, calling upon the help of many spirits. She works closely with a full repertoire of spiritual helpers, who choose to help her. The shaman's continually expanding experience sets up pathways of trust and alliance between spiritual helpers, facilitating a trust that links different realities. She is able to mediate between the everyday world and the unseen realms, becoming a bridge of living Spirit.

Shamanism is distinct from other magical and visionary techniques because it is part of the shaman's soul that makes a spiritual journey, flight or voyage between the worlds. Methods of divination, mediumship or healing may have *shamanistic* elements, but they are not technically shamanism unless such a spirit journey takes place and the knowledge, healing or help brought back is implemented in our world. Shamanism is used by indigenous peoples the world over. Many retain ancient techniques, and others have adapted ancestral skills for new situations.

World Shamanism

In most people's minds shamanism is now associated solely with North American nations or Siberian peoples. But it exists in many other places as well. Circumpolar peoples from China to Alaska continue to practise it, despite the overlay of Christianity or Marxism, while Central Asian shamanism from the Middle to the Far East continues underneath the teachings of Islam and Buddhism. Areas of India, Africa and South America retain many shamanic practices as part of their mainstream spirituality.

Some of the following shamanic names, drawn from worldwide cultures, indicate the extent of shamanism around the globe:

bhopa – Hindu – shaman
hatali – Navajo – medicine person
awenydd – Welsh – inspired one
mudang – Korean – female shaman
noaide – Saami (Lapp) – shaman
gongsai/jinpo – Zhuang (Chinese) – male/female shaman
angaqoq – Inuit – shaman
sangoma – Zulu – shamanic healer
dhami – Nepalese – shaman
curandero/a – Central American – male/female shamanic healer
llapo – Tibetan – oracular shaman

The ancestors of Western peoples also used shamanism, but the shaman's role became fragmented, subsequently devolving upon a multitude of people, including priests, storytellers, healers, judges, diviners. In most cases, the essential shamanic component was lost, although individuals and scattered families have retained intrinsic shamanic practices in their hereditary skills of healing, mediumship and divination; some social pockets have also retained certain skills and still guard certain shamanic doorways in collective folk-customs. A close study of European folk-customs and archaic spiritual practices reveals that shamanism is well rooted in many European countries, although this evidence is frequently overlooked or discounted as a manifestation of atavistic superstition or witchcraft.[1]

Shamanic traditions around the world developed according to the kind of societies in which they were found: nomadic, pastoral, hunting. The movement of animals or the behaviour of the elements were critical factors in existence and different needs affected the kinds of shamanism which developed. Environmental factors and ways of life shaped the spiritualities of early people.

Ake Hultkrantz believes that it is natural 'to regard shamanism as one of the strongest powers behind the historical formation of religions'.[2] Although it can manifest as a spirituality, it is rarely manifest as a religion in the Western sense. It most often appears today as a healing practice within a religion. In parts of Central and South America, for example, *curanderas* (shamanic healers) call upon both Catholic saints and indigenous gods, while in Tibetan Buddhism the ancient, pre-Buddhist deities are invoked to enable oracles and healing. In some places shamans provide certain ritual and healing functions for their society which are not met by the predominant spirituality of that people or region. Shamanism is the servant of all traditions.

The Calling

This book doesn't attempt to be a historical or anthropological survey of shamanism, but it is important that the vocation and work of shamans is properly contextualized here. Shamans are always chosen for their role by the spirits of the universe, for shamanism is not a self-elected vocation: so the one who determines to become a shaman as an ego-enhancing exercise will not succeed. Shamanism may run in the family or one shaman may become teacher to one or more spiritually elected candidates.

When someone is called to be a shaman, he may attempt to avoid the calling for the very good reason that shamanism is one of the most demanding of vocations, the shaman being available simultaneously to the spirits as well as to future clientele. This avoidance may also spring from a fear of dealing with spirits and the otherworlds they inhabit. The creative basis for shamanism shows itself clearly in such situations for, like the repression of creativity, the avoidance of a shamanic calling usually results in a massive loss of power or soul, frequently leading to life-threatening illness. This 'shamanic illness' is generally cured by a full acceptance of the spirit-dictated vocation.

The training of shamans is usually undertaken by both spirits and human teachers who are themselves shamans. The apprentice learns by assisting the qualified shaman and so integrates her own growing shamanic knowledge with practical implementations of techniques and the reactions of clients to specific treatments. The acceptance of trainee shamans by their community is critical, for they cannot practise without people.

Why Do People Consult Shamans?

People need shamans' help for health, work and relationship problems, as well as for making ritual sense of changes in life-patterns from birth to death. They may also have difficulties that have mysterious origin, perhaps arising from their ancestral inheritance or from a curse. In response to these needs, shamans seek out solutions, cures, rituals and information from the spirits in the otherworlds.

Contemporary manifestations of shamanism reflect the changing needs of society. Many of our present needs are similar to those of ancient and indigenous societies – health, work and relationship problems and making sense of life patterns – but we may also add the needs produced by Western urban life: the need to address the soul-loss which manifests as incompletion, meaninglessness, alienation, addiction, self-mutilation, lack of self-esteem and loss of vision. Modern medicine has found solutions to many physical illnesses, while modern psychology attempts to heal what it sees as mental illnesses, but the subtle illnesses and imbalances are largely ignored or marginalized, nor are their needs addressed by the major religions who do have the apparatus to discern spiritual cause and effect. It is left to shamanism and a host of complementary therapeutic disciplines to address the soul.

Modern shamanism addresses contemporary problems and helps us reforge our primal belonging to the earth by providing rituals and healing practices. The creation of rituals by shamanic means re-empowers those disempowered by religious ceremonies which alienate rather than reconnect. The immediacy of walking between the worlds and of implementing what is discovered there re-authenticates each individual's spirituality.

Misconceptions About Shamanism

Shamanism is a primal spiritual practice that has somehow survived into our time. This survival has been ensured by the *usefulness* of shamanic skills. If ancient techniques are lost it is because they are not so useful. People simply do not consult ineffective shamans and they soon have no clients, no income and no status in society. Chandra, a Nepalese *dhami* (shaman), speaks humbly about this:

> '... a man can learn many things from his failures, but failures can create uncontrollable needs and weaken his soul. For that reason, a dhami must always bring satisfaction and success to the people around him, even small successes, for only then will the souls gain strength to take a next step.'[3]

This philosophy of small, incremental successes is central to shamanism which, since it deals in spirit, is very much concerned with 'keeping the spirits up'. While shamanism can produce dramatic and immediate results, the subtle and gradual organic changes that it brings are more enduring and more comfortable when we ourselves have changed. Human nature is a creature of habit and old habits die hard, as we all know.

This leads us to a clarification of certain misconceptions about shamans. One of these concerns the alleged charlatanism of shamanism. All shamans

25

work in the context of their society, wherein their practices are performed publicly. Like any showman, the traditional shaman will accordingly 'play to the gallery', utilizing illusions and sleight of hand to enhance the healing or seance. Many people have assumed that the use of such tricks must significantly devalue whatever shamanic work is done or mask a complete inability to heal.

Some early anthropologists who studied shamanic cultures were of the opinion that shamans were epileptic, since they seemed to behave in hysteric and irrational ways, often falling to the ground. This view has been abandoned by most academics, although it was still popular until recently among Soviet researchers to whom any truck with spirits was evidence of fraud or mental derangement.[4] In working with spirits, shamans frequently experience intense shaking and physical agitation; since it is difficult, if not impossible, to remain upright once soul-flight has begun, shamans usually sit or lie down suddenly. I cannot find any evidence for the allegation that shamans are hysteric, weak-minded or nervous individuals: on the contrary, living shamans demonstrate a balanced, well-integrated and creative personality that has to be well-grounded in order to perform shamanic healing.

Some people have acquired the notion that, because some shamans utilize cross-dressing in their spiritual work, they are homosexual or transvestite. Shamans can be of either sex and of heterosexual or homosexual orientation: sexual orientation does not determine the ability to shamanize. There are distinct shamanic traditions of a woman taking on a male spiritual persona, or a man taking on a female one and dressing accordingly: this is in accordance with the principles of non-duality, not sexuality. A male spirit may work through a female shaman, just as a female spirit may work through a male one.

Traditionally, many shamans are perceived as 'tricky' or 'mischievous'. While it is true that many people are fearful of those who wield or mediate otherworldly powers, it is also true that most shamans have a sense of responsibility towards their clients. The playful or trickster behaviour of the shaman is often an attempt to lighten the serious nature of much of the work, as well as to keep open the ways between the worlds. The entry of the clown, the *heyoka*, upturns the normal order of things, permitting authority to be mocked and confusing the barriers between what is possible what is not. In the midst of this licensed holiday from the normal is a sacred opening that allows healing and transformative experience to take place.

Shamanic teachings are entrusted to those who love the universe and wish to be in its service, but there is always the chance that some unscrupulous student will use it for herself. Unethical shamans occur, as do corrupt judges and mercenary doctors; self-serving practitioners who offer public service are to be greatly feared, for they have no disinterested compassion to balance their skills. Most societies make distinction between shamans and sorcerers. A shaman *co-operates* with the spiritual worlds and their inhabitants, beseeching their appropriate help; a sorcerer *manipulates* the spiritual worlds and seeks to command their inhabitants without their advice. This book is concerned with shamanism, not sorcery.

Shamanic practice goes hand in hand with rituals of purification, as well as prayers for assistance and thankfulness to the spirits; these remind the shaman that he is not solely responsible for bringing about changes. Such rituals keep the shaman in a balanced awareness which sustains ethical practice. The 'habitual intuition' by which shamans live and work is developed by drawing upon the web of knowledge amassed by experience and perception; it is maintained by the daily practice of sacred tradition.

Shamanism Today

We now seem to stand near a perilous abyss of understanding where the sacred culture of many peoples currently practising shamanism may be forgotten or overwhelmed by a blanket Westernization. I say 'seem to stand' for shamanic knowledge is never utterly lost, since we need only make the soul-flight to recover information and methods. We are also aided by a factor which I believe is superintended by the otherworldly guardians of wisdom: before any massive crisis which destroys ancestral networks of remembrance and understanding, there is usually a movement to record and remember what is threatened by loss. As the second-century traveller, Pausanius, toured the sacred centres of Greece recording indigenous spiritual practices prior to the institution of Christianity as the state religion of the ancient world, and as antiquaries like John Leland (c.1503–32) recorded the ancient sites of Britain prior to the destructions wrought by the

Reformation and industrialization, so many anthropologists explored and recorded shamanic cultures in the twentieth century.

During the last one hundred years or so, an anthropologist's visit to an primal culture has often heralded the demise of that culture. But with more sensitive approaches and methodology, modern anthropology has redressed the balance and brought us knowledge of many unknown practices so that the precious heritage of sacred shamanic knowledge has been recognized and recorded. So far shamanic knowledge has not been codifiable in the same way as the humanities or philosophies have been, but it may well find greater cogency in this century.

Shamanism is an experiential practice; knowledge of spirits and otherworlds stems alone from shamans who journey thither: it cannot be fully comprehended or annotated by theoretical anthropologists, only by those who experience this for themselves. Fortunately, many anthropologists now approach shamanic traditions as students, often becoming apprenticed to living shamans. Foremost among these practical anthropologists is Michael Harner, who was a student of the Amazonian Jivaro Indians. He has utilized knowledge of this culture and of worldwide shamanic traditions to form the Foundation for Shamanic Studies, which teaches core or non-cultural shamanism worldwide. Such centres have reintroduced shamanic ideas and practices to Western culture. We might view such developments as third wave shamanism: the first wave belonging to primal peoples and discrete cultures, and the second wave to the admixture of shamanism with other spiritual traditions. We do not yet clearly know how this Shamanic third wave will affect the West, but its methods are already rippling out faster than the ethics and social context of shamanism can be understood and integrated.

'Shamanism' is rapidly becoming the most over-used and misappropriated word of the current era. Too many people read a book, attend a workshop and become 'instant shamans', or else rejig their therapeutic training and add the word 'shamanic', in the hope that this will align their work with the current fashion. Shamanism is in danger of becoming warped out of context. Imperfect understanding, cultural reclamation and exposure to unrelated 'new age' techniques often devalue what is a worldwide tradition with local specialities.

Shamanism isn't a therapy, although it may have a therapeutic effect. Psychotherapists of many kinds may wish to append the role of shaman to their list of skills but, although analysts may study clients' dreams and visions, they do not act as shamans, since they do not accompany clients on journeys or journey on their behalf. Especially dangerous is the teaching of shamanic techniques without a firm grounding in any ethical or personal spiritual practice. The learning of shamanism cannot be compared with learning to draw or speaking a foreign language: shamanic knowledge comes with a set of responsibilities towards the universe. Working with any form of power requires a long training and a broad practical experience. Apprenticeship to a shaman is not easy in Western culture since, to learn from a living shamanic tradition, the student must assimilate an alien cultural tradition. After training, the student's task is then to see how the teachings can be applied to her own culture, without disrespecting the teaching or bewildering clients or students.

The reasons why Western people are seeking shamanic wisdom and traditional knowledge are not difficult to understand. Urban living has eroded the ties of land and clan, and distanced us from our sacred heritage. The overwhelming response among white, spiritual seekers to indigenous cultures, especially the North American kind, comes from a deep need to belong to a tribal family where sacred wisdom is revered rather than traduced.

When we first encounter the attitudes of indigenous people, our Western viewpoints are turned upside-down, for among them money is irrelevant to status, the oral teachings have a stronger validity than the written word and the messages of the otherworlds are received with respect. Where Western science attempts to manipulate the physical universe, 'native science is a way of bringing people to a higher knowledge ... to the still, quiet place'.[5]

Often, in an attempt to reach this kind of holy simplicity, Westerners have striven to become like indigenous peoples, to live like them and imitate their customs. Though this emulation usually derives from someone's heart-felt urge to change their life, there can also be a kind of spiritual dishonesty about it. Those without a spiritual fire often warm themselves at other hearths until they understand how the spark is kindled, but ultimately they must return to their own hearth and make fire there. Once the fire is burning, it must be fed with local fuel. Such is the challenge of this book: to kindle the sacred fire and feed it until it warms your whole life, then to discover how to keep it burning with what is to hand. Spirit is catching, and it alone will show you how to respond if you are sensitive to the way it blows.

How To Start

How, then, can anyone who lives outside a traditional culture receive a shamanic training?

Each culture has its own roots, songs, stories and traditional wisdom in which sacred heritage lies encoded. The effect of the shamanic path is to place our footsteps in those of our ancestors, to reconnect us with the universe, to become purposefully part of it once more. Each person has ancestral guardians and spiritual teachers who stand ready to guide them: it is these who will help you if you decide that this is your path. While this book will not make you a shaman, it will set your footsteps on the shamanic pathway and help you become a walker between the worlds. When we accept the reality of other worlds and have travelled between them, our attitudes to daily life will change. As we become aware primarily of the inter-relatedness of all that we do, think, are, we will no longer be able to disregard the subtle urgings of Spirit and power within us.

☙ Practice 1: Grounding

In ancient times, few people actively sought out a shamanic vocation; their innate caution taught them to keep both feet on the ground, not to spin off dancing with the spirits. Today, shamanism is new and exciting, and many people positively desire to propel themselves into the otherworlds and get 'high'. Shamans may visit otherworlds to gain information, healing or advice in order to help people, but to do so they *need to come home again*. Finding out where home is is essential, which is why you should regard this practice as essential information (see also Part 4).

Perform grounding after all shamanic work, returning gently to yourself.

The following things will earth or ground you:

Breathing calmly and evenly
Bringing to mind mundane purposes
Bringing your awareness back to your body, mind and emotions
Eating or drinking
Gentle humour
Being outdoors and becoming aware of your surroundings
Recording your experiences
Taking time and space to assimilate what has been experienced
     before rushing into the next activity

Create your own grounding sequence, based on your own needs and reactions. After any shamanic work, ensure that you are ready to perform ordinary tasks, especially driving, in a safe way.

✋ Practice 2: Recording Practices

Essential knowledge and personal shamanic experience can dissipate like evanescent dreams unless it is recorded. After performing the practices in this book, permit yourself assimilation time.

Sit and write down your experiences, however vestigial or wacky they may seem. Enter into the experience with all your faculties: How did it make you feel? What was the most salient feature of the practice?

Do not worry if you cannot understand the experience right away; fragmentary information is often referenced again in subsequent practices. Some experiences make no sense for months or even years, and so your record becomes a very special way of assimilating understanding.

In your notebook record journeys, dreams, drawings, doodles and thoughts. If you are a pictorial person, you might prefer to draw pictures of your experiences, or if you are a verbal person, record them on tape.

**Permit yourself to enjoy and learn
from your experiences!**

2. THE SPIRIT OF THE UNIVERSE

All things are full of Gods and Powers.
– Epictetus

The threefold gifts or dimensions of shamanic work are spirit, power and ecstasy. In shamanism we become the filaments of Spirit, using the bridges of power and ecstasy to mediate between one world and the other.

Spirit is like a subtle aroma which permeates all things but which is not detectable to our physical senses. In the practice of shamanism, as in our everyday mystical interface, we are continually reminded that Spirit is everywhere. The daily wonders of weather, the seasons, gifts, synchronicities and patterns encompass our lives in an ever-changing yet connective dance. We instinctively know that these things are not random occurrences, yet we feel that neither are they ultimately dictated as fixed and immovable: a creative chaos threads the complexity and simplicity of the universe. If we acknowledge Spirit, we also acknowledge the existence of an unseen reality, 'subtle reality', which exists alongside the physical reality of our tangible existence.

For the modern person the acceptance of another reality is the most radical challenge of shamanism. There is no easy way to come to this acceptance, as any instruction that something exists beyond our physical senses is contrary to the values of contemporary society. The walker between the worlds may find that a provisional acceptance of subtle reality 'as if' it existed is a necessary bridge to this work.

Animism, Religion and Mystical Experience

Shamanism is often defined as 'animism': a world-view in which everything has its own spirit or 'anima'. This is vastly different from the currently received monotheistic basis of Western belief which sees one god, the architect of creation. Can only one approved story of Spirit explain what we know of the worlds, both seen and unseen? It would seem unlikely.

Indigenous shamanic responses to Spirit are and have been various; some have resulted in the formation of major religions focusing on a single deity, while others have remained pragmatically animistic. Shamans were the first to manifest images of Spirit, the first to mediate between the unseen worlds and our world. The many forms of Spirit underlie the deities venerated through the world, although monotheism does not strictly recognize any fragmentation of Spirit.

Subtle Reality

Each major religion has its own mystics who keep open the lines of communication between the worlds, but these are little spoken of and are reserved for 'professionals', not the laity for whom the subtle reality of the unseen has been subsumed in a welter of ritual practices which veil the glory of Spirit. In our society, such professionals have become the official guardians to the door of spiritual knowledge, those whose words must not be questioned.

The experience of mystic and shaman are comparable, if we regard mystical experience as communion with otherworlds. The similarity of common shamanic techniques worldwide, without traceable connections or transmissions to account for them, begins to make sense if we realize that every shaman born has travelled in and learned from the otherworlds and their inhabitant spirits. However, the result of the scientific world's dismissal of subtle reality and the churches' insistence that only their versions of subtle reality are authentic is twofold: some say that there is no subtle reality at all and others that subtle reality is more diverse and accommodating than religions have indicated. Some people have explored the latter proposition themselves and proved it to their own satisfaction, but what of those who believe there is no subtle reality? These are a strange tribe, the first of their kind in the history of world anthropology. We live in extraordinary times when people disbelieve in spiritual worlds and beings. This total disregard for subtle reality makes it very hard for the mystics and visionaries who perceive it to live in our society. I am not speaking of people of extraordinary gifts, but of anyone who experiences mystical insights and knowings on a daily basis. The common, mundane nature of mystical experience is one of the best-kept secrets; its neglect and cover-up has given us a society in which we have no framework for speaking about our mystical perceptions – be it a sudden impulse or synchronicity, the urge to write a poem or song, or a vision of immense beauty.

Spirit

Shamanism is best understood not as a religion, but as a way of life. While it acknowledges that Spirit is in all things, its manifestations are not generally worshipped in some formal religious way, although there are indeed many ceremonies to reverence Spirit. Shamanism doesn't require us to give up our religion. When Margaret Umlazi, a Christian Zulu now working as a *sangoma* (shamanic healer), first received the call to shamanize she asked a wise *sangoma* about this very matter. Her response was: 'You do not have to give up Jesus to be a *sangoma*; the more sources of power you have at your disposal, the better.' Accordingly, one of the images on Margaret's wall is a picture of Christ.[6]

When Spirit calls us, it totally changes our lives. In past eras, many people received the help of a shaman but few wished to become one. When the call to shamanize arises, it is often severely resisted; eventually, the candidate submits since resistance becomes life-threatening. This seemingly coercive spiritual call should be regarded in the same light as when an artist says, 'I must create or die!' Spiritual conversion works along the same lines. We can look at the example of St Paul who converted from being an ultra-conservative, Christian-hating Jew to the primary missionary of early Christianity; he heard the voice of God on the Damascus road, was stricken blind and lay immobile for three days; he could only be healed when he acknowledged the will of God (Acts 9). In exchange for his healing, Paul had to dedicate his whole life to Spirit.

If we ignore Spirit, we immediately become imbalanced and lose touch with reality. We fall into disease, separation and disharmony. To reconnect with reality, wholeness, connection and harmony we must acknowledge the Spirit in all things. This does not necessarily mean becoming a strict religious believer, although it might do, but it does involve a recognition that *Spirit is reality* and the willingness to inhabit that reality.

This last statement cuts diametrically across the grain of received Western understanding because modern Western belief comprehends 'reality' as 'that which we can see and touch, that which is genuinely existent and true'. The gradual erosion of the totality of reality has left many people suspicious and distrustful of Spirit. This is especially so since the authority of Western religion has begun to decline. Having dictated

34

how and what people should believe for thousands of years, orthodox religions are now being rejected as authoritarian and manipulative. In truth, for many centuries Western society has ignored the validity of Spirit which is within all things.

One of the reasons that shamanism is so popular at this time is because people are seeking to restore their spiritual authority. Rather than believing in just one story about Spirit and making it their personal myth or 'story to live by', they look for their own spiritual connection. The re-empowerment of our spirituality is essential, but it must never again be at the expense of so much suffering and manipulation. Human beings hunger for absolutes and ultimate definitions of all kinds because they seem to create a cosy certainty. This is why fundamentalist religion is so attractive: it has no moral ambiguities, only straight, clear lines of action. But Spirit cannot be policed or regimented in this way, which is why people of spirit, of all disciplines, are often the first against the wall when an outbreak of fundamentalism seeks to overwhelm individual and creative expressions of spirit. The Cultural Revolution of China, the purging of artists in Cambodia, the slaughter of educators, artists and people of spirit in former Yugoslavia, the persecution of actors and others under the McCarthy regime in USA – all are horrific examples of fear of Spirit's power to bring harmony, connection and peace.

Spirits

Shamans work with Spirit, yet they each have their own helping spirits. Just as a mirror may be shattered yet each shard still give a perfect reflection, so must we understand the spirits of the universe as the refractions of Spirit. The refractions of Spirit are discernible even in what we consider to be the monotheistic religions: the ninety-nine holy names of Allah and the Islamic angels, the kabbalistic aspects of Yahweh in Judaism, the trinitarian aspects of God and the myriad saints in Christianity. But they may also appear in any form which has shared some part of the life of the universe: the spirit of a human, tree, animal, stone, star, place; even objects of organic origin, such as musical instruments, toys, masks, pictures have their indwelling spirit. (You can read about the different forms of spirit in Chapter 3.) Anything that has or will share the universal life has Spirit: Spirit is in everything that has or will share universal life.

Spirits are not usually apprehendable by the physical senses; they have their own volition or power; they do not have to be believed in to be experienced. Spirits have their own vitality. When shamans co-operate with spirits, they do so to help reveal or restore the harmony between all things.

We are unique in world history in that we have ceased to believe in the indwelling *numen* or spirit of all things. It is only our children who recognize this spirit and honour it in their play. The Greeks called the indwelling inspirational spirit the *muse* or *daimon*; the latter (pronounced day-mone) has been relegated from our language and its true meaning is not reflected by the associated word, demon. However, we still dedicate newborn children with the spirits of saints, by giving them their names, hoping that the virtue of the saint will protect and inculcate the child. The names and spirits of heroic and philanthropic people are associated with hospitals, sports associations and welfare foundations in the same manner.

You are full of spirits: many special magics, secret skills and creative gifts. These make you uniquely yourself. Spirits visit us: some stay with us, others are just passing through. It depends on whether you are a willing host/ess and are interested in playing with your guests. Co-operating with the spirits is very important. Many people spend lives of misery denying the gifting powers they were born with.

Spirits are the shaman's teachers and helpers; no shamanic work can be done without them. Shamans love their spirits; spirits love their shamans.

Creative Spirits

To acknowledge our spirits is not the dire business that the movie world and fundamentalism have warned us against. In the movies, loving spirits rarely make it to celluloid: evil spirits are much more marketable. In fundamentalism, controlling people's freedom is of central importance, and so all unauthorized spirits are automatically considered to be demons. But consider the spirits that assist a master cellist. This instrumentalist has probably been born with the spirit of music in him. He has cultivated his gifting spirit by going to classes as a child and delighted in the power of his cello to voice the inspiring spirits of composers. He may have sought out supreme technicians of the cello, courting their help and apprenticing himself to their skills. At last, he emerges as a virtuoso in his own right. No-one hearing him on the concert platform doubts that this accomplished instrumentalist has full trust in his spirits to help his fingers over the finger-board and to sustain his bowing hand. No-one would wish those spirits to go away.

And yet, we are often supremely frightened of our own creative spirits; we neglect them and cause them to migrate. We lose our power when we lose our creative spirits. Many of us are bludgeoned out of our creativity by life's circumstances, some of us actively avoid our creative spirits because of the unsettling feeling of a roller-coaster that they set up in our lives. Perhaps we realize instinctively that if our spirits are to abide in and work with us, we are going to have to do something active about it.

Any discussion of spirits inevitably brings up the question: are they safe? We have grown up in a culture which permits only the existence of its *own authorized spirits* – we call them saints, God, the Virgin, and so on. Some religions, especially Christianity, have denounced ancient cultures so relent-lessly that indigenous wisdom and beliefs have come to be seen as sorcery, and their gods and spirits regarded as devils. In Brazil this process has been creatively reversed. The *orishas* or powers of *candomblé*, a syncretic fusion of Yoruba (West African) religion with Catholicism which flourishes in and around Bahia, are daily presences and inspirations. A woman may feel close to the strong warrior goddess, Iansi, associated with St Barbara, saint of lightning; a man may feel the indwelling presence of the God Shango, asso-ciated with St Jeremiah. In *candomblé*, each 'son or daughter of the saint' learns to welcome the presence of their indwelling *orisha* in ecstatic dancing, drumming and singing, during which they may become one with their spir-it. *Candomblé*, like Cuban *Santeria* or Haitian *Voudun*, has successfully restored its native spirits to centre stage, while still retaining the Catholic personas of these spirits.[7]

Finding Our Guardian Spirits

When we first go seeking our own guardian spirits, we start our search in familiar territory, looking for *helpful spirits* of benign intent. These helping spirits, who are disposed to be our allies and with whom we probably have connection, already know and see our search for them; they wait only to be invited or approached.

Many people associate subtle reality with illusion and have no trust in it or its denizens. You may wish to 'test the spirits to see if they are from God' (I John 4, 1). But the only way you can do that is first to meet them. The surest way to proceed is to use all the common sense you would show when meeting any new acquaintance: a short and formal meeting, followed by a deepening process of sequential meetings.

This process of trust takes a long time to establish. Consider any long-term friendship which you have and you will understand this. When we first journey into subtle reality, we steer blindly unless we can trust at least one spirit-friend.

Meeting the spirits may not be easy. A radical deprocessing of Western attitudes and expectations is often required before we can journey in soul-flight or gain the help of spirits. The workshop-tourist's demand for quick results is not always gratified: after all, why should her guardian spirit appear on demand this particular weekend, if she's ignored subtle reality all her life? Shamanism is not a quickly learned craft.

If we go looking for our helping spirits with fear and suspicion, then we make our journey more arduous and prone to paranoia. The nature of Spirit is neither good nor evil; the different refractions of Spirit are vortices of energy, like electricity, wind, fire or water. A shower may bless the garden and a flood may destroy it: does that make water good or evil? The gradations of power in spirits are all expressions of Spirit.

The major part of a shaman's duty is to deal with spirits on their own terms, acting as a mediator and sometimes director of spiritual energy. It is usually a matter of inappropriate rather than 'evil' spirits: of clearing out or extracting unwanted accumulations of spirit from one place or person where they are causing blockage or illness, rather than of exorcism and banishing. For example, we call wandering human souls 'ghosts': they are not evil, usually just lost. A shaman's job is to help these souls pass to their appropriate place in the otherworlds. Some spirits of place can be rather like errant children, both mischievous and disruptive. A shaman would seek to discover why they were behaving this way, possibly as a result of human disrespect to the site in question, and to calm the disruption. Many of life's problems result from spirits colonizing a vacuum which has been left by human neglect. The etiquette of co-existence with spirits is something we learn through walking between the worlds.

Permit yourself to listen to your creative spirits.

3. THE POWER OF THE UNIVERSE

In a society which is rapidly losing touch with the strictly codified subtle realities of state religions, many people are drawn to shamanism as a means of exploring those realities for themselves. One of the most attractive features of accessing subtle reality through shamanism is power, and unfortunately rather more people are drawn to the power of shamanic techniques than to the power of Spirit itself.

Use and Misuse of Power

Shamans believe and work with the power of Spirit, which sustains, changes and flows through all things. This power of Spirit is the vital energy of the universe – it is life. Shamans bring life by reconnecting the broken links of power or by removing blockages which impede its flow.

Like Spirit, the word 'power' has problematic associations in our language. It bears the connotation of 'authority', usually of the dictatorial or censorious kind. In this book, I am talking about the shamanic power of life, the vital energy of Spirit which runs through all that is. At no point am I talking about power as a mode of violence or tyranny.

In the Amazonian culture of the Desana Indians it is believed that the quantity of energy or power is fixed and that 'man must remove what he needs only under certain conditions and must convert this particle of "borrowed" energy in a form that can be re-incorporated into the circuit'.[8] By misappropriating power for manipulative ends, our society has lost its spiritual authenticity. By taking power for selfish ends, we can cut ourselves off from the reciprocal circuit of Spirit and power. It is no wonder that we are spiritually gasping for breath.

Power flows through all of us: it does not 'belong' to us, but is a vitality common to all. It comes into us, passes through our being and moves on again. It is always entering and leaving us, like our breath. To speak of 'possessing power' is as ridiculous as trying to own the air in our lungs. By all means, try to keep 'your own air' in your own lungs, if you can: you will only succeed until your next exhalation! Through this metaphor, we begin to understand how it is futile to hoard our share of power. When the pathways of the Spirit are blocked, power cannot flow. Those who have kept the pathways open are feared by those who have not, the latter often harbouring jealousy of any creative skill.

The cosmic web which connects all life is like an electrical grid: each part of it hums with power. Wherever disconnections and blockages occur, the power cannot flow. No one being distributes this power; all beings are responsible for keeping it flowing. We each share in it in the same way that everyone swimming in the sea shares in the water: some bodies displace more water than others. It is not apportioned equally, but is available to all.

Those who are spiritually aware are generally perceived to be 'powerful' in the sense of being livelier, more integrated and less unbalanced than others; they may achieve more in a shorter time, be more open to ideas and therefore more resourceful. Being a 'powerful person' does not necessarily make you stronger, healthier or more successful than others; but it will make you better aligned, assured and humbly part of the universe. The more pathways we walk through the worlds, the more power-cables connect us. But to whom more is given, more is also required.

Our power, our vitality, derives from many sources: from the light of the solar system, from the nourishment of foods, from having a secure environment, from supportive and loving relationships, from cultural and creative nourishment of our souls, from spiritual engagement with the universe. When any of these channels is fractured, we begin to lose power. We can choose to relinquish them through neglect or unclear motivation or by giving away our share to others. This happens, for example, when we unhealthily abrogate our self and our needs for the sake of someone we wish to impress. We may unwillingly relinquish our share of power to someone who is coercive or dominating, who has discovered how to play with our emotions. We can lose power by being threatened, cajoled, invaded, overwhelmed, whether by people, accident or trauma. In all instances, our natural power-cables connecting us with the cosmic web are fractured and power begins to leak away. The resulting power-loss may lead to illness, soul-fragmentation or sometimes death. A person lacking power will be dispirited, tired, frustrated, and generally disengaged from daily life. Only by re-sourcing the power of the universe can she build up her resistance.

A song often sung in spiritual circles tells us that 'where there's fear, there is power'. Our power is often locked up by fear, which causes blockage, illness and disruption to our lives. The poet Rainer Maria Rilke wrote that our deepest fears are like dragons guarding our deepest treasure. Dealing with fear requires forthright courage. Many people feel it is easier to live with the self-imposed controls of fear than to experience the liberation of the power that lies beneath the fear. Shamanism cracks through such restraint and puts us in touch with our power treasury. (Ways of restoring power and vitality are dealt with in Chapter 8.)

There is much talk of 'empowerment' and 're-empowerment' in esoteric training circles, as though this were the end product of such training. Many people are drawn to shamanism because it seems to offer them instant empowerment. By walking between the worlds we may indeed enhance our vitality and power, but we do well to remember that this is only an incidental effect, that shamanism is not a therapy and that deeper commitment and responsibility are required. A true appreciation of how we receive and give out power in accordance with the laws of the universe only comes when we live in alignment with those laws. The realization that neither we nor our species are the mainspring of the universe will keep our practice ethical, as will the necessity for thankfulness and proper reciprocation.

Like Spirit, power is non-dual: it is itself, but it can be misplaced. The shaman's duty is to reconnect and restore broken power-lines, as well as to remove and re-circuit inappropriate accumulations of power. Such work is not done indiscriminately or without recourse to the cosmic web of power: the circumstances surrounding any shamanic action are first investigated in both physical and subtle reality to discover whether a course of action is appropriate.

It is only by consulting the whole universe through the networks of Spirit and power that healing connections can be re-established. Wherever one part of the cosmic web is healed, power is restored to the whole web, benefiting all.

Permit yourself to draw upon and share the power of the universe!

4. THE DANCE OF ECSTASY

The experience of shamanism leads to a sense of non-duality where the contradictions of life are dissolved and replaced by a primeval, paradisal wholeness; where memory is restored to the forgetful, unity is given to the separate, transmutation flows to the stagnant spirit. The soul, having partaken of the otherworlds, experiences total freedom and bliss. This sense of non-duality is called ecstasy.

Ecstasy sounds dangerous, chaotic, uncontrolled. Our society encourages us to be in such rigid control that very few people now experience ecstasy as an everyday thing. The abandonment of dance, the joy of sex, the freedom to enjoy life to the full are the common heritage of all, yet perhaps only a few young adults enjoy these to any degree. But we must distinguish between this and the shaman's experience of ecstasy which is purposeful, not recreational; he journeys forth for the benefit of others, not for the personal thrill of the ride. For him, ecstasy may result from sharing in the non-duality of the cosmic web.

Except in dreams, most mature adults have lost the key to subtle reality; they are imprisoned in a cage of physical reality, doomed to walk the mundane round of existence without sparkle or soul. The prisoners of physical reality are often controllers, who have difficulty going to sleep, who find it hard to delegate duties and who may have problems in situations where deep trust is required, such as learning to swim. These people are not closed to Spirit by any means – they often yearn for some tangible token that Spirit still flows through their lives – the problem is, they just can't let go of physical reality long enough.

Soul-journeys to otherworlds are fuelled by the use of rhythm, sound and movement which propel the shaman's soul into subtle reality. Such journeys require relinquishing the same amount of control as you would need to swim or sleep successfully. Anyone who has learned to float knows exactly what I mean here. The way to float is to let go and trust the water to support you: try and take control of the water and it is easy to get into a panic. However, those who learn to trust water become skilful and successful swimmers, able to go where they please, using a variety of strokes. Shamans are similarly able to journey because they learn to trust and enjoy the sensations of journeying.

Shamanic ecstasy propels the soul-flight to otherworlds, but this does not mean that the shaman abrogates his will or self-discipline. The combination of disciplined control and ecstasy results in the alchemy of shamanism. For the shaman is an alchemist, facilitating changes to substances, lives, emotions and souls through the alignment of power and Spirit.

Ecstasy helps us escape from our earth-bound reality and opens doors and windows into freedoms which society usually bars shut. It enables us to see resourceful and spiritual ways of working out seemingly insuperable problems. Our culture has associated Spirit with stricture and rigidity; consequently, it neglects Spirit, is ignorant of how power flows and fails to understand how ecstasy can be more than recreational.

If we are alive to the Spirit and power within us, then the non-duality of ecstasy can be the vehicle of our lives.

☙ *Practice 3*: Mapping Your Spiritual Journey

Look over your life so far and map the course of your spiritual journey from birth to the present. Take a large sheet of paper and draw your journey, noting where Spirit has inspired you and touched your life. Your journey may not be a straight line – it might curve back on itself like a labyrinth or spiral. Include mystical experiences where you were touched by Spirit, visits to places of beauty and power, books, music, inspiring people, insights and thoughts, and so on.

These events, influences or experiences may not be specifically religious or conventionally mystical: if Mickey Mouse has changed your life, if watching a tree cut down has altered your spiritual perceptions, then include it in your map. Review your spiritual itinerary: what patterns, significant factors and connections do you see? Which features are continually repeated?

✹ *Practice 4:* Sources of Power

You are a living terminal of the universal power-house. Many power currents and cables flow into and through your life. Review your present life-style and assess the sources of power that you consciously and unconsciously draw upon. These might include the foods you eat, your emotional relationships, your cultural influences, your spiritual sources. Take a large sheet of paper and draw a spider's web chart, with yourself at the centre and with these lines of power leading into and out of the middle. Now follow one of these lines back as far as you can go. For example: if you have written down 'fruit' as a source of physical nourishment, explore the source of fruit: apple tree, earth, rain, sun, and so on. If you take back all the power-lines to their source, you will make an interesting discovery about the nature of power and Spirit.

✹ *Practice 5:* Unzipping Your Passion

Our lives are wound with prescriptions – don't, can't, mustn't. The restrictions which bind us have often arrived unannounced or may have been the result of circumscribed periods in our lives when such rules were a necessary survival mechanism; whichever is the case, we are often too screwed up to enjoy life at all. Allowance and permission are the first gifts we can give ourselves to help restore the flow of universal power into our lives. Sometime this week, do something you really want to do for the love of it: swimming, walking, reading a novel, eating chocolates, buying a nice thing you want but don't need. Give yourself permission to enjoy this, take time to appreciate it. Don't sanction something just because it incidentally gives pleasure to someone else – expedience and self-effacement are not what this is about.

Although it may seem frivolous and unnecessary, this practice is a valuable way to bring the zest and freshness back into your life, especially after a period of denial. You may also need to reinforce this practice by finding a friend who encourages you to reach into the originality of your soul and do something unusual, uncharacteristic and fun on a regular (but unregulated) basis.

Permit yourself to be recreated by your passions!

5. THE COSMIC WEB

Without any doubt there is something which links material energy and spiritual energy together and makes them a continuity. In the last resort there must somehow be but one single energy active in the world.

– Teilhard de Chardin S.J. *The Hymn to the Universe*

This book invites you to become a walker between the worlds. To do this, you need to know just where the thresholds of those worlds are and how to cross them. They are not difficult to find.

The doorways and pathways lie all about us. As children, we knew them intimately in our secret play; like Alice in Wonderland, we explored the multi-dimensional complexity of the cosmic web, which was inhabited by spirits with whom we played. The tragedy of growing up is that we are seduced into giving up any contact with the web, to join the adult world where people are largely disconnected from it. When Dylan Thomas wrote 'Rage, rage against the dying of the light', I believe that it was this creative illumination, our connection with the web, that he meant. As adults, we lose our easy access to subtle reality, except through dreams or through meditation and other spiritual practices.

The all-pervasive nature of Spirit connects all things in a cosmic web of relationship. When we become aware of it, we feel the flow of power and ecstasy within us; when we separate ourselves from it, we feel depressed and uneasy. When we say, 'things just flowed along that day', or 'it was just one thing going wrong after the other', we are expressing our connection with or disconnection from the cosmic web. Many people have dedicated their lives to pursuing this feeling of unity and connection. In the midst of an ashram, monastery or retreat, it is easy to feel our connection. But shamanism is not about acquiring a self-absorbed sense of well-being for our personal nirvana, it is about reconnecting our physical world with the rest of the web and helping realign whatever and whoever has become separate from it, then, with the help of spirits, mediating between physical and subtle realities. This involves a personal exploration of the otherworlds, where they are, what they contain, how their inhabitants relate to us and understanding what personal changes need to be made to be able to work in this way.

Soul-fragmentation

Western society allows us to be aware in our body and in our mind; it sometimes permits us to be creatively aware; it gives no such spiritual allowance to our soul, parts of which have become homeless and wander unsatisfied, seeking shelter in whatever place seems safe. The West has become increasingly soulless, driven by the need for economic survival, seeking satisfaction in fatuous and hollow pursuits, and avoiding spiritual challenges by promoting quick-fix political solutions.

Throughout the world, shamanism recognizes that human beings have a multiple soul consisting of several parts. The number of parts varies tremendously: some cultures recognize two or three parts, others several more. In traditional societies, soul-parts are held to reside in different areas of the body – in the blood, hair or breath – and to be able to travel forth at will, as in dreams or to visit a loved one far distant. In this book we will be talking about the way these composite soul-parts can become involuntarily ejected, stolen or lost. We each have multiple soul-parts which usually function in complex and efficient ways: they enable us to live ordinary lives and we are not usually aware of them. But if a soul-part becomes ejected due to the shock of an accident or through traumas such as divorce, burglary, rape or bereavement, we suddenly become aware of having mislaid something. An inability to heal or recover or function as we once did is the signal of soul-loss, or more accurately, soul-fragmentation.

Each part of our soul needs to be with us, to enable us to pay proper attention to the different dimensions of our lives: to be emotionally aware, to give love, to appreciate what is true and beautiful, to respect the boundaries of others and ourselves, to discern danger. If one or more soul-part is missing, we begin to find some of these things difficult or impossible.

Soul-fragmentation can happen to societies and groups as well as to individuals. The signs that this has happened in the West are clear to see in the sabotage of community and national programmes, in the meaningless violence, addictions and self-mutilations of our society. In many ways our society resembles a long-caged animal in a zoo, lacking self-respect or purpose for living, declining at the end of its chain – a prisoner of one reality. The shamanic task is to restore self-respect and a sense of life-purpose to both individual and group by retrieving the lost soul-parts.

Reconnection

By seeking reconnection with the cosmic web and exploring it, we are not trying to escape the confines of our physical world; by walking the ancient pathways, we are not striving to enter the past. Shamanism wants only to sing the soul back home, so that the primal harmony of the cosmos may be re-experienced by all. When shamanic students first encounter some part of the cosmic web, beholding its unity, beauty and harmony, they weep tears of joy and recognition mixed with tears of regret for wasted time and opportunity. Nothing can prepare us for the flood of remembrance which flows into our being when we perceive the web and realize that we too are connected.

It is for this reason that shamans journey, that artists paint and sculpt, that musicians play, that poets sing: each practitioner upholds his art, her skill, in order to keep those doors of perception open, that others may be led upon the pathways of power, ecstasy and life to behold the web and to be become a part of it. It is for this reason that we must uphold the imagination as a faculty of the soul, to keep our own imaginations brightly polished to refract the luminous and all-pervading beauty of the cosmic web. If we resonate with the web, we will immediately be able to perceive what brings nurture and inspiration and be able to reject whatever is artful, spurious and self-seeking.

Our background and education are still very much rooted in the inheritance of the Age of Reason, which forswore religion and otherworldly realities as pretence and superstition. Since the 1960s, the tide has turned and we are beginning to understand and reaccept the validity of subtle reality.

Scientists, physicists and cosmographers have sought to express the interconnective nature of matter with time, space and dimension in a variety of ways: from the parallel universe theories of Brian D. Josephson, through the divine milieu expounded by Teilhard de Chardin, to the cosmic wormholes of John Archibald Wheeler. Such theories of our universal interconnection parallel those of shamanism, and scientists and shamans agree that specific techniques of consciousness can make us more aware of such relations. A growing understanding of cause and effect, both physical and subtle, is being expounded by the new science; this echoes the shaman-ic need for reciprocity, for we do not only receive power and benefit from connection with the web, we also give back thanks and power in return. If we refuse to share with Spirit the result is usually separation from Spirit.

I believe that we in the West are ready to comprehend the cosmic web once again. New technology and communication networks have interlinked our physical reality in the last fifty years. Now the work of restoring the net-work of our subtle reality must begin. We have started to listen to shamans and indigenous peoples who respect the cosmic web and already interact with it. Our major drawbacks as 'civilized' and literate people are our very urbanity and literality; we need the wisdom of the web-keepers. We have lost our sensitivity and perception of subtle reality, we easily throw off any understanding of it, gravitating towards the familiar ground of mundane reality. We have been conditioned to be separate, disconnected and proud of our independence.

The Three Worlds

Our disconnection from the web is increased by the absence of any subtle reality cosmology. Indigenous peoples see the inter-relationships of the cos-mic web as complex and various. In contrast, our perception of otherworlds and states is very unsophisticated. We have inherited a narrow set of cor-relatives in speaking of the otherworlds: *up* for heaven, *down* for hell.

Throughout shamanic traditions worldwide, the subtle worlds which lie within the cosmic web are described as zones of activity and function. Perceptions of these zones vary, but the most common model is a three-tiered series of worlds (see opposite).

The Three Worlds diagram is a model, not a representational map. The Upper, Middle and Lower worlds are experienced as real and complex, not as flat and two-dimensional. They are interpenetrated by a central axis –

The Three Worlds

The Upperworld

The Middleworld

The Underworld

The Cosmic Web

The cosmic web surrounds and connects all that is,
interpenetrating the three worlds, multi-dimensionally,
from all angles.

49

sometimes called the pole, pillar or ladder of the heavens, or the *axis mundi* – or, as here, by the great tree. The image of the central tree is a universally compelling one, for its roots draw upon the depths of all that has been, its trunk rises up in strength in the present moment and its fruits soar into the heights of potent futurity. This is the major highway along which shamans travel between the worlds.

The three worlds are encompassed by the cosmic web which must be imagined as interpenetrating them, multi-dimensionally, from all angles. The image of the cosmic web shown on p.49 cannot convey the vigour with which it can be accessed from all points within this cosmological totality. Like a safety-net, the web surrounds and connects all that is, whether in physical or subtle reality.

As we walk between the worlds, the intersecting filaments of the web are close at hand. Even if we travel at speed in soul-flight, our allies and helpers are there to remind us and help us reorient ourselves. As we explore the otherworlds more thoroughly, we will find other connecting ways between the worlds; we may also discover further worlds within worlds. Some cultures envisage three further worlds in each zone, making a total of nine; others recognize seventeen or thirty-three or ninety-nine. We will not be making so complex an exploration in this book, but will use the three-world model. (It is expounded fully in Chapters 4, 5 and 6.)

The three worlds are part of all cultures worldwide, even in Christian Europe. We see it reflected in Dante's *The Divine Comedy*, in which Dante is accompanied by the classical poet Virgil on a tour of a lowerworld, defined as Hell, and of a middleworld, defined as Purgatory, and led by Beatrice and other female allies into an upperworld, defined as Paradise. Each of Dante's worlds has nine levels, but this is not precisely analogous to the shamanic three-world model. Rather, it is a dualistic and Christianized diminishment of the ancient tradition of the three worlds.

Walking between the worlds, we begin to understand the original dynamics of inner space for ourselves, without the overlay of restrictive theology. We are already aware of the physical reality of the Middleworld, which lies about us in everyday life; some of us may be familiar with the subtle reality of the Middleworld, so adding another dimension to our three-dimensional perception. The Middleworld reveals the relationship between our physical world and its subtle appearance in many ways. When we stand aimlessly in front of a shelf in the supermarket, trying to recall what it is we need, we only have to send a soul-part home to the kitchen to check, and we remember! In a journey that has taken less than a second, we have moved from one side of reality to the other.

We are drawing on the rich and sustaining power of the Underworld when we reach into our memories, when we use our deep instincts, whenever we want to access primal foundations. When we are challenged and put on our mettle to defend something we love deeply, we have to sink our roots deeply into the Underworld to draw upon the power of that realm and suddenly we have the strength to speak and act with power.

We also come into contact with the bright illumination and mercurial flow of the Upperworld when we access connective patterns and ideas, when we evoke sources of universal wisdom or when we seek out new ways of working. When we say we got a creative idea out of the air, for example, we mean we reached up high into the branches of the tree of ideas to fetch down the enriching fruits of the Upperworld.

Although most people experience connection with the three worlds and access the cosmic web in some way, few do it consciously or with repeatable skill. For most of them, only the physical reality of the Middleworld is real: they may experience the sudden closeness of a far-distant friend or pick up a sense that they should not travel on a particular road, but these feelings are put down to coincidence or imagination, not to the impinging of the subtle reality of the Middleworld. Similarly, people who sense a dead relative guiding them, or who feel that they are being instructed by an eminent figure such as Plato or Marie Curie, have no sense that they have had contact with spirits from the Under or Upper worlds.

One of the reasons why early anthropologists assumed that many shamans and indigenous peoples were schizophrenic or mentally unstable was because they could conceive of physical and subtle realities simultaneously – a skill which the anthropologists no longer possessed. We are in no doubt when we are thinking, imagining, recalling or dreaming – we can switch perceptual modes skilfully. But these skills can decline through our growing dependency upon the visual media and our neglect of subtle perceptual modes. If we add to this a complete dearth of words to describe

51

mystical or otherworldly states and take away any social framework in which such states can be discussed, it is no wonder that subtle reality and its inhabitants have been expelled from our culture. Yet, when they are exposed to it for the first time, many people are amazed at how easily and speedily shamanism works.

Any attempt to codify or understand the immensity and connectedness of the universe can only be an approach. Some approaches have gone further and defined the universe so completely that these definitions – religions, philosophies and political trends – have been enjoined as binding and oblig-atory, so that to disbelieve in them has been a criminal or heretical act. Shamanism has no desire to impose a rigid definition of reality upon anyone: it is happy to accept a loosely associated framework of regionally various experiences which have resonance, harmony and connection.

On the Threshold

As you stand on the threshold of interconnection with the web, you may be wondering about the advisability of shamanic work. It is common to be afraid of stepping through the veil between the worlds: What terrors will you experience? What dangers will you meet? Be assured that your innate common sense, instinct and perception will not abandon you as you walk between the worlds; please take them with you. The unknown is not evil, it is just unfamiliar. Just as when you travel to a foreign country, you will have your own guides who know where you are going and speak the language. This book is unfolding gradually to prepare the way, so that you will become incrementally familiar with the layout of the landscape and features of the three worlds.

Those who travel fearfully, always suspicious of those they meet, always expecting problems, usually encounter them. Those who travel with pur-poseful intention, who keep alert and treat those they meet with respect, usually become good travellers. Healthy caution should always be tempered by a trusting heart. Fear in shamanic work usually arises from a lack of trust, in our selves or in our spiritual allies. Absence of self-confidence stems from loss of power and self-esteem which are endemic in our dependent and passive culture. But if we start with familiar landmarks and become acquainted with our helping spirits, we will walk between the worlds safely and in growing wisdom.

A Bushman trance dancer described his journey through the cosmic web like this:

'I enter the earth. I go in at a place like a place where people drink water. I travel a long way, very far. When I emerge, I am already climbing threads. I climb one and leave it, then I climb another one … You come in small to God's place. You do what you have to do there … Then you enter the earth, and you return to enter the skin of your body.'[9]

That is all that is required of you: to go forth, to listen and communicate and to return upon the cosmic web. In the next part we will explore the practicalities and dynamics of how you do this.

✋ Practice 6: The Cosmic Web

Sit somewhere you can be private and uninterrupted. Consider the physical reality networks in your life: the people, places, work, activities, group memberships, and so on. Draw a chart showing how these influences interconnect.

In another session, consider the subtle reality networks in your life. This is more difficult, requiring you to go deeper into yourself and who you really are. You might include the unspoken or unacknowledged connections between yourself and others, the connections between yourself and other beliefs or group-associations, the lines of connections that link you with other species of life, with those who are dead, the effects of your activities upon those not yet born. Draw an interconnective chart of these influences upon yourself. Superimpose one chart upon another – where are the significant connections?

In a follow-up session, sit outdoors in a private spot, once during the day, once during the night: both times, consider how you impinge upon the cosmic web. Compare your findings. What have you learned?

✋ *Practice 7:* Wishing True

Review any old wishes you've made in the past, discarding and cancelling them if they are no longer desired. For example, your childhood yearning for a rocking-horse, your adolescent desire to meet a pop-idol, your adult wish, uttered in anger, that someone might drop dead. These wishes are taking up links in the cosmic web and therefore within you: to cancel them, just reverse them aloud, for example, 'I no longer wish for a straighter nose.' If you wish to cancel forgotten desires you might now regret, say so out loud and with intention.

You may want to make a new wish, or to reinforce an old one. Before you envisage what you want, consider how it would change your life, what repercussions it would have on any living creature now alive or yet to come, how it will shake the web. This is not an exercise in cosmic manipulation or selfish desires, but in attuning to the power which runs through the cosmic web, and learning to trust and respect it. If your wish, and it doesn't have to be a personal one, stands up to scrutiny, now describe it and make it exciting to yourself with all your senses. Send your wish out into the universe on free wings, without reserve. Without trying to manipulate the manifestation of your wish, bring it to mind regularly, but let it be free to manifest if it wants to, remembering that things don't always come to a satisfactory conclusion on our terms.

**Permit yourself to experience the cosmic web as only you
can experience it!**

CHAPTER 2

The Shamanic Journey

*People must believe what they can, and those who believe more must not be
hard upon those who believe less. I doubt if you would have believed it all
yourself if you hadn't seen some of it.*

        – George MacDonald *The Princess and the Goblin*

1: OTHER DIMENSIONS

*Through the simplest alterations of consciousness, we can enter a world of
living interaction and unity.*

        – Holger Kalweit *Shamans, Healers and Medicine Men*

The feature which identifies shamanism and sets it apart from mediumship,
channelling or other forms of spirit-communication is the shamanic journey. By means of the soul-flight, shamans actively seek out the help of spirits, visiting and communing with them in the three worlds.

    The idea of the shaman travelling through other worlds is outrageous to
many people – a fantastic illusion at best, an imaginary fraud at worst. Yet
throughout history, there are examples of this from all cultures. The Italian
Franciscan ecstatic, St Joseph of Cupertino (1603–63), was often seen in
two places at once; the Hasidic *tzaddikim*, the spiritual masters of kabbala,
were able to make the *kfitzas haderech* or miracle journey, appearing to peo-

ple in need many miles distant. Even people with no training or aptitude send out a soul-part when a loved one is in need and have actually been seen or felt by them. These are all instances of Middleworld journeying.

To understand the shamanic journey, we have to comprehend the soul. Westerners generally perceive the psyche or soul as the unit of the personality, while the spirit is seen as the immortal unit which continues after death. In the mystical philosophy kabbala, the human soul is threefold: the *nefesh* or 'animal soul' which bears the vitality of life, the *neshemah* or 'the breath of God' and the *ruach ha kodesh* or 'spirit of enlightenment' which acts as a bridge between the two.[1] For the Kogi Indians of Columbia, *aluna* or 'the generative intelligence' of memory forms a bridge between the human spirit and the universe.[2]

The shaman skilfully uses different soul-parts to divine the universe. When she journeys, those soul-parts governing the body's involuntary maintenance system (circulation and respiration, for example) are left behind to guard the body, while those that go forth into the otherworlds journey out. This method of soul-travelling has never been forgotten and is frequently used involuntarily by those whose lives are in danger or who are subject to shock. When the anaesthetized patient on the operating table perceives himself lying there, this is called 'a near-death experience'. The soul of such a patient may travel further and experience entering paradise or meeting dead relatives. In the Western Mystery tradition, when a magician journeys countless miles to learn something, it is called 'astral travel'.

Shamanic journeying is distinct from the near-death experience and the traumatic soul-ejection since the shaman always enters the otherworlds voluntarily and purposefully by specific routes, travelling through already-mapped terrain and encountering familiar spirits. Although these journeys may unfold in a variety of sequences, they are not randomly undertaken.

Shamans journey to the otherworlds in a different state of consciousness from that which we experience every day. Human beings live by varying their modes of awareness quite dramatically, according to their needs. Major forms of awareness include the following:

Total absorption (no sense of separation between self and other,
· as in mystic rapture)

Intense concentration (playing a musical instrument)
Vigilant awareness (when driving or searching for something)
Day-dreaming (voluntary fantasy)
Ordinary awareness (walking along, performing simple tasks)
Drifting consciousness (involuntary when ill or sleepy)
Hypnosis (reduced awareness, involuntary actions can be suggested)
Sleep (of varying densities of consciousness)
Unconsciousness (coma, involuntary life-functions only operative)
Death (cessation of consciousness from a physical viewpoint)

Drugs may enhance consciousness or diminish it to varying degrees. The use of trance-inducing drugs among traditional shamans cause, the suppression of bodily awareness but a heightening of soul-awareness.

The consciousness of a shaman while shamanizing has often been described as 'trance' or 'ecstasy', which may be very misleading, since 'trance' implies reduced consciousness and 'ecstasy' indicates an exalted and rapturous awareness. These expressions have been coined by non-shamans since they are descriptions of how shamanism *appears* to the observer: the shaman dances and sings loudly (ecstasy); the shaman falls to the ground and lies motionless (trance). Neither expression is really accurate. I have already mentioned the ecstasy which arises from a unitive, non-dual experience of the cosmic web but this is not always a feature of the shamanic session: fear, expectation, joy, wonder, uncertainty and trust are experienced as well.

Sourcing

To describe the condition by which shamans enter into soul-flight through the three worlds, Michael Harner has suggested the phrase 'shamanic state of consciousness' or 'SSC',[3] which is better than 'trance' or 'ecstasy', but I prefer a simpler term: 'sourcing', which is the nearest I can get to describing the experience by which we enter the otherworlds. A source is an original fount, usually where water or primal wisdom arises; when we enter the otherworlds to access spiritual wisdom, we are returning to the source of Spirit, power and ecstatic non-duality.

During sourcing, the shaman actively and purposefully seeks out and returns to his source – in one of the worlds – remaining totally aware of the experience he is having and trusting that all his body functions will operate automatically until he returns. During sourcing, the shaman may be unaware of things happening in the room, but not so unaware that he could not return to ordinary consciousness if necessary, say, if fire broke out. Certainly, some traditional shamans may reach so deeply into their source that they remain journeying for many hours: this is a rare occurrence, a condition we can confidently define as trance.

For shamans, sourcing is a primary mode, done at will when the need arises, for at the source help is to be found. Sourcing is like plugging into an electrical socket and being filled with an energy and illumination which, though it is all about us, is seldom experienced in normal ways. It is a way of deeply rooting ourselves in our centre. When we have lost our awareness of that centre and seek to return to it, we are 're-sourcing' or finding our spiritual centre again.

During sourcing, a shaman's consciousness expands to comprehend not only the everyday world but all its spiritual forms too; it expands to journey into otherworlds, moving freely. Sourcing utilizes the soul's awareness which is frequently dormant or 'unconscious' in everyday life.

Sourcing is a form of intentional consciousness, wherein delight, intense concentration and involuntary receptivity are simultaneously experienced. For, although the shaman may decide to visit one of the worlds to seek out a helper, she does not direct the journey. Her helpers will take her to different parts of the otherworlds, show her things of which she is previously unaware. While at the source, she may speak in languages unknown to her and access many forms of knowledge not in her personal database.

The Sequence of a Shamanic Session

At this point it is probably useful for you to have some sense of the sequence of a shamanic session.

1. *A need or purpose* underlies all shamanic work. No shaman sets off randomly into the otherworlds without a good intention or an issue to resolve. The issue

may be framed as a question: 'How can love be restored between me and the friend with whom I have quarrelled?' or as a request for advice: 'Please show me what steps I must take next in this matter.'

2. *Preparing the place* where the shamanizing is going to happen comes next. This is usually indoors or, if outdoors, under shelter in a very remote place. The sacred dimension of the place and what is to take place within it is ritually realized by cleansing and intentioned preparation. External intrusions and interruptions are insured against.

3. *Inviting the spirits.* The shaman asks her spirits to come and help her, usually by song or speech, maybe also with dancing or ritual offerings of, for example, sacred smoke or grain.

4. *Sourcing.* Consciousness is re-tuned to the cosmic web by shamanic singing, dancing, rattling or drumming. This can be performed by the shaman herself or the rhythmic sound-source may be continued by an assistant. When the shaman is ready to journey, she sits or lies down. Thanks to modern technology, it is now possible to journey quite deeply with the aid of a headset and drumming tape. The repetitive rhythms, cadences and movements all help the shaman reach her source.

5. *The journey* or soul-flight begins when sourcing has been successful and the shaman becomes overwhelmingly aware of the pathways which lead to her intended source. Her soul follows her usual routes to reach one of the worlds where her spirit helpers advise and counsel and help her to find solutions to problems. The sequence of this journey is various and can last from ten to forty minutes. Examples of typical journeys are given on pp.79–81.

6. *The return* from sourcing is just as important. If an assistant has been providing a continuous sound-source with drum or rattle, he will take his cue from the shaman's hand signals, body language or breathing when to change the rhythm to sound the soul's coming home. If a drumming tape has been used, then after 20–30 minutes of drumming the call-back signal will sound, calling the shaman's soul home. There is a brief period of readjustment to ordinary consciousness during which the shaman assesses the information or advice gained.

7. *Thanking spirits and helpers* is never omitted, since it is by their help alone that solutions have been found. Again, offerings, songs or dances are often performed here.

8. *Imparting or implementing* the advice gained on the journey is the final act, manifesting otherworldly help in a practical way.

This schema gives a broad outline of one possible approach to the shamanic journey; shamanic sessions which involve working with clients or larger groups unfold in different ways.

Engagement

Shamanism requires a balance of relaxed awareness and concentrated perception; it is not a passive activity. The will is operative so that the shaman can choose to return at any time, exercise his usual common sense judgements or make decisions during the journey. The experience of many such journeys inevitably alters the character of the walker between the worlds who truly interfaces with the cosmic web, bringing greater spiritual and emotional stability as well as a physical steadfastness and mental resolve which totally refute the notion that shamanism renders the practitioner fey or otherworldly. If, however, the walker between the worlds goes as a mere otherworldly tourist, without engagement, the same cannot be said.

Folk-wisdom represents this symbolically in the story where two daughters are sent out to find a treasure. The younger daughter relates compassionately with the beings she meets on the way and they aid her quest so she returns successfully with the additional gift of speaking gold and silver. But the elder daughter, desirous of similar success, tramps relentlessly over and through all the beings she meets, receives no help from them and returns without achieving her aim, and with the consequent gift of speaking worms and spiders.

We take who we are and what we have accumulated with us into the three worlds. Of course it is possible to travel thither as a mere observer, as some kind of theoretical exercise, but this is not the shaman's way. It is like studying the art of painting and buying brushes, paint and canvas but never creating your own picture. Unless we engage with the otherworlds and become involved with their inhabitants, we cannot walk the web with any compassion or understanding.

We turn now to the dynamics and techniques of sourcing.

☙ *Practice 8:* Modes of Awareness

One day this week, make a note of where your consciousness is focused from when you rise until when you go to bed. Be relaxed and not over-analytical in this, making a sample collection of random moments of the day.

Example: 8.45am intense concentration in rush-hour; 11.35am daydreaming about me and Andrea on holiday; 2.40pm strong empathy with Roger who collapsed at his desk with heart trouble; 6.30pm mystical oneness with blackbird's song in twilight garden; 11.10pm drifted off to sleep worrying about tomorrow's presentation, which spiralled through my dreams all night.

Note what was happening during these moments, how easy it was to move from one mode into another and what was happening to your body, mind and emotions during this time.

2. RIDING THE SPIRIT WIND

When I practised drumming and chanting ... an unusual merging of mind and feeling took place, drawing me downward to a beginning of something. As I trusted its vertical pull, it took me to the fundamental elements of life.

– Carl Levett *Crossings: a Transpersonal Approach*

This account by the American psychologist Carl Levett who studied with an Indian shaman, closely describes the feeling of the beginnings of sourcing. Sourcing can also be accompanied by irresistible waves of power such as are experienced in childbirth, a dissolution of all else save the rhythm, brightness and vision of power. In sourcing we become everything, we enter everything, and everything becomes and enters us simultaneously, in the same way that a labouring mother and the baby coming forth from her womb are also one in the cosmic birth struggle. I have used the image of childbirth because our first entry into the otherworlds is a real birth, where we are recreated and introduced to our forgotten spiritual home or source. The awe, terror and wonder of that birth are never to be forgotten.

While working on this book, I had a long, lucid dream in which the spirits told me how any person can access inner space, whatever their cultural or educational background. I was told that four factors are necessary:

1. The stillness   2. The container
3. The companion   4. The story

These were explained to me as follows:

1. The primal *stillness* of our alert but relaxed attention must underlie all travel in inner space. It is usually attained by the simple process of stilling the body's tension, the mind's activity and the heart's desires, and by focusing the soul's attention. The stillness is discovered through the sound that reaches the silence; it may be attained through physical motions which bring their own internal stillness such as in certain martial arts, dance-forms and music-making. The stillness seeks the still centre of our being from which we journey forth to our source.

2. The *container* refers to the place whence we start to journey, as well as to our destination. This includes the interaction of time and space, as well as of knowledge of the pathways which lead us into the cosmic web. Our container can be as simple as an undisturbed room in which we recreate the directions of the universe according to our geographical location upon the earth and the time of year, by our evocation of the required elements and spiritual powers. In all instances, we focus upon our physical location, our connection with the earth on which we live and upon the seasonal gateway which creates the opportunity for our journey.

3. The *companion* refers to the spirit or ally who accompanies us. The companion is our guide on our journey and we travel nowhere without one. To gain a companion, we must make an initial contact in special circumstances. This is described in the next chapter.

4. The *story* refers to the impulse for our journey, the reason we are travelling, and the answer which is completed or mirrored in inner space. Take the example of my student, Fiona, who was adopted as a baby and wants to make a connection with the ancestral qualities she has inherited. Her physical reality research has drawn a blank: her partial story may be completed by means of a journey to the ancestors. Our story is very important and concerns motive and purpose. None of us can function without some engagement and knowledge of our story. No journey can begin without a good purpose. Indefinite purpose creates mean-

dering journeying where the story is fragmented or meaningless. (We will explore the ways we arrive at our story in the next chapter and will discover how to understand it more deeply in Chapter 7.)

There are many means of sourcing available to us. Traditional shamans attain passage to the worlds by the following means:

1. Rhythmic or percussive instruments (drum or rattle), resonant and sustained sounds (bowed and stringed instruments, voice, and so on).
2. Motion: dance, shaking, swaying.
3. Consciousness-altering plant medicines that are inhaled or swallowed.
4. A mixture of all or some of these.

These methods involve the engagement of the senses of sound, touch, taste and smell to bring about sourcing. Physical sight is normally obscured by a mask or blindfold or by closing the eyes, thus enabling 'the inner sight' to be fully operative. During sourcing and the journey itself, the other subtle senses are awakened and fully employed: intense tastes, smells, sounds and feelings are also experienced along with extraordinary visions.

This book does not deal with hallucinogens as a means of sourcing because these should not be used in shamanism without the presence and guidance of a teacher who knows their potency and effect, and who is personally experienced in engaging with the spirits of such plants and in travelling the pathways which lead from them. In a society such as ours which regards drug-use as recreational rather than as sacred medicine, the walker between the worlds is better off using more simple and equally effective methods which have no side-effects.

Eye-covering

The first aid to sourcing is an eye-covering: a simple scarf which doesn't impede your breathing will do. Dim light or darkness is required for this work and, while it

An Eye Fringe

is possible to journey in bright light, it is very difficult to begin sourcing without an eye-covering. If you are going to shamanize by movement or dancing, then an eye-fringe is helpful since you are able to see your feet, but your field of vision is still darkened.

The Rattle

The common instruments of the shaman are percussive ones like the drum or rattle which produce repetitive sounds. The shaking of the rattle represents the life-spark itself. It is the first toy given to babies in many cultures; instinctively we understand the importance of the 'voice' of the rattle which 'speaks' in the hands of the infant. It can be equally effective in the hands of a shaman.

Even if you intend to use a drumming tape for shamanic journeying, you should acquire at least a rattle since it can be used when a drum is inappropriate. The rattle is a primary aid to sourcing. It is used in a variety of ways to evoke power, to accompany power songs and dancing, to speak to the spirits of a sick person by being shaken over them, to divine and seek out information. Its body represents the immensity of inner space, the vast womb of the universe, and its handle represents our connection with it. As the seeds, stones or fragments within the body are agitated, their motion, velocity and sound re-constellate the networks of the cosmic web within our remembrance and perception.

Among the Desana Indians of the Amazon, the cosmic symbolism of the rattle is even more dramatically obvious: the gourd represents the womb, and the handle represents the phallus, while the tiny pieces of quartz crystal within the gourd represent the energy of the universe. When the rattle is shaken in darkness, the crystals spark against each other and illuminate the darkness like stars through the slits in the gourd.[4]

Rattles are used throughout the Americas, while shakers, clappers and noise makers of different kinds have been used all over the world. The ancient Egyptians and modern Copts use metal *sistra*, while ancient Irish vision-seers used branches from which bells were hung. Sometimes a rattling sound-source is part of the shaman's costume with metallic bells, jingles and ornaments sewn onto the robe or belt.

It is quite easy to fashion your own rattle and there are also many kinds available from music supply shops and ethnic stores. Choose one with a handle for easier use. Listen to its voice: it should be pleasing to your ears, with a sharp, bright sound which is capable of many subtle changes, depending on how it is shaken. Avoid those big fat gourds which sound as though they are full of waterlogged cigarette butts. My husband was given a pre-Columbian clay rattle which had been broken and mended many times and had no voice. We filled it with tomato seeds and resealed the top with clay and now, though very delicate and used only for planting cere-monies, it has a strong voice for our own times.

The Drum

Drums are used worldwide for ceremonial purposes, but the shaman's frame-drum, played with a beater, is the most useful kind of drum for sourc-ing. It is constructed from a wooden frame over which an animal skin is pegged, tied or tacked. The frame may be taken to represent the universe and all that is, while the skin can symbolize the energy, power and spirit of the cosmic web; the beater may represent ourselves, while the different rhythms of the beater or drumstick represent the many pathways between the worlds which we set up by our interaction with them.

The frame-drum is played all over the world in the Middle East, North Africa, Europe and the circumpolar regions, as well as in the Americas. Drum symbolisms and usage vary considerably across the world, but some of the most interesting are found in Lapland among the Saami people where the drumskins are decorated with complex designs depicting the landscape of the otherworlds, and symbols of the shaman's spirits, pathways and helpers.[5] These drums are also used for divination.

The drum is one of the most powerful instruments for sourcing. It com-pels attention as its steady beat and body-moving rhythm build into a sus-tained, resonant song. It is no wonder that Siberian shamans call their drum their 'horse'. As the drum gallops, so sourcing begins and the soul is carried away upon its quest.

Drumming 'allows shamans to align their brain-waves with the pulse of the earth'.[6] Surveys relating brain-wave patterns and drumbeat frequencies have been made, suggesting that theta waves of four to eight cycles per second relate to shamanic sourcing, as well as to dreaming and sudden insights.[7] Theta waves are actually accessed not only by the rate of the drumbeat, but also by the harmonics of the notes produced by the beater against the drum-head. This subtle web of harmonics is appreciable in any instrument, whether it be percussive, wind or stringed.

When listening to a drum, the journeyer listens not to the tap-tap of the drumstick but to the resonance of the drumskin and the music that it makes. Concentrating solely upon the drumbeat often *impedes* sourcing.

Around the rim of your drum a galaxy of sound is awaiting to be revealed. The rainbow harmonics which a drumskin can emit, hollow out our ears in many different ways: I have known a single drum sound like a symphony orchestra, birdsong, a choir, a speaking voice, fireworks and even siege cannons on one notable occasion! The true harmonics of any drum cannot be appreciated until the skin is 'drummed in' and warmed up. In ancient Sumeria as well as in modern Voudun, drums were given names at special dedication ceremonies, because they receive their souls at this time.[8]

If you decide to buy a drum, do not buy the cheapest. A good drum is worth spending money on. Bear in mind the following: most animal-skin drums go flaccid in damp weather and will need heating; a very heavy drum is impossible to hold up for long without damping the resonance by resting it upon your body or the ground; a single-headed frame-drum is most portable and useful for this work. Animal-skin drums have the best and most responsive voices; vegetarian and vegan shamans can use synthetic-skin drums which are widely available.

Other sound-sources may be readily used to the same effect: it is reported that a Saami shaman, temporarily without his drum, picked up a firkin lid and beat it with his knife.[9] Natural sounds, such as water flowing or dripping, repetitive bird calls, wind soughing in trees, the clattering of reeds, the waves of the sea, windchimes or attuning to the heart-beat can and have been used with different effects. Natural sound-sources are better than synthesized sounds. While it is possible to journey without sound, attuning to the rhythms of breath or by swaying, the sourcing is generally not so deep. Using such sounds or silences for sourcing is best attempted when you have first learned how to source using rattle, drum or voice.

I have used a variety of different things for the purposes of sourcing, especially singing and stringed instruments of many kinds; at need and without any shamanic equipment, I have even used the sustained motor-noise of fans or cars, and even a pencil on the back of notebook!

All sound has vibration. Remember that all live sourcing-sounds are likely to be overheard by others; drumming is especially pervasive through neighbouring floors and walls. Use of a drumming or rattling tape with headphones is a good compromise in urban situations, but do not become too dependent on canned sounds; give yourself a good live sound journey at least once a month. If you use a sourcing tape, ensure that it has a good clear call-back signal that you can recognize. Suppliers of sourcing tapes and CDs are given in the Resources section, p.263.

Dance and Song

Rattle and drum are often accompanied by singing, dancing or both. These are often regarded as auxiliary aids, yet they are also primary ways to sourcing. Dance has always been a means of accessing the otherworlds, especially when whirling or spinning are paramount. We are more familiar with the social aspects of dancing, but many of these have their roots in communal ceremonies which reconnect people to their cosmological origins. (We shall be looking more at the shamanic nature of dance in Chapters 4, 5 and 6.)

Our voice expresses our soul, and its tone, timbre and mood mirror our being to the universe. The burdens, sorrows or repressions of people can be heard in the restrictive and unreleased nature of their voices.[10] Most people are aware of this truth and are consequently self-conscious about their own voices because they are so revealing. The burdens of world-sorrow may cling to the human voice yet, when we sing to the rattle or drum, when we seek to commune with our spirits and give them a voice, something quite miraculous occurs. A massive vocal release can be registered by the listener as the voice drops its cares and enters into the chorus of the universal song. We have few social frameworks in which we can sing and, unless there is some alcoholic lubrication to encourage them, most people prefer not to sing, so:

Permit yourself to use your free singing voice!

Rattles and drums may be wonderful ways of sourcing, but your own voice travels everywhere with you; it is your own free gift and a major means of sourcing.

The human voice seems to have become ashamed of itself since the substitution of the written tradition for the oral tradition. Once, all laws, myths, customs and histories were stored in memory and recited aloud. Among indigenous peoples, the oral tradition still has primacy. For them, the utterance of the strict truth is a tribal necessity, since the sacred teachings are imparted by the memory-keepers by word of mouth or in long incantations which are nothing less than a formal recreation of the world. These teachings, garnered from the otherworlds by a succession of walkers between the worlds, are commonly recited as an act of healing. Among the Navajo, such chants are immensely long, often lasting many nights; they must be performed with exactitude or the chant becomes invalidated.

The use of chanting, where the voice is often mid-way between speech and singing, is common to shamanism. Specific chants are taught to shamans by their spirits; these chants are regarded as sacred regalia, to be held in trust by the shaman and her successors inalienably. Chants of healing, of welcoming the spirits or of calling upon the powers of the universe soon become part of the sacred regalia of any walker between the worlds. These are the songs by which you will sing the wandering soul back home, and, in so doing, also help to restore the human voice to its rightful task.

Shamanic Assistants

This book has been written for use by a lone person, but shamanism has always been practised in a social context and the shaman invariably has a companion or assistant. For example, the Saami noaidi often journeyed to a women's choir which maintained the sound-source during his spirit-flight. One or more would watch over his body while he sourced, while the others accompanied him and guided his soul back home again.[11]

You may wish to practise these ways with a friend. If you do so, ensure that your companion is as fully instructed as yourself. If you are going to make a journey and send forth part of your soul to the otherworlds, then you want to be confident that your physical and spiritual well-being are in

70

good hands. Your companion must be able to sustain the sound-source competently and continuously, for he is responsible for the depth of your sourcing. If you're not sure how long you need to journey, then prearrange a hand signal to indicate to your companion that you've concluded. Make sure that the call-back signal is clearly distinct from the regular sound-source rhythm, so that you are called home safely.

Remember that all instruments used for sacred purposes should be treated with respect; they are the voices of the spirits and the vehicles of your sourcing. They shouldn't be used for mundane or frivolous purposes. When you have chosen a drum or rattle and have introduced yourself to your instrument as described in Practice 9, you may wish to dedicate it to shamanic work in a simple ceremony.

Sourcing enables us to ride the spirit wind, to fly free upon the cosmic web and walk between the worlds. It is a powerful way of working which should be treated with respect and in appropriate times and circumstances, especially since the transfer of consciousness from mundane to otherworldly during sourcing is often sudden and shocking. One minute here you are drumming, rattling or singing; the next, you are away, intensely aware of other worlds and beings. This is why it is so important to have a clear grasp of your purpose and a full knowledge of where you intend to travel to before you start. In the following practices, ensure that you fully understand this before proceeding.

☙ *Practice 9*: Rattling

Take a rattle with a handle and experiment with it. Try shaking it at first, using only a small wrist action. Try shaking it 2–3 times a second for full effect: this is a rough estimate which you will adjust for yourself. Stand with eyes closed or covered, letting the rattle speak. Try it loudly and softly; shake it deliberately in straight strokes, shake it spirally with circulating strokes – note the sound changes. Now stop and formulate your purpose, which is – to meet and acknowledge the spirit of your rattle. Rattle for at least ten minutes and go with the sound, letting whatever impressions strike you unfold like a story or an imagined landscape. If you have a strong desire to move or sing with the rattle, do so. You may encounter spirits of the plants, trees or minerals from which your rattle is made. Thank and praise them. Write down what you experienced.

✋ *Practice 10*: Drumming

Take a drum and beater and explore the drumskin: which parts of the skin have the best dynamics and resonances? You will find that the area near the frame's edge is more musical than the middle. How hard or soft do you need to beat? Experiment with tempo, using slow deliberate strokes of 1 beat per 2 seconds, moderate strokes of 1 beat a second, faster strokes of 2–3 beats a second. When you know your drum a little better and the skin has been warmed up from use, cover your eyes and stand with the drum and beater in a safe space. (It is important that any delicate or dangerous objects are clear of your space.) Stop and consider your purpose, which is to meet and acknowledge the spirit of your drum. Drumming is a very strong way of sourcing which may take you very deep, very quickly, but keep your purpose in mind and follow the unfolding of any images, patterns, impressions or sounds without dissecting them. If yours is an animal-skin drum, you may encounter that animal's spirit. Thank it for giving its skin for this purpose, listen to its voice, acknowledge its help and wisdom. You may wish to move, dance, sing or call as you drum; allow this happen.

✋ *Practice 11*: Singing

You may already have sung or chanted in the practices above, in combination with rattle or drum. This time, you will chant without any other aid but darkness. Sit upright, cover your eyes and put a finger in each ear. Now take a deep breath and sing or chant a lovely open O in the middle and comfortable region of your voice. Let the breath come easily through the hole of the O, allowing your lips to vibrate gently as you do so. The sound is centred deep within you. Breathe in again and repeat, this time taking one finger out of your ear. Get used to the free vibration of your own voice until you can chant without covering your ears.

Now bring to mind the cosmic web which permeates the universe. With eyes covered, gradually allow your voice to describe the cosmic web in

sound, in whatever way it wishes to; change the note if necessary – if words
or syllables also come then let them. Focus entirely upon the cosmic web
and how you sense it, not upon your voice. If the results do not seem coher-
ently song-like, don't worry: this is not a voice competition. Maintain this
for at least five minutes. You may find that your own 'chant of the cosmic
web' arises from this, a power-song which will help remind and reconnect
you with the web at times when you are feeling less connected. Record this
as best you can, on tape or by simple notation.

3. THE MIRRORED MESSAGE

*I see everything all at once, without the delays of succession, and each detail is
equal and equally lucid ... Yet even as I look, as if to remember forever this pristine
world, already the forms become modulated into meanings, cease to be forms.*
— Maya Deren *The Voodoo Gods*

This account by a white initiate of the Haitian shamanic tradition exactly
expresses the experience of shamanic perception, which is subtly different
from mundane perception. It is with the heightened perception of an artist
or poet that the shaman experiences the otherworlds. A simultaneous transmission of a great knot of imagery or material is common, as is a sense of
being part of an enormous collage whose details are each clear and distinct,
yet also inter-related. This inside/outside vision is common to all seers.

In Gaelic tradition when the seers see the physical reality and the subtle
reality simultaneously, it is called *do shealladh* or 'two seeings'. The
Hawaiians call this *papalua*, 'double vision' or 'double knowledge'.
Fortunately, most of us do not possess this ability in ordinary life, for the
involuntary stimulation of the second sight is a terrible affliction as well as
a great gift. In shamanism, during sourcing, it is possible to have specific and
voluntary sight of the subtle reality which surrounds a subject, whether it
is the true cause of an illness or the hidden motivations surrounding a project in which we might be involved. It is to obtain such knowledge that
shamans seek to enter the otherworlds; for though shamans may also be
seers, most cannot achieve the 'two seeings' without the aid of sourcing.

We access the otherworlds for knowledge, healing or help. All knowledge

is discoverable in the cosmic web of the worlds: the earliest human understanding of the universe was brought about by shamans accessing the cosmic
web. Whatever is unknown may be found within the web.

Before sourcing begins, the shaman must assess the needs and possibilities, for the results of the journey are dependent upon the purpose which
underlies it. One of the earliest purposes for journeying may have been
hunting, for locating herds of animals by shamanic means. This is still done
among the Inuit, where the shaman living in the ice-locked Arctic regions
will journey to the Goddess of the Sea in times of hunger, requesting that
she unlock the game penned in her house that the people may eat.[12]

In times and places where there were no books, no prior bodies of
knowledge concerning the world, the shaman was the major means of discovering the unknown. It has been suggested that the widely separated
islands of the Oceanic Polynesian triangle may have been colonized as a
result of the *ariki* or shaman-chiefs shamanically journeying. By imbibing
the narcotic *kava* (*Piper methysticum*), they discovered navigational courses
in subtle reality which were then followed in actuality, across wide,
unknown seas.[13] How many of the ancient world's staggering achievements
have been suggested by the spirits through shamanic journey? The precise
cosmological alignments of megalithic monuments such as Stonehenge,
Callanish and Avebury, and their technically arduous construction, have
been much discussed, with a host of explanations ranging from giant
builders to alien construction companies from outer space posited to detract
attention from the real issue: that human beings somehow conceived the
idea and physically achieved it.

Governments rarely invest their country's resources and talents in the
exploration of something which, because it is not physically apprehended, is
presumed to be non-existent. This is why we have highly sophisticated
technological and scientific knowledge, but almost total ignorance of subtle
reality. For the shaman, the realms of subtle reality are as full of mystery and
wonder as physical reality once was to our ancestors. Our society now lacks
the simple, daily structures by which our world and the otherworlds are
bridged. We are curious about subtle reality, but few people are technically
accomplished enough to find out how it works.

We are used to thinking of knowledge as an empirical thing, which should be gained for its own sake, as a theoretical adjunct to our cultural achievement. Subtle reality may be studied by para-psychologists in a purely scientific way, but it does not yield its secrets to theorists, any more than the heart of music can reveal itself to musical mathematicians, who quantify notes and measure vibratory ratios. Subtle reality reveals itself to shamans because they journey into it with real needs. This enables them to become true technicians of subtle reality. Such shamanic technology is often derided by theorists for its imprecise and subjective nature.

The writer Alan Ereira recounts the story of an Amazonian shaman who had heard an alarming radio report of a then current world situation and was very worried by it.[14] The way he interpreted what he heard was that two men called USA and USSR were fighting over a prostitute called Israel who was giving birth to bombs which would destroy the world. With his shamanic peers, the shaman worked hard to lock the bombs inside a spirit ice-mountain where they could cool down. The shaman's interpretation of events is simplistically symbolic in our eyes, nevertheless his shamanic action was successful because he had understood the nature of the world's need.

Framing the Question

The motivation for our journey is of paramount importance. If our intentions are clear, then our sourcing will be apposite: we will be patched into the cosmic web in ways which help heal and reconnect. If we decide to make a journey just because we haven't done so for a while, without a purpose, our sourcing will be aimless and the journey without cohesion. It is as pointless as setting out in your car without any clear destination.

While shamanism can and does provide solutions to everyday problems, it is particularly helpful in issues which seemingly have no mundane solutions. If you have a headache, then you can take some aspirin, but if you keep running a traumatic incident over and over in your head, then you need a different form of help. Similarly, if someone with whom you've had a misunderstanding died last week, you have no mundane means of effecting reconciliation. The analgesic of psychotherapy may be able to help you cope with such difficulties, but it is rarely able to communicate actively the powerful and effective answers of Spirit.

The ways in which we frame our purpose are important. Regard each quest or question as a key to one of the doors which leads between the worlds. Does your key fit the keyhole? You will be asking or seeking advice of your companion spirits, so the purpose must be a clear one, worded as exactly as possible. The following guidelines are offered to help you frame your question (see also page 198).

1. *What is at issue?* For example, 'organizing my time'.
2. *What kind of help are you requesting in this issue?* For example, 'How can my free time be organized more effectively?'
3. *If it involves others, frame your purpose so that benefit accrues to them, not only to yourself.* For example, 'How can the free time which Felix and I have be organized in mutually beneficial ways?' Ensure that your purpose is not manipulative, as in 'How can I get Felix out of the house so I can enjoy myself?'
4. *Is your question simple enough?* If your issue has many correlatives, frame your question to include them all, or journey on each individual item in turn: 'In what ways can I learn swimming, French and cycling in my limited free time?' It is wise to stick to one issue at a time rather than tacking on peripheral issues to the main agenda. If your issue is complex and the phaseology would be too unwieldy, you can frame it like this: 'Please advise me about organizing my time.'
5. *Is your issue open to spiritual help?* If you frame your question thus: '*How can I create more time in my crowded schedule?*' you have closed the issue by asking only how *you yourself* can make changes. A better way of putting this issue would be, 'In what ways *may time be made* in my crowded life?'

The shamanic journey gives us a new slant on intractable old problems, proffering solutions which may afterwards seem obvious. In Practice 12 (p.85), you are invited to create your own journey checklist.

What is Journeying Like?

We do not journey alone. During sourcing, we call upon our spirit companions to aid us and we always travel with at least one ally wherever we journey. Our trust in our shamanic allies is our lifeline, ensuring that we do not become lost or confused; they help us to make firm decisions and encourage our good judgement.

What is journeying like? It is not unlike lucid dreaming wherein the dreamer is enabled to become interactive with the dream, rather than a mere passive observer of events. In journeys, different scenarios or sequences often appear distinct, like the acts of a play, with different locations and characters, but usually they are purposeful just like mundane journeys.

Our abilities during journeying become subtle: we can fly through the air, swim under the sea, change shape or size, travel at super speeds, experience timelessness or the superimposition of different times and places. All the dimensions familiar to you from folk and faery story are here borne out in personal experience.

Trusting the journey that you take is sometimes hard because we have been brought up to believe in only physical reality. Common reactions are: 'I'm making this up!' 'Did I put that jaguar in the tree?' 'I must have an overactive imagination to see that!' People who are alive to archetypal symbolism are often disbelievingly astounded by their own archetypal experiences.

Shamanic journeys are not to be confused with journeys using guided imagery, where a scripted scenario or inner landscape is recited by a leader and meditatively travelled through by listeners. Most often, these non-traditional scenarios are invented ones. However, traditional use of the actual journeys of shamans and mystics has been used effectively as training models in hermetic and religious schools. The paths which follow the kabbalistic tree of life are one example, as are the pathways of the Tibetan bardo, which teach the ways between life and death. In my own Celtic tradition, I sometimes use soul-leadings, traditional scenarios and stories, to help lead less experienced students to specific locations and teachers. Such work is helpful as a means of way-showing: outside the main framework of teaching, it is not intended to be slavishly reproduced and followed to the exclusion of personal experience.

The shamanic journey unfolds in its own ways, without script. But that doesn't mean to say that, as the walker between the worlds, you are without any map. In Chapters 4, 5 and 6 we will familiarize ourselves with the three worlds, and the way-marks, doorways and pathways which take us thither.

Some students begin to enjoy shamanic journeying for its own sake, becoming virtual journey-junkies who zip between realities like otherworld tourists, trying to lap up all the sights and experiences, especially at the start of their shamanic work. Regulate your own practice by keeping your journeying to around four to six journeys a month; this way, you will be able to better understand and assimilate your experiences. Your spirits will help you, but if you are always asking their advice yet not allowing any time to implement it in your life, then you are hardly accepting or validating such help. The shaman must be able to bring information, healing and power into our world in ways that actually inform, heal and empower. Unless this happens, all shamanizing is a waste of time. The implementation of advice is very dependent upon your understanding and intepretation of your journey. But to ignore or neglect advice is disrespectful to your allies.

Shamanism is not a one-way street. Journeying is not a good form of escapism. If you journey merely to avoid your problems and to enjoy a little otherworldly sight-seeing, you will surely encounter your mundane responsibilities in their subtle forms. Indeed, your spirits may place these encounters in your way, in order to help you deal with them. This also happens if you have failed to implement properly your allies' advice before going to make another journey: they may overturn your new issue in order to encourage you to deal with the last one.

Paradox, riddle and cosmic humour thread the shamanic experience with zany sparks of light. Many students of shamanism are thrown by its random humour and sharp paradoxes. In direct opposition to the physical reality norm where we work seriously and play playfully, shamans learn to play seriously, and to work playfully.

When the spirits appear as divine clowns, they do so in order to make us vulnerable. Excessive self-awareness or a bloated ego preclude sourcing, and therefore, we must learn to forget ourselves, to empathize deeply with our spirits, letting our separate selfhood sink down like an ebbing tide.

When we source, we draw upon the imagination. Our society has taught us to distrust the imagination as a source of illusion. In shamanism we must understand that *imagination is a faculty of our soul*, just as our sense of touch is a faculty of our body.

When our ordinary modes of thought and comprehension are turned on their heads, we are able to access lateral thought and universal understanding. This new approach imparts rich gifts and ingenious solutions.

Some Journey Examples

Here are some sample journeys, drawn from my experiences and those of my clients, to give you a flavour of their variety, wisdom and humour. In this journey I asked how the spiritual and the everyday worlds can be practically combined.

I arrived in the Middleworld and found myself a little up my tree where my teachers and animals sat on the platform of a tree-house. I asked my question and was shown a garden through a tall hedge. Within were four tall, strong faery women of statuesque beauty and dignity. I was told that they came to protect us from soul-loss. They said we were not to let anyone take the power of Spirit from everyday life, for we were all guardians of Spirit. We were to defend the indwelling spirit of all beings. Then I was shown the stars and the zone of Sophia, the atmosphere which shrouds our earth. The faery women instructed me to tell people that we must send up our deepest aspirations for the universe nightly to this boundary of the earth's soul that all beings might imbibe, dream and be nourished by the common pool of loving thoughts gathered there. We must bless the elements, and be aware of the messages of our bodies daily. We must dance to help keep our sense of connection between the worlds. If we maintained these things then all beings would learn to see these connections. The blessings of the elements were repeated to me in this vision:

Blessed be the precious and preserving air, by which we are given life.
Blessed be the precious and preserving fire, by which we are warmed.
Blessed be the precious and preserving water, by which we are cleansed.
Blessed be the precious and preserving earth, by which we are sustained.
Blessed be the precious and preserving spirit that is within and around me.

In accordance with instructions, I subsequently published this journey in our quarterly newsletter and shared it with students as a spiritual invitation for all to participate in the work of the faery people.

The second journey recorded here was taken by Malcolm, an independent film maker, whose urgent question was: 'In what ways can I next earn money?' He had been unemployed for a few months and was getting desperate.

A very confused journey to the Upperworld where I encountered water buffalo grazing at the tops of trees near a Disney castle. I asked my teacher my question and he rode with me on Cloud Horse (Malcolm's guardian animal) to the cave of the sun where I was bathed in liquid gold. This was very consoling as we had ridden through bewildering images of violence and birth. Afterwards we came to the most perfect house on a hill. Here lay the salamander or dragon which I'd seen in my morning's dream. It seemed to guard remembrance of my earthly home's security and enchantment.

Cloud Horse then took me to the Middleworld where I entered a world of wacky cartoon thirties gangsters. I asked who they were and they declared themselves 'the media mafia'. I had to fight them. In the ensuing chase, I went up a spiral staircase where I saw a beautiful woman looking out across a skyline for something. Time slowed completely. I followed her gaze which became like a lighthouse's beam, only solid. Cloud Horse and I trotted across it and found a clock with animals on it, rather than numbers. It was at four o'clock, represented by a camel.

I asked my question again and the camel said I would be working next in animation, but that I wouldn't be contracted again until next April. I went crazy then and demanded to know how I would live. For answer a seagull flew from the clock-face and started scavenging. My teacher appeared on the skyline and bade me go back.

Malcolm found this difficult to interpret. Subsequently, he realized that he was indeed scavenging just like a seagull, doing odds and bits of freelance work for different companies, including preparing storyboards for a stop-frame animation short. He signed his next firm contract the following April, which was a long nine months after this journey. He got through this time by trusting his allies and continuing to journey for strength and help. The journey had been helpful in providing timeless and continuous support when he was confused, and suggesting that he should not be over-proud at accepting whatever crumbs of work came his way.

The third journey is also work-related. Janet took up her shamanic studies with great enthusiasm and on her journeys received strong instructions that she should pursue her studies even further. She was also contemplating a return to work and had been offered a long-desired post at her *alma mater* university; however, she was worried that it would interfere with her shamanic work. Her question was: 'Should I take up this position?'

My journey took me to Egypt, along with my animal. Most significantly, I met with one of my inner guides, the goddess Sekhmet. As I looked at her I was taken by complete surprise as the snake which sat prominently upon her sun-crown came alive and grew in seconds to fill my entire field of vision. He mangled and then devoured first my face and then my entire head. I recovered quickly only to find myself transformed into a sleek and beautiful lioness with two heads.

One head was ravenous and hungry, and tried to pull my entire body backward in her search to relieve her hunger. The other head, quiet and serene, ignored the agitated movement and kept her eyes focused on the blinding light before her, beyond the temple. It is her movement that quietly, without effort, brought the lioness to merge with the light.

Janet interprets her journey as follows: 'I take this to be a re-enforcement of my commitment to study shamanism. I have been turned into various animals on journeys but this particular lioness with two heads seems very significant. The one head looking back to my former position, and the other looking forward to a new, though as yet unmanifested, career. That the goddess should have to mangle and devour me in order that finally I see clearly what my uncertainty is about is very much in line with my training. Sekhmet gave me very clear understanding of my real insecurity of moving ahead into the unknown. The hungry head seeks the security of a known situation, hence its seduction.' Sekhmet is a lion-headed goddess, and being transformed or having one's body altered is a common shamanic theme. Janet subsequently turned down the offered post and is continuing to explore many different aspects of shamanism.

You may be surprised at the amount of trust and credence placed in their journeys by these walkers between the worlds. We are so used to validating advice only if it is given by experts, that such seeming self-reliance seems shocking or impertinent. We are not obliged to follow the advice of our allies, but our journeys do inculcate a deeper sense of authority for our actions if we try to do so. As you will see from these journeys, trust in our spiritual allies and knowledge of the three worlds are intrinsically required before we set out walking the worlds.

Some Journey Problems

Before we continue, I would like to offer some help for those who experience a failure to journey. Some people find journeying very difficult and unproductive. The causes are most often over-expectation and an inability to let go of conscious control. If you are a person who is used to a very structured life-style or if you live in your head more than in your body, journeying is quite hard. A very few people cannot journey at all but that does not stop them from living a life that is connected with the universe.

Others often fail to read the signposts and identify them as such; such people believe they have not journeyed when in fact they have. Misleading expectations that journeying is something terribly exotic are often the trouble here, for journeying usually unfolds so organically that the margin between dream or mind-wandering is difficult to establish. In such cases, *treat everything you experience during the period of your journey as information.* If you spent the whole time touring your garden or being shown a plant, then ask yourself how this experience related to the journey's purpose.

Here is a quick check list of possible journey problems:

1. *Nothing is happening.* What's happening in the nothingness? Record your experiences, however vestigial. Maybe only one bit makes sense. Relate *any* feelings or impressions to your issue.
2. *I experience things episodically or erratically, not staying in one place for very long.* Sometimes first journeys are like this. When you learn to let go and trust the experience, the 'story' will begin to join up, though it will still have distinct scenes.

3. *I become easily distracted and end up thinking instead of journeying.* Check physical comfort and minimize sound-sources that are likely to distract. For example, take the telephone off the hook or ask children to play more quietly. When you feel yourself drifting, check in with your guardian animal.

4. *I fall asleep when I journey.* Check that your time is a good one. For example, it's not at the end of day or when you are emotionally fraught. Normally if you sleep during a journey, the call-back signal will wake you; if your sourcing is very deep, you may pass from journeying into a deep sleep from which you will awake.

5. *I keep getting the same experience.* Have you dealt with the agenda of previous journey/s? How is the experience related to your journey's purpose?

6. *My experiences are so interesting that I don't get any further.* Don't analyse things during your journey, just observe, interrelate or act and pass on.

7. *I have difficulty coming back.* Check that you can recognize the call-back signal and practise grounding methods (see pp.30–31) before journeying again, or ask a friend to drum and call you back. In extreme cases, set up a muffled alarm clock in the same room, but not right next to you.

8. *My spirit helpers don't talk to me.* Check if they are showing you things, using body language or speaking directly to you without words. Communication may be head to head or heart to heart, rather than by speech.

9. *I can't go down my Underworld opening* (see Chapter 5). If Underworld journeys are too difficult; choose an ordinary reality location as your starting point and journey outwards from there, taking a Middleworld journey. People with claustrophia, unhealed birth-trauma or deep-seated anxieties may find Underworld journeying impossible.

10. *I'm sure I'm making all this up.* The ease with which most people journey disconcerts them; surely it should be more complicated that this? Most people are able to slip straight into journeying but find difficulty accepting what they experience. Accept this ease with the unconditional gladness with which you greet a fine day, as a great gift.

11. *My experiences seem very two-dimensional or colourless.* Many people with good mental control find it hard to let go enough. Allowing sourcing to happen is often unconsciously resisted. Try changing your method of journeying from a passive to an active one – dancing and singing rather than lying down.

12. *My head is full of babble.* Distractions happen to us all. The trick is to forget yourself, and indulge your willing suspension of disbelief: we are all used to for-

getting ourselves when we watch a film or a play, identifying ourselves with the experience of the characters before us, so you are already able to do this. Breathe, concentrate on the harmonic vibration of your sound-source, bring your purpose to mind and watch for the next part of the journey. Become more aware of what you are physically experiencing in your journey location. Ask your allies to help you focus.

13. *My 'book of dreams/symbols' says that dreaming/seeing teeth means 'great loss'.* Correlate your findings closely with *your own experience* and the intention of your journey. Don't worry about what Big Walking Bear says, or what Jung wrote, or what your therapist told you – *your* experience is the final arbiter!

14. *I lost/forgot my animal as I journeyed.* Losing or forgetting an animal is usually a sign of ungroundedness. Read Chapter 4. Always travel with one ally, keep checking for their whereabouts, and ask them to help you.

Finally, if nothing seems to be happening, check whether you are not trying too hard. Rest, do something else and try again another time. In our busy world sometimes rest and sleep are more important than just one more task. Remember, there are no correct ways of sourcing or journeying, only many ways. The procedures outlined here are guidelines only. Whatever you experience when you journey will be unique to you; no-one can direct what you experience on a journey, it will unfold in its own way. Any attempt by yourself to direct events will usually be immediately apparent: the energy, verve and organic nature of sourcing will become two-dimensional and vague. How we understand the results of our journey will be explored in more detail.

Permit yourself to experience and welcome the unexpected!

✋ *Practice 12:* Journey Checklist

As you have been reading, you have probably thought of many issues which are currently thronging your life on which you need advice, help or healing. Shamanic methods of answering questions or seeking help should be used only if ordinary methods of inquiry and help have been sought first. It is respectful to ask for help when all these have been exhausted. Make a list of your current concerns; these may include some of the following:

Issues about work, relationships, spiritual vocation or direction, health.
Mysterious occurrences: 'Why do I always faint on planes;
     how this can be prevented in future?'
Issues where there is a lack of power or Spirit.
Issues where there is inappropriate or unbalanced power.

If you notice that many of your issues lead back to one source, then that is probably your most important question. You will have opportunities for journeying on other issues as you proceed and we will explore further how you can best find help.

♨ Practice 13: Relaxation

Journeying requires good relaxation combined with clear and alert attention. If you suffer from problems with sourcing or journeying, you have probably omitted to relax first. Relaxation is something we all theoretically recognize but seldom personally implement. Lie down on a firm surface, with your head and knees supported by cushions. If your space is limited, lie on the floor on your back with your shins and feet resting on a chair or settee. Be physically comfortable. Breathe in deeply and allow your body to fill with power-giving air. Breathe out deeply, allowing tiredness, tension and worry to pass out into the universe to be recycled as new energy. Feel the universe breathing you in and out. Breathe into all parts of your body, until you feel a warm looseness in your limbs. Feel the love and power of Spirit permeate your being. Let your focus go from yourself and experience the filaments of the cosmic web holding you up.

Fears and Expectations

When you contemplate your first shamanic journey certain fears and expectations may arise, not unlike those that people have when considering their first driving lesson. Here are some common anxieties that first journeyers experience and some strategies and advice on how to handle them.

85

1. *The journey method feels too open-ended.* How will I experience anything without outside guidance? The prospect of taking a journey without a known format can seem overwhelmingly frightening and exposing. This often stems from fear of taking authority for the experience that you have or from a long dependence on structure to provide context and format. If you can dream, you can also journey. Your responsibility is to ask the question, find and stay with your allies and allow them to help the journey unfold.

2. *How will I know if I'm doing it correctly?* On your first journey, there is nothing to compare your experience with. There may be no yardstick but the input of your question and impulse of your strong motivation will keep your experience authentic. Be assured that the way that it happens is the way that it happens. There is no one right way, no set of predetermined co-ordinates.

3. *What will happen if I don't know what to do?* Remember that, even though you may not have formally met any of your allies yet, they already know and support you. Ask for their help. Focus upon the mission for your journey. If you've met one of your helpers, ask their assistence and follow their advice. Ask for the help that you need.

4. *Just reading the instructions, I find I'm already mapping out my journey ahead. Is this right?* It is common to anticipate the first journey. As with a dream, we don't know what is going to happen next, we just follow its unfolding. Let this happen for you and focus more on your mission than on your pre-set scenario.

5. *Will I get lost?* This fear can be overcome by spending lots of time considering your start point before you begin: this is where you are going to start from and return to. Before launching off into your journey, explore it thoroughly and acquaint yourself with its qualities. When journeying, stay with your guardian animal and keep your question forefront in your consciousness.

6. *What if I meet something scary that I can't handle?* This is very unlikely to happen. Journeying is most often a very organic and ordinary feeling when we begin. Remember that it is your guardian animal's job to help you avoid dangers or difficulties when journeying, not yours. If you are alone when something challenging happens, use your common sense, otherwise trust your allies to guide you safely.

7. *I'm more used to accessing subtle reality by meditation or some other means: will journeying work for me?* You will find journeying different. If you are a good meditator, you will need to be more proactive in journeying. Don't expect

things to come to you: rather you need to go and meet them. Listen to the sound-source and allow it to move you. Follow the instructions here, rather than relying on the methods you have been taught in other disciplines.

8. *What if I get petrified by fear?* Use the actor's old stage-fright trick: get your fear out of the equation by focusing strongly upon your purpose in journeying, on the purpose not the fear. Repeat your question to yourself as you journey.

9. *Will I go into a deep trance?* No, you will be too busy remembering your instructions and receiving information and impressions. The call-back on your sound-source tape or CD will ensure your return.

10. *How will I remember all the instructions?* Read the information you need in this chapter and Chapters 3 and 4. Run through this checklist before you begin:

- ❧ Exclude light and prevent possible interruptions.
- ❧ Formulate a short and simple question. For example, 'Please give me help and power with … *(your issue)*.'
- ❧ Repeat your question or request for the journey aloud.
- ❧ Go to your start point with the intention of finding your guardian animal.
- ❧ Keep asking for help from spiritual helpers if difficulties arise.
- ❧ Actively seek your guardian animal.
- ❧ Ask all animals you encounter: 'Are you my power animal?'
- ❧ Accept the one whose answer/body language says yes.
- ❧ Then ask your finalized question in its correct phrasing.
- ❧ Enjoy the rest of the journey.
- ❧ Conclude the journey at call-back.
- ❧ Return with your guardian animal.
- ❧ Announce your return to physical reality by saying, 'I'm back in the room.'
- ❧ Record your journey in writing or on tape.
- ❧ Discover what connections you can between the journey and your issue.

CHAPTER 3

Spirit Helpers

There are two things a person must do for him or herself: find a teacher and choose a friend.

– The Talmud

1: KEEPERS OF MEMORY

It is absurd for men to vaunt their superiority over the animals when, in matters of great importance, it is they who are our teachers: the spider for weaving and mending; the swallow for architecture; the swan and nightingale for singing.

– Democritus

When we begin to journey into the three worlds, our first task is to find and be befriended by otherworldly allies, spirits or helpers. These will be our guides and travelling companions for all future journeys that we take.

Many spirit helpers already stand by you, waiting to be called and recognized. You may work for years with some, others may pay only fleeting visits. If you look through your own address book, you'll see different kinds of people listed there: close friends, acquaintances, family, experts, companies, contacts. Your connections with spirit helpers will vary as much as your contact with the people around you. There will always be the very special friend, the circle of close friends who support you, as well as a wider network of companions and associates upon whom you call at need. You will need and find very many kinds of allies in your journey experiences: mineral, plant, animal, human and non-human.

Our Animal–Human Kinship

Animals connect us to the ladder of life-forms which leads back through time. They are the guardians of pre-human memory, inheritors of wisdom and teachers in their own right. Western philosophy often regards animals as 'just' the bridge between other life-forms and human beings, with humans at the head of the evolutionary triangle and the food-chain.

The animal world is dependent upon both the mineral and plant realms for its existence. Animals and humans inherit the cellular and genetic treasury of both mineral and plant realms but they have complex brains and organizational behaviour. Animals have mobility, which most plants and minerals lack, and they form family relationships. Animals and humans are very close in kinship as the Koran (Surah VI) reminds us: 'There is not an animal that lives on the earth, nor a being that flies on its wings, but forms part of communities like you.' Fish, insects, birds, reptiles and mammals are closely related, only developing when earth conditions are suitable.

Our attitudes to animals are very revealing. Sentimentalization and exploitation are forms of animal abuse which purposely diminish their innate power and increase our own. The Malaysian Chewong people have a sacred law forbidding humans from teasing or laughing at animals: one wonders what they would make of Disneyland, performing circus animals or genetic manipulation.[1]

Many domesticated species live with us as pets: where the individual spirit of the animal is respected, we can learn much from each other. However, the captivity and servitude imposed upon wild animals is less easy to tolerate or excuse. The word 'animal' derives from the Latin *anima* or soul, as if to remind us that human beings are also animals who have souls. Animals are infinitely patient of our human clumsiness, our inability to read clear sensory signals and to comprehend the simplest soul-communication. The great naturalist, Konrad Lorenz, wrote that it is 'animal politeness' never to stare another animal in the eyes; he himself always gazed at his animal friends with soft, unfocused eyes that encompassed their whole being.

Many people find using any part of an animal for nourishment or clothing repugnant. Vegetarians and vegans are rightly repulsed by the lack of true reciprocity between ourselves and animals, whom we regard as a commodity rather than as living beings. Factory farming and inhumane slaughter reflect the desacralization of our society and our separation from the cosmic web. People frequently ask whether meat-eating and shamanism are compatible. There is no single answer to this; it depends on many factors. Our teeth proclaim us to be an omnivorous species, whose ancestors have eaten many food-stuffs in order to stay alive. It is our attitude to our food that counts. If you eat meat, you should acknowledge the animal's sacrifice; if you eat vegetables, it follows that you should do the same. If you live in the polar regions, like the Inuit or the Saami, then the vegetarian option is not available; you are totally dependent upon animals for food and clothing since no vegetation grows for the best part of the year.

In his expedition to the Iglulik Eskimos in 1921–24, Knud Rasmussen reported one hunter as saying, 'The greatest peril of life lies in the fact that human food consists entirely of souls. All the creatures we have to kill and eat, all those we have to strike down and destroy to make clothes for ourselves, have souls, as we have.'[2] Indigenous peoples who live by hunting or fishing cope with this realization by employing rituals of respect and gratitude; they use every part of an animal, they do not kill breeding animals or those with young, they do not kill more than they need.

In our own time, animals are acting as important teachers, patiently enduring and revealing the truths which humankind is ignoring: that each life-form has its purpose in the universe, that certain wise memories are in danger of being lost from physical reality if we continue to eradicate certain species, that human beings are also animals, dependent upon and part of the food-chain.

We regard our human species as a totally different order of beings. However, we are merely more developed members of the animal world. Animals have formed the basic template of human existence in both shape and behaviour, but humans have further developed these: we have turned from quadrupeds into bipeds, and we have learned how to combine not just in family groups but in other social relationships. Humans have developed brains which not only reason, but can communicate and influence their environment, but we still have to learn how to interact with other species in a responsible way.

Within humankind we can see traces of many life-forms: our bones have the density of the mineral world; our internal organs have the liquidity and cellular structure of the plant world; our outer physical shell betrays traces of earlier animal species in our scale-like skins, in our nails and hair. Our brains have the mineral realm's ability to create crystalline order, the plant realm's ability to intuit and broadcast meaning in our sphere of influence, the animal realm's ability to hunt and to desire. We could not have acquired these traits and abilities without the prior forms of life.

Many naturalists have begun to approach animals as kin rather than as objects of study, so that the ancient cycle of spiritual relationship between humans and animals is being re-established. Most tribal groups associate themselves with a particular animal who is viewed as a progenitor or guardian. During the rites of passage of many indigenous peoples, including those of North America and Africa, young people discover their particular guardian animal, and learn its lessons.

Animal Helpers

Shamans work with animal spirits in a variety of ways. Each has a primary guardian animal, often called a power animal, because it guards our power and resonates to our own distinct nature or energy vibration. A guardian animal is our guide between the worlds and the companion who helps us on journeys, supporting our quest. Just as human beings are not alone in physical reality, neither are shamans alone when they travel to the otherworlds. No shamanic work is undertaken unless the shaman can raise the help of at least one spirit; she may work with more, but she will never pass into the three worlds without a helper.

Many of us already feel a strong resonance with a particular animal, and it is possible that it will be encountered when we go to find a guardian animal for shamanic work, but this does not necessarily follow. The kinds of animals which people acquire as allies are various. There is a good deal of confusion about this. Some people assume that they can shop around for the animal of their choice: when you meet your guardian animal, you will find that it is the other way about – the animal chooses you! Some people expect an imposing or 'noble' animal to turn up and are very disappointed when, instead of an eagle, they find themselves companioned by a rodent. All animals are equal upon the cosmic web: none is better or worse than another, only possessed of different powers and skills. In your shamanic work, you may require the senses of a bat rather more than you need the grace and strength of a tiger.

In seeking a guardian animal for the first time, some species are less suitable as primary helpers. It is not usually desirable to have an insect or reptile as a guardian animal; this is due to no negative quality in reptiles or insects, but because a primary animal is usually one that is nearer in kind to our human condition.

The chain of evolutionary life shows that our nearest cousins are mammalian and it is these who most often appear and offer themselves. However, there are notable exceptions: some people have bird, fish, reptilian and insect guardian animals because of certain special skills they are able to mediate in their shamanizing. Such individuals are often less easy to be with: not because they have any negative intentions, but because the primary nature of their power-current feels less human, less mammalian to other people. Bird-people are often visionary, fish-people often explore hidden or submerged principles, snake-people often facilitate transformations, insect-people often work in subtle organizational and networking ways. Such people often become outstanding specialists in their shamanic field, but they also need to work upon their mammalian and human relationships in order to manifest what they mediate in helpful human ways. Bird, fish, reptilian and insect helpers usually come along when the walker between the worlds is more experienced, or is learning specific healing techniques.

There are many books and divinatory systems available and these attempt to define the qualities of guardian animals in human terms; they are often supportive to our understanding, but remember that your personal experience and inter-relation with your animal is more important than the definitions of others.[3]

☙ *Practice 14:* Seeking Permission

Human beings usually take the physical parts of other living beings without asking permission. Thoughtless use of living beings creates blockages and imbalances, and merely compounds the current notion of the world as a convenient packaged place. Before taking any part of a living being, whether you are picking a plant, pruning a tree, milking a cow or taking a chicken's eggs to eat, be present in spirit to that being. Ask and listen before taking, seek permission and offer thanks for that being's sacrifice. It is the habit of some indigenous peoples to offer saliva or a hair from their heads, a song or some other offering as a token of exchange before plucking a herb or lopping a tree. If you take, be sure that you also give back.

This practice may be also used when seeking to use some part of a being which is no longer living in physical reality, such as the feathers, pelt or horns of a road-killed animal. Before utilizing any parts of a dead animal, it is good to make a journey to its spirit and seek permission, since its spirit would be part of any shamanic equipment that you make. Similarly, if you are going to make use of the subtle essences, the very spirit of plants for sacred or healing purposes, permission is essential. Asking permission should not be used to show your enlightened spirit to others; it is a private act of politeness which becomes habitual and creates a reciprocity between all beings on the cosmic web. If our need is expressed, permission is more often granted than denied; if you experience a massive 'no' to your request, go back and examine your true needs. Sometimes a reciprocal service will be asked of you, so be prepared to maintain your side of the agreement.

**Permit yourself to join the living network of the
cosmic web as a kindred soul.**

2. THE GREEN WORLD

When you can see each leaf as a separate thing, you can see the tree; when you can see the tree, you can see the spirit of the tree; when you can see the spirit of the tree, you can talk to it and maybe begin to learn something.
– William J. Bausch *Storytelling: Imagination and Faith*

Several thousand species of grasses, trees, herbs and other plants clothe our earth: we take their spectacular variety for granted, using them to provide us with food, medicine, shelter and clothing, responding to the beauty of their flowers and scents.

Our Plant–Human Kinship

The life of plants is still mysterious to most of us; we fail to understand that plants are also alive, that they have spirits. Scientific research has proved that plants have their magnetic force-fields, that they are sensitive to their surroundings and to the treatment they receive.[4] These findings have been greeted with derision among those who do not acknowledge their relationship to the green world, so that 'talking to plants' has become a byword in lunacy. Yet the amazing results of human communication with plants is a fact in both Findhorn, Scotland and Perelandra, Virginia, where plant-life flourishes contrary to all human expectation.[5]

Elsewhere, a terrible human expediency governs the way in which we regard plants. The widespread use of chemical pesticides to control plant growth and deter parasitic insects is achieved at a cost, for it tampers with the food-chain, poisons the soil, kills off micro-organisms and causes degeneration in the immune systems of all life-forms. Dr Jerome Weisner, science counsellor to President John F. Kennedy, reported that 'Use of pesticides is more dangerous than atomic fall-out.'[6] The eating of organically grown food-stuffs is thus not a luxury or a fad, it is a necessity for healthy living.

The effect of abuse upon the spirits of plants is incalculable. Human beings are now reaping the harvest of long-term chemical intervention by suffering increased immune-system failure, rising rates of respiratory diseases and a widespread allergic response to basic food-stuffs that have hitherto been our staple diet.

In order to convince governments to prevent the destruction of the once vast Amazonian rainforests and the unique habitats that are found only there, ecologists have promoted the medicinal value to humankind of the many plants which grow there. But the green world has its own dignity and status; it deserves to be respected for its own self, not just as a pharmacy for human survival.[7]

Psychotropic Plants

Many traditional societies use psychotropic plants in order to achieve mild ecstatic states for recreation, just as the fermented and alcoholic derivatives of plants and their fruits are used socially all over the world (except in Muslim countries where they are forbidden). But the shamanic use of plants for sacred purposes is a different matter and traditional shamans never employ them without good preparation and strong intention.

Throughout time, the strong spirits of ergots of barley and rye, hallucinogenic mushrooms, narcotic poppies and vines have been used to source the otherworld. Sacred traditions speak of the properties of Soma, of the transformatory Holy Grail, of the sacred drink which inspires and initiates.

However, few people in the West have ever been instructed in the use of psychotropic substances as a means of shamanic journeying; we do not have elders who can teach us the pathways, dangers and benefits. It is for this reason, and because our own society has a recreational and selfish attitude to drug-taking, that I have never advocated drug-use in combination with shamanism. It simply is not necessary, since other journeying methods are readily available. Traditional shamans may know how to journey by these means and be able to adjust dosage to the metabolism of each individual and help rescue souls from bad experiences, but in contemporary society we have no such traditional knowledge, and the dangers of using substances whose effects and powers we have not been called to learn is immense. Recreational use of hard drugs is a form of self-abuse which, combined with an ignorance of otherworldly realities, can lead to extreme soul-loss and death. During drug-use there is a great danger of being lost out in otherworlds. The dissociated and disoriented manner of the seasoned drug-user is a fair indication of the soul-erosion that goes on; unhealthy dependencies lead to irresponsible and criminal acts which injure the delicate web of life.

Plants for Food and Healing

How did our ancestors first discover the properties of each plant? The only method seems to have been physical experimentation, since there were no books to consult. But we may conceive of another way: that shamans sought communication with the spirits of the green world and received the knowledge through sourcing and journeying. My respect for our ancestors who were taught the uses of powerful and poisonous plants by the spirits is immense. This traditional lore has been handed down to us and the core healing remedies are still derived from this ancestral spirit-derived knowledge. Despite the addition of complex pharmocological products to our medicine cabinets, we still need this ancient knowledge to heal our ills. For example, we still use the anti-rheumatic qualities of willow (*Salix alba*), the anti-depressant power of St John's Wort (*Hypericum perforatum*), the digestive qualities of peppermint (*Mentha* × *piperita*), and these are still components of orthodox and homeopathic medicines alike, simple and powerful wisdom from the plant spirits. Plants heal, scent and nourish us every day.

Myths speak of the mighty spirits of the green world who instruct humans in the use of these substances, to institute agriculture and to harvest food and inspiration from the use of plants. These myths are particularly strong in the Americas, which have retained memory of these spirit-contacts. The abundant plants of the Americas now appear on tables worldwide: tomatoes, potatoes, maize and squash, not forgetting chocolate, which is appreciated everywhere. We should remember, too, that the primal use of tobacco was and is for sacred, not recreational, purposes.

The distillation of plant and mineral essences to form an alchemical tincture is the process by which the true 'elixir of immortality' is obtained, for they reconnect us with the cosmic web. The gentle plant essences, like the Bach Flower Remedies distilled in the county of Oxfordshire where I live, are invaluable ways of working with plant spirits. Essences are now made all over the world, including California and Australia: check your local health shop. Such plant and flower essences are non-addictive and can help us slow down the accelerating pace of human life so that we may appreciate the spiritual wisdom of that plant.

Trees

Trees are the giants of the green world. Their wisdom is recognized in all societies, many of which look on them as teachers who store and disseminate knowledge. One of the earliest means of recording knowledge was by using the language of trees. The names for the letters of the Irish alphabet derive from trees, and the ancient Irish *filidh*, the vision-poets, preserved secret teachings by means of inscribed strokes in wood, known as *ogham*.[8] Many methods of divining employed trees. The association of trees with language continues in our own time, with the use of wood-pulp to make paper; without trees, we would not be able to read books or newspapers. The compressed memory of aeons is part of a tree's inheritance.

> 'Living matter is stored information in the cells and in the genes ... there is more information of a higher order of sophistication and complexity stored in a few square yards of forest than there is in all the libraries of mankind. Obviously, that is a different order of information ... It is the information that has been flowing for millions of years. In this total information context, man may not be necessarily the highest or most interesting product.'[9]

The clear-cutting of trees for timber and wood-pulp products, and the damaging deforestation of the earth, assisted by acid rain from toxic chemical emissions, seriously affects all life-forms. Vegetation exists by photosynthesis whereby carbon dioxide is combined with water using energy taken in from sunlight by chloroplasts, which produces oxygen as well as the plant's food; animals breathe in oxygen and breathe out carbon dioxide, thus there is an all-important chain of dependence. The tropical rainforests maintain the planetary environment by evapotranspiration, pumping water back into the air, causing cloud condensation; these clouds reflect back the sunlight which would otherwise heat and dry up the regions beneath.[10] Plants are therefore a bridge between mineral and animal life-forms. We are finally discovering that we cannot tinker with the green world without detriment to the earth.

✋ *Practice 15*: Harvesting Seed

One small seed is a storehouse and memory bank and can become the progenitor of many plants. The potential seeding capacity of any plant or tree is enormous. In wild places some plants flourish unchecked, but around inhabited places few plants have this ability. Human beings have encouraged

flowering species and cultivated the plants which supply their table or pharmacy, but have eradicated others as weeds. Discover which indigenous plant
species are threatened with extinction in your area and acquire some seed
which will flourish in your soil-type, climate and habitat. It is important that
you use seed which has been produced your region and is not imported.
Also ensure that if the plant is not self-pollinating, you raise both male and
female varieties in the same place. Rare plant seeds are available from specialist suppliers, which are usually listed in gardening journals and herbal
supply chains. Check that your local soil conditions are appropriate.

On a windless day, hold the seeds in one hand, shake your rattle over
them with the other, closing your eyes and allowing the rattle to speak with
the seeds. Sense the way in which these seeds are connected to the cosmic
web and listen to their voices, communicate always with the spirits of the
seeds. You may receive a power-song from the seeds which you can use
when planting.

When the weather and season are correct for planting, prepare the earth
carefully, singing or chanting a song of preparation quietly. Make a bed for
the seeds with the care you would use for putting a child to bed. Rattle over
the earth; include rain, wind and sun in your song. Plant the seeds sparing-
ly and tend them as they grow, protecting them against insects or birds
which find them tasty, using natural and organic methods. Watch the
growth and flowering as the year unfolds, and be ready to harvest some of
the seedheads when they are ripe, leaving some on the plant to disperse
naturally. Store the seeds in a special pot; share them with friends to plant
in their gardens. This method can be used whether you have a garden or a
window-box.

✋ *Practice 16:* Plant and Tree Wisdom

The nineteenth-century Rabbi Nachman of Breslov said, 'How wonderful it
would be if one could only be worthy of hearing the song of the grass.'[11]
Using shamanism we can, for it is not just humans who talk to plants, but
plants who talk to us. Contacting the spirits of plants can be done in both
physical and subtle realities. Choose a healthy, living plant or tree and study
it carefully in its own habitat. Greet it and listen. Be present to it in spirit

and, without deep sourcing, ask it to share its wisdom with you. You will find that plants, especially trees, live at a much slower rate than animals. Thank the plant and record your impressions, cross-checking these with a book or someone who knows the properties of that plant.

When you have become proficient in journeying, you can extend this practice to journey to the plant through your Middleworld entrance (see Practice 23) in order to meet its spiritual form in a much more powerful way. Again, go with the intention of asking for wisdom or knowledge, and how it should be applied. Always listen carefully to what the spirits tell you. If it is appropriate, ask questions about usage: Which parts of the plant are to be used – root, leaves, flowers, stem? What is the purpose of plant? How is the plant to be prepared and administered – internally or externally? What advice does the spirit of the plant give you that is non-medicinal: you may receive a song, ritual or dance, for example, which is the primary way of healing.

I keep a regiment of herbals and plant-identification books on my shelves in order to cross-check everything I'm told by the plant-spirits themselves. I haven't yet been led astray, but the golden rule with all identification is: if you can't identify it or it looks remarkably like a poisonous species – DO NOT USE IT. Never prescribe for someone else, unless you are a medically qualified practitioner.

Repeat this practice with different species of tree and plant. Some will become close allies in your work; keep parts of these plants in your shamanic bag (see Practice 62).

Insects

Because the human response to insects is often revulsion, insects are regarded as evil. People wonder why insects were created since they seem to have little usefulness. However, insects may be tiny, creeping things, but they are also very powerful. Their functions vary tremendously. The winged pollinators are the long-range messengers of the insect world, while burrowing and other recycling scavengers transform the earth. Insects and plants are interdependent – plants evolved into new forms as a result of insect pollination.[12]

The insect plant-helper (see below) has a close association with one or many plants to whose spirits you may journey when you are more experienced. An insect helper lends its highly developed senses to the shaman, helping her home in on specific plant usages and the correlations between the plant qualities and a healthy ecological balance in all beings.

Universal shamanic healing practice reveals that spiritual intrusions in a sick body often appear to subtle reality vision as insect-like in form. I believe that they appear in these guises in the sick human body in much the same way that insects seem to form 'disposal squads' in the garden, eating up what is diseased or wasted. In human healing, the shaman will extract such spiritual intrusions and attempt to rebalance the sickness with the help of his spirits, but this is advanced work that goes beyond the scope of this book.

✋ *Practice 17:* Insect Plant-helpers

Plant-helpers are healers. If you want to work extensively with plants as a healer or herbalist, you will need to contact an insect helper to teach you plant wisdom, since insects are the bridges between plants and animal life. Shamans will sometimes journey in the shape of their insect helper in order to seek out the best plant or herb for a specific illness.

The following method will help you find an insect–plant alliance if you are drawn to plant medicine. This is advanced work which appears here by virtue of its subject matter: do not attempt this practice until you are very proficient in otherworld journeying and have acquired and extensively worked with guardian animals and teachers *in all three worlds*.

1. With your guardian animal, journey to a plant you've already visited. Commune with the plant's spirit and, together, call out for an insect helper to assist you in plant work.
2. Ask any insect if it is your helper. Follow the instructions for accepting or refusing as given in Chapter 4.
3. The way you accept your insect is different, however: to cement your alliance, both of you eat a small portion of the plant, *in subtle reality*. Thank plant and insect.

4. Do not bring your insect helper back into your world. If you require its help in everyday situations, call it up through gentle sourcing.

3. STONE PEOPLE

I can see with the eyes of a stone, and think with its thoughts, and feel with its layers and strata.

– William Mayne *Earthfasts*

A few years back I met with a Cree medicine woman who was a stone companion: most of her spirit allies were stones. Her greatest desire was to be worthy to become of one the stone people herself: a wish which would baffle most people today as they consider stones to be dead. Yet vegetable gums and other substances harden to become minerals, as coal and amber do. Even animals and their impressions can become hard and fossilized as stone. Life-forms evolve, die and return to the earth, retaining memory: they take on other life.

Our ancestors have accorded special qualities to different forms of stone throughout time. We have valued precious stones and used them for their healing and prophylactic properties. We have reverenced sky-falling stones – meteors – as gods: Moslems still pray facing Mecca where the Black Stone, a meteor once venerated as a goddess, is set in the Qa'aba. We have set up monoliths and circles, places of meeting, worship and dancing which endure across millennia. In Britain, we hang up stones with holes in them, called 'hag-stones', to bring health and luck, to ward off the evil eye.

Myths reveal strong belief in the spiritual virtue of stones. In the Germanic versions of the Grail legend, the Grail itself is a green stone which falls from Lucifer's crown. In Hindu scripture, Vishnu, the preserver, wears upon his chest the jewel, Treasure of the Ocean, which manifests itself in all that shines: the sun, moon, fire and speech. In Gnostic scriptures, the pearl of great price is the image of the soul.

Metals and minerals also have their spirits. Smiths and metal-workers have always been regarded as magicians, capable of transformatory processes. The work of alchemy is to understand the universe through the transmutation of matter, working specifically with metals, through the gamut of lead to gold. Gold has been seen as the revitalizing energy of the sun as well as the blood of Mother Earth, as the final perfection of matter. Greed for the economic value of gold has degraded this ancient belief. Alchemy is truly the art of becoming allied to the full spectrum of life-forms, from mineral to spirit worlds. Classical alchemy was closely related to the unfolding path of the spirit. Many alchemical texts read like complex shamanic journeys, where the alchemists have become aware of the spirits of the minerals with which they worked. The Egyptian alchemist, Zosimos, experienced a vision of seven planetary stages each guarded by the spirit forms of metals.[14]

Minerals form the basis of our planet's structure. All life draws nourishment from the mineral realm. Although they appear to be inert, dense matter, stones and minerals are capable of imparting essential life; this is evident from studying anyone suffering from mineral deficiencies – when the appropriate salt or mineral traces are supplied, that person's energy becomes revitalized.

Stones, metals and minerals are responsive to certain forms of sound. Tibetan singing bowls, which are used in meditation, are alchemically made of the seven metals and create a medley of rainbow sounds in which the overtones of the universal music can be heard. Such bowls (now rarely made of such precious metals) can become powerful bridges between the worlds. The shaman's costume invariably has pieces of metal sewn into it which jingle and vibrate as he dances.

Aldous Huxley wrote: 'Precious stones are precious because they bear a faint resemblance to the glowing marvels seen with the inner eye of the visionary.'[14] The present preoccupation with crystal therapy may seem a modern invention, but crystals have been used for shamanic vision and healing for centuries. North American medicine bundles contain crystals. In North Asia, crystals were believed to cause rain and were called 'rain stones'. Mongols dried crystals to prevent rain, while the Altai people smoked them in fires and the Yakuts threw them up to the sun. Elsewhere crystals were used to heal, by impregnating the patient with the essential energy of the universe.

Crystals are like radio transmitters, which receive information and pass it on. They store energy and power in exactly the same way as microchips. They also act as amplifiers of such energy and are therefore very powerful.

Stones and crystals have spirits which must be respected. To draw upon their essential qualities without permission is to be spiritually manipulative. Very few crystal-healing teachers or books seem to mention this: they are more interested in the techniques and what they can achieve.[15] The whole-sale mining of crystals and their indiscriminate use is an unfortunate feature of the West's spiritual materialism.

The Cherokee teacher, Dhyani Ywahoo, speaks truly when she says:

'... misuse of crystal energy can be as destructive to the physical and light bodies as the use of drugs. Many of the so-called "enlightened crystal teachings" can potentially kill a person. It is especially dangerous to place crystals upon one's energy centres or to sit within certain configurations of crystals without having established stability of mind and purity of action.'[16]

Crystals mirror our actions and thoughts directly onto the cosmic web; they amplify any imbalances within us. If we remember that, we will always use them with respect.

Stones, metals and minerals are attuned to the essential structure of the cosmos; they also permit us to become tuned to the universe. The whole of modern technology is based upon this premise, as we rely upon the micro-chip to store and retrieve memory, and on fibre-optics to exchange information. Shamanic reality becomes manifest every day all around us.

👋 Practice 18: Consulting the Stone People

Hold any stone, mineral or gemstone: study its surfaces and texture; with your eyes closed, feel the creative power and life within it. Be present to it in spirit.

You may wish to sing or rattle to begin a gentle sourcing while holding the stone, with the intention of meeting its spirit and seeing if it is willing to become your ally.

Consult this stone ally through journeying to ask what nature of help or qualities it possesses, and whether you may have permission to use these in your work.

Remember to give thanks.

✋ Practice 19: Learning from Crystals

If you are drawn to work with crystals, select a clear quartz crystal or other stone that has not been used by anyone else. Cleanse it by leaving it for one complete lunation (mooncycle of 28–29 days) in a dish of crystal sea-salt out of doors and exposed to the elements. Holding it in your hand, make a journey to meet the spirit of the stone and ask if it willing to be your ally. Ask what it can teach you and how it is to be used. Keep your crystal wrapped or covered when you are not using it.

✋ Practice 20: Becoming the Earth

Earth is the seedbed for all growth. We can place dead things in soil and the processes of nature will break down their constituent parts and essences to create new life. All that we eat grows in this earth: we are the earth. Middle Eastern and other myths speak of humans and animals being made out of clay, fashioned by gods who breathed life into us. We also call soil 'humus', the word from which humility is derived. Soil is not dirt, it is the humus of which we are all made. Indigenous peoples ensure that all animal and plant residues are returned to the earth, where they can decompose into humus and re-enter the life-cycle. All organic matter can help make compost which we can spread upon the earth in our gardens to enrich what we grow.

This practice is useful in acclimatizing you to a new environment or country, helping put you in touch with the spirits of that region in the quickest possible way. Go outdoors and find a patch of earth which has not been polluted by chemical waste or fertilizers. It doesn't have to be a pretty place, just somewhere where the soil has been left to be itself. Touch the soil and greet it. Pick up a palmful; with closed eyes, smell and feel it. Be present to its spirit. Grind a little finely between your fingers and taste some, then spit it out. Now sit and be with the earth of that region, gently sourcing through chant or song. Allow impressions from the soil to emerge in your song in sounds or words. Return home and journey to the spirit of that patch of earth and ask it to be your ally in acclimatizing to your new place. This practice will be greatly aided if, in the first few months of your move, you start to include a majority of locally grown food-stuffs into your diet.

4. FAERIES, GODS AND UNICORNS
No god is without animality, no animal without humanity,
no man without a part of divinity.
– Alain Daniélou *Shiva and Dionysus*

All cultures have called upon or been visited by spirits which are not nor ever have been human: mythic animals, faeries and deities are the most common. These spirits have subtle reality forms which inhabit the three worlds; they manifest in physical reality in many different ways, seen by children, visionaries, seers and prophets, apprehensible to shamans and those who have attuned themselves to forms of subtle reality.

As you begin to journey through the three worlds, you will encounter a variety of such spirits and they may become your allies and teachers. This chapter attempts to introduce you to them and how they operate in a shamanic way. We will be meeting human spirits, heroes, saints and ancestors in Chapters 4, 5 and 6.

Mythic Animals

The appearance of mythic animals while you are shamanizing should not be treated as a breakdown of your reason, nor indeed as an occasion to vaunt your prowess. Mythic animals sometimes appear as occasional helpers in certain situations. Unicorns, dragons or phoenixes are beasts who solely inhabit subtle reality and so their wisdom is primarily about understanding otherworldly concepts: such beasts symbolize pristine archetypes, and they come as teachers to assist us to pass over and through, to transcend or transform. The knowledge of the unicorn and dragon occurs worldwide, indicating that unrelated civilizations have envisioned and encountered them in subtle reality. They often appear depicted as heraldic supporters of royal shields or as guardians of national institutions, testifying to the fact that their powers are recognized and their protection sought.

Extinct species of animals also become inhabitants of subtle reality only, although they do not usually join the ranks of mythic beasts. Recently extinct animals rarely appear as allies: I believe that they are busy coming to terms with their new subtle reality state. Certain forms of extinct animals appear to us to warn us that we are approaching a crossroad or threshold. Although they rarely appear as primary helpers, their wisdom or support is often synchronous.

Certain climactic, seasonal and social changes may bring us into reso-nance with animals no longer living on the earth. The widespread dinosaurophilia due to Michael Crichton's book, *Jurassic Park*, is a case in point: carnivorous raptors of the Jurassic era may invade our dreams with awe and fear, but they also subtly reflect the saurian nature of our ravenous consumer society. Few would want a dinosaur helper, but one such extinct species may appear in popular consciousness to teach the lesson of greed to living species who sometimes seem hell-bent on extinction themselves.

Faeries

When we work in the Middleworld, we frequently encounter faeries. Although they have been reported as very small, they have also appeared as very large: these size variations are due to the unlimited dimensionality of the cosmic web, which cannot be defined by human concepts of space and time. Our ancestors were careful to acknowledge their faery neighbours, to offer them food and goods and to be vigilant about not trespassing or build-ing on faery dancing grounds, assembly points or pathways.

Faery lore is found the world over. The Pakistani *bitan* (shaman), Ibrahim of Altit, describes his experience with the faeries or *peri* thus:

> 'Ordinary people can't see the fairies. But who sees them? First of all, the *bitan*; and after that, the *pashu*, the seer. Between people and the fairies, there is a veil … We pour millet [over the offering] and worship the *peri*. We do *barayo* [calling and requesting]. At this request, the fairies begin to gather during the night.'[17]

The alliance between faeries and humans is well attested. Practical methods of contacting and co-operating with faery allies are given in the book *Earth Light* by R.J. Stewart, who has a wide personal experience of the faery world.

Reports of faeries abducting children or coming as lovers to human adults are commonplace. People have even reported living among them, or being taken into their dwellings. Nowadays, with the increasing noise and industrialization of our world, the faeries are less often encountered and talked about and these reports have become blamed on UFO abductions!

Faeries and elemental spirits often have close association. If you are near the sea, do not be surprised to see mermaids, mermen or naiads in your journeying. Likewise, gnomes and dwarfs appear near caverns and mountains and sylphs and salamanders in cliffs and in fires; tree-elementals or dryads will be found in forests.

Deities and Teachers

The dance of the deities upon the cosmic web causes great disquiet among those who practise spiritual totalitarianism, only allowing the existence and authority of their own gods, and regarding all others as disobedient spirits who do not conform to the rules; yet many primal deities and spirits remain embedded in our regional cultures, retaining their power and connection with our world.

We may understand deities as wavebands of power, having different frequencies and qualities, but all deriving from the universal web of the cosmos. People worldwide have interfaced with deities and they have often reported startlingly similar experiences. For example, we can appreciate the close links between the Christian Virgin Mary, the Chinese Kwan Yin and the Tibetan Tara, to whom the devout go for last-ditch assistance as well as for daily motherly support. The appearance and myth may be dissimilar, but their common pattern is like a waveband signature which cannot be mistaken.

Many critical junctions in the cosmic web are marked by a mixture and meeting of powers. Most often deities take human shape but they may appear as a mixture of species. For example there are Hanuman and Ganesh, the Hindu gods with monkey and elephant heads, the Egyptian gods with ibis and cow heads, Thoth and Hathor, and Dionysus and Christ who appear as men and as wine.

It has been frequently pointed out that people create god in their own image. It is in our best interests to seek out the spirits which are most beneficial and resonant to our path. Where deities have not been relegated to the scrap-heap, they often prove to be powerful sources of assistance. In Tibet and Nepal, for example, the pre-Buddhist land spirits are not relegated to infernal regions but are actively sought out by Buddhist practitioners as guardians and supporters of the dharma. They act as threshold guardians who maintain standards of spiritual behaviour.

You may not end up working with existent god-forms but you will certainly encounter their archetypal frequencies in different ways, usually when you go to find your teachers in the three worlds (see Chapters 4, 5 and 6).

The idea of a spirit teacher is not the same as a mediumistic spirit guide who 'controls' the operator, nor like a discarnate spiritual guru to whom you show unswerving obedience. Walkers between the worlds seek teachers and allies in order to learn how the web is walked. We enter into alliances with spirits, not to become passively dependent upon them, but for a mutually beneficial friendship. There is a great sense of companionship and collegiality in the spirit world, through which we are enabled to become aware of a wider potential which transcends boundaries.

Spirit teachers and allies know the specifics of subtle reality, which we do not. They will guide, inspire, encourage and teach us; they will also show good discernment, rebuke us and pull our legs when we become pompous. They will not become spiritual dictators who tell us how to run every aspect of our lives, although we may indeed consult them when we have problems which we cannot deal with. They will not take those problems away, but they may offer solutions which we then implement. Spirit teachers will remind us of neglected shamanic duties or promises, but they are not nannies.

Why should gods, spirits, mythic animals and faeries bother themselves with humans at all? The answer is that they all lack something which human beings have: mortality and the continuum of physical reality life. Just as we humans seek experience of subtle reality and so increase our knowledge and understanding, so the non-human spirits wish to experience physical reality. The descent of gods to earth and to mortal forms can be seen as their spiritual progress. The greatest 'saviour deities' are those who, like Osiris, Demeter, Rhiannon and Christ, all enter into the human condition and take the initiation of mortality.

Truly, humans and spirits are the initiators and gatekeepers of each other's realities. We learn from each other and grow together in understanding. Our capacity for teaching our allies about physical reality should not be underestimated: this is often a humbling experience as the shortcomings of human nature become apparent, but at least we are attempting to reconnect our different spiritual kindred in a more loving way.

Questions About Your Spirit Helpers

As you start to use this book practically, certain issues and questions may arise about allies. These are the most common:

I'm unhappy about trusting my helper/s.
You may have an innately reserved or distrustful nature, but this problem occurs most frequently with those who are dependent upon a dualistic spirituality, whether they practise its ideas or not. As in life, you just have to trust some people: bus-drivers, pilots, dry-cleaners and dentists may be fallible human beings but we have to trust them or we wouldn't venture out of the door. We always retain our free will. If a piece of advice strikes you as inappropriate, or if your allies suggest something you aren't ready to implement, you don't have to.

My helpers don't come when I call.
There may be a good reason for this. You may be unprepared through tiredness or illness. You may have lost power and need to re-source yourself. Ignoring your helpers' advice may lead to a temporary breakdown in communication until you have implemented it. Persistent neglect of your helpers ranks with not calling up your closest friends; they will understand if you have good reasons not to, but sheer wilful neglect presupposes lack of mutual respect.

My helpers don't talk to me.
This problem arises most often in relation to our animal/s. Just because animals don't speak in physical reality doesn't mean to say that they can't in subtle reality. Most spirits can and do speak, while others are of a similar

school to the mime-artist, Marcel Marceau: their body-language speaks volumes. Words may not come out of their mouths: they may speak directly to your heart so that you are aware of receiving their response. Another reason for non-communication may be that *you* are doing all the talking. Conversation is a two-way street, so allow space for response.

I feel that I am answering myself.
When we begin to source, it is often not very deeply. It is sometimes hard to distinguish between our allies and our own thoughts. Concentrate on being present to your helpers, don't analyse whence advice comes but be thankful and receive. Some days, communication will seem trite; on others, the secrets of the universe explode through every pore of your being.

How can I be sure that the figure I meet is really my ally or teacher?
This common fear arises from a real disquiet about our potential for self-deception. Use the same common sense and instinct about a spirit which proclaims itself your ally as you would for checking out any human. Your particular allies will usually appear well-defined and full of vitality and significance for you. You may well have already encountered an ally in a dream or vision, so it will be familiar. Animals shine with health and are glad to see you. Spirit teachers are notably matter of fact and down to earth; they do not appear as portentous beings in puffs of smoke, spouting upholstered wisdom. All true allies have the eyes of integrity and trustworthiness. You will know your ally is an ally as you know a best friend is your best friend. Our allies choose us, not we them; the kindred companionship that springs up can only be experienced.

I see figures in cartoon, not in real forms.
This experience sometimes happens to people with missing soul-parts, especially those who are living their lives at someone else's behest or vicariously through a partner or children. Such people often see cartoon worlds as well. When the soul-part returns, or the life-style is changed, then subtle reality is resumed. *Note:* Helpers will sometimes assume cartoon-like attributes in order to make a special point: check the context and see if this is the case. (For more about soul-loss, see Chapter 8.)

I can't see my teacher's face.
The form is hazy or keeps changing. It may take a few visits to see your
teacher's face with any clarity. Our spirits try to help us by taking the forms
we can most easily work with. Our fear or anxiety can cause fluctuating or
hazy images. But just as a blind person can instinctively recognize someone
who is familiar without having to hear or see them, so we too can distinguish if this ally is the same one we met last time: their qualities and general feel will still be apparent even if the form is not yet settled down.

How can I have a teacher who is a spiritual leader?
A sense of awe, outrage, astonishment or unworthiness can often accompany the realization that one of your teachers is a spiritual leader, a saint or
god. You may have turned your back on your childhood faith only to find
that a venerable rabbi or Moses appears to be your shamanic mentor. Spirit
can appear in any form, and will assume the shape most able to approach
us. Sometimes, after a period of working with such a figure, a less archetypal or more approachable teacher, who is easier to relate to, may appear. We
often encounter primary spiritual figures of this kind as threshold guardians
of our spiritual lineage; see p.179.

Can I have a shamanic ally who is a living person?
No, this is not advisable. We sometimes encounter living people during
journeying: usually it will be someone who is an important inspirational fig-
ure or a person who is mundanely involved with you. When a living exem-
plar touches your life, you enter the special alliance of their spiritual lineage.
Such a bond is actively part of many spiritual traditions from the Apostolic
Succession of the Catholic Church to the transmission of wisdom from
Tibetan lamas to their pupils.

Respect for living teachers is as much a feature of shamanism as it is of
other pursuits: sports personalities, artists, musicians and writers who are
living exemplars of their craft may act as catalysts to constellate fresh
teachings, but shamanic allies will be animal, ancestral or in spirit form. If
people with whom you are having difficulties appear to you, then this may
be relevant to your quest or it may indicate that it is time that you sorted
out your differences.

How many helpers can I have?

While we all start with one animal and one teacher, your growing experi-ence in the otherworlds will lead to closer acquaintance with new helpers. Some will become very close friends, others will become professional allies who drop in when certain issues need dealing with; there may be gaps of months or years between the appearance of some. In practice, you will find yourself working towards having one very dear animal who accompanies you everywhere, a bunch of animals who have specific alliances with you, and a teacher or helping spirit in each of the worlds, as well as the acquain-tance of other spirits. There is no standard acceptable number or right kind of ally.

My guardian animal has changed.

Be aware that the changing of the guard happens from time to time: instead of your usual swan, for example, you may find that a wolf turns up when you start sourcing. This may indicate that your training is entering a new stage, or that the demands of your everyday life require a different kind of companion. There is usually a sense of being handed on to another ally, and a feeling that the cosmic dance has entered a new rhythm for you. When you consciously sense this change, then you are ready to learn something new. Your old animal may turn up again after a brief period, or become integrated into a small band of helpers and teachers. You need to ask some helpers for assistance: they are like friends who see you having difficulty but don't like to intrude. Often when we have taken a life-changing decision new allies turn up.

Sometimes I feel that I become my animal/teacher.

In walking between the worlds, we enter into deep states of non-duality where the boundaries and borders of identity become blurred. Many people experience flying or galloping as their animal, or feel that their teacher has become superimposed upon them. The longer you work with spirit helpers the closer the identification; you feel part of that animal family, allied to this tree-clan, and as close to your spiritual teachers as a daughter or sibling. But when your allies lend you their subtle reality bodies, then rejoice and be thankful, for it is a great honour and deep lesson!

I keep encountering a challenging spirit who won't let me pass.
Many allies appear as challengers. We tend to regard this as aggressive and threatening, yet we must learn to respond truthfully to such challenges when we journey. Many challengers guard thresholds to ensure that you understand where you are going and what your journeying there will mean. Always check your guardian animal's behaviour; if it seems totally calm and unconcerned, then rise to the challenge. If, for example, you encounter a giant with a staff at a threshold, ask him questions: 'What are you guarding? Why aren't you letting me pass?' If he asks you questions, respond, earn your right to pass by a friendly wrestling match if necessary. Be advised by your animal. If it counsels swift flight, then flee! We must learn to use the same kind of discrimination in subtle reality as we use in physical reality, employing our native caution and gut-response. You have free will, and don't have to accept everything as right for you if you are not ready. If, however, you are consistently blocked and challenged on your journeys, it may mean that you need some interventive help: consult a shamanic practitioner.

My ally/teacher won't tell me his/her name/gender.
Some animals and spirits do not identify themselves by names. I have known my fish as 'Fish' for over 20 years, but we have a perfectly intimate relationship. One of my teachers is known to me simply as 'Skeleton Woman', but she knows her stuff. Some allies are very chummy, while others reveal their nature more gradually. The gender of your animal can sometimes be unclear or can change: let it be what it wants to be. The appearance and gender of some teachers may also change, especially if they first appear in an archetypal 'wise teacher' form. One client of mine has a teacher who changes gender according to the nature of the issue on which she is journeying. Learn to perceive the identity of your allies in subtle ways.

I have just had a most extraordinary encounter with my ally: I hardly like to share it.
The experience of consuming one's animal or having sex with one's teacher is very common in journeys and can be extremely disconcerting. Be assured, your sexual fantasies are not taking over your life! When eating or sexual

encounters occur in this way, view the experience as an important assimilation of spiritual power. Your animal or teacher is sharing his power with you
in the most intimate way. We have to see the assimilation of ourselves and
our helpers in the light of the old Mystery Traditions, where the cooking
and consuming of the deity – be it Osiris, Dionysus or Christ – is ritually
shared. The human mind finds it very shocking, but this is what is at the
basis of the mystery of spiritual power-sharing. The literature of mysticism
reveals that union between worshipper and deity is commonplace. St Teresa
of Avila experienced the visitation of an angel:

> 'In his hands I saw a long golden spear and at the end of the iron tip I seemed
> to see a point of fire. With this he seemed to pierce my heart repeatedly so that
> it penetrated to my entrails – he left me completely afire with a great love of
> God. The pain was so great that I screamed aloud, but simultaneously felt such
> an infinite sweetness that I wished the pain would last eternally.'[18]

So might a virgin speak of the first night with her beloved! Whether we look
East or West, mystics and shamans everywhere speak of the ecstatic union
of themselves with the object of their worship or practice. Tibetan
Buddhism has a vast literature relating to the mystical relationship between
practitioner and tutulary deity which underscores this. Be assured, you are
privileged to have experienced such non-dual kinship.

❦ *Practice 21:* Inner Companion

When you were a child you probably had a secret, inner companion with
whom you conversed. The invisible friend may have inhabited the body of
a special toy. Bring that friend to mind; be spiritually present to him/her.
What wisdom did you learn? What kind of kinship was between you?
Through gentle sourcing, speak to that friend now and call up that deep
intimacy of spirit. Ask your companion to please prepare the way for you to
walk between the worlds, to alert your guardian animal, allies and teachers
that you will be coming to meet them soon.

116

The Middleworld

One touch of Nature makes the whole world kin.
    – William Shakespeare *Twelfth Night*

1. THE MOTHER PLACE
There is no state or condition more holy than the Earth.
    R.J. Stewart *Power Within the Land*

The earth is more than our physical home: it is the mother place, the matrix of planetary life, the locus from which we enter the Middleworld, the Underworld and the Upperworld. Since 1969, we have all been granted the privilege of seeing the physical reality of our planet as it looks from space: you would think that this would make it an even more precious place, but this has not generally been the case. For many, the earth is all that there is, for they have blocked out any consciousness of otherworlds. And yet they continue to abuse the only home they know. Only crazy people, or those who no longer feel safe within it, wreck their home. Only crazy people try to kill their mothers.

Throughout primal world cultures, the earth has been envisaged as possessed of a female and motherly spirit, whom people have been taught to honour, whose natural laws they have been taught to uphold. This view is now alien to the West. Technology has given the impression that Nature is now our servant. In the Middle Ages, Nature was often portrayed as a traipsing drudge, Dame Kinde, a simple, willing slave for the use of humankind, a degrading image inherited from the late Classical view of the *anima mundi*, the World Soul, as an impressionable and vacillating woman. This diminishment of the great Mother of Life underpins the Western vision of Nature and the natural world in which we live. Such desacralization is tempered by the shamanic, animistic view, which invites us to see the holiness and spirit in everything that is.

Environmentalists and deep ecologists concur that the old stories and myths of the earth are no longer adequate to the situation. The scientist, James Lovelock, has sought to restore the old view of the earth's spirit as Gaia, the ancient Greek Mother of Life. This redefinition has brought about a greater response and environmental concern than any consideration of the earth as a scientific phenomenon, comprised of inert matter and gases, could have done.

The Earthly Paradise

At some deep level, we each have an inbuilt sense of the perfect earth of the 'Golden Age', before everything went wrong. Countless myths relate how we lost communion with the earthly paradise, with Eden, the Fortunate Islands, with Avalon. Each loss is associated with the apple, fruit of the tree of the earthly paradise. We mourn its loss, as we mourn our disrespect for Nature, not understanding why things went wrong and half-hating ourselves for it. These myths have been conceived of as memories of earlier times when simple, primitive peoples flourished without benefit of civilization. Yet the 'Golden Age' is nothing less than a memory of Middleworld, within whose subtle reality the perfect pristine earth remains. Reconnection with the subtle reality of the Middleworld restores us to the 'Golden Age': we have never really lost anything.

Our separation from subtle reality has been so complete that we have told ourselves complex myths of how we came to be orphaned from goodness; ever since, we have ceased to even recognize the thresholds between the worlds for what they are, and have posted fiery angels or fearsome monsters to bar the ways. Our ancestors were well aware of the simultaneous realities of the worlds: some they experienced themselves, others were considered to be the province of shamans. Some ways became so completely covered by superstition and avoidance that no-one walked between them save priests: such blockages have caused massive planetary sickness and have severe consequences on the soul-health of all beings.

Discovering the Middleworld

In our enthusiasm to start journeying into subtle reality, we have to bypass centuries of rubble made up of fear, hope and thwarted possibilities. In seeking to rediscover the thresholds where we can walk between the worlds, we have to remember that although we have lost most of our sensitivity to spirit, we have also lost much of our innate caution and spiritual discrimination as well. We need the help of our allies to assist us to walk between the worlds, just as our allies need us to implement the healing which centuries of neglect have rendered necessary. No human being can, singly and alone, reconnect and bring healing between the worlds.

The Middleworld is our anchor-point, our starting place, our foundation. The Middleworld has two appearances: the ordinary physical appearance of the material world which we experience with our five senses, and the subtle appearance or spiritual reality which we appreciate with our subtle senses. Both are real. Each inter-relates with the other.

We may regard these two meshed realities by comparing a photograph and a painting of the same object. The photograph shows us the physical reality, while a good painting will show us something of the subtle reality as well, the spiritual form which is veiled by the physical form. Seers are born with the ability to see both realities at the same time: most shamans do not have this ability, but consciously access the subtle reality of the Middleworld through sourcing and journeying.

In everyday life, we become aware of the subtle reality of the Middleworld in many different ways through the faculty of our imagination, spiritual awakening, shock or loss of the familiar. Dante likens the beginning of his cosmological journey *The Divine Comedy* to being lost in a dark wood. Great thinkers, scientists and humanitarians have all entered into and partaken of the Middleworld's subtle reality: Einstein, Marie Curie,

Gandhi and others have journeyed deeply beyond the physical realities of the earth, impelled by compassion for its needs, to find pragmatic and implementable solutions. But for every one person who makes this journey there are many more who will not or cannot, through ignorance or fear: they remain the prisoners of one side of reality, their lives become one long avoidance of subtle reality in which imagination is shunned as dangerous, where the emotions become betrayers, where rigid control and strictly linear thought patrol the borders between realities.

Generally, we already skilfully move about within and interact with the energies of the subtle reality of the Middleworld in our daily lives. The unregarded synchronicities of life reveal this: without any conscious prior warning, a mother returns home early to catch her child's phone call from overseas, a man takes a sudden detour on a planned route and meets up with the business opportunity he really needs, a family decide not to take a flight which subsequently has an accident. These are all incidents where individuals have received messages from subtle reality. Many non-shamanic people are already skilful Middleworld travellers in subtle reality. We have all 'checked ahead' to intuit whether a garage is open, a friend already arrived at a station, there is any milk left in the fridge, where a lost object is located, where a parking space may be found: we automatically do a mini-journey, sending out a soul-part to check.

We journey to the Middleworld in order to deal with the present issues, with life on earth now. However, you may find yourself travelling forwards and backwards in time, especially if you are dealing with issues involving sequence and frequency. Middleworld journeys might also include travelling to a sacred site, to a sick friend, to a place far distant from you.

The Middleworld is being exhaustively worked by many people in psychotherapies at present; much of what passes for 'guided fantasy' or 'visualization' unconsciously accesses this world by getting clients to visualize their favourite recreation spot, or by calling up situations or helpers which can heal. Many people cannot face or are frightened of the Underworld or Upperworld, so it is the Middleworld that is often their prime means of healing. Middleworld journeying often liberates immediate potentialities and stirs up stagnant situations.

120

Inhabitants of the Middleworld

Beings encountered in the Middleworld include the elementals, in Western tradition called: gnomes (earth), sylphs (air), salamanders (fire) and undines (water). These may appear in other forms as dryads, fairies, elves, brownies, house spirits. The beings encountered here are terrestial entities, guardians and spirits of place who are concerned with the smooth running of the planet.

The female spirit or *juno* of the Middleworld is the Earth Mother or *anima mundi* who is known by many names: her champions often manifest as heroes and heroines who do not die, like King Arthur. The male spirit or *genius* of the Middleworld is invariably the Green One, appearing as a god of the fields and woods, as Pan, Shiva, the Green Man. Sometimes the *juno* and *genius* appear in partnership, as a pair of deities or as Faery Queen and King. Guardian animals of places may also be encountered here, often those which appear on the heraldic shields of countries, like the Lion of Scotland or the Eagle of America.

The Middleworld can be the place where we can increase our facility in a skill or learn a new skill that would be useful to us in our daily lives. A form of this method of learning is often used by sports people, dancers and practitioners of martial arts when they rehearse their skill without moving their body, thus creating 'skill-lines'.

Interaction with the Middleworld activates the central pathways of our central cerebral cortex and allows them to collate and bridge the separate hemispheres in resourceful ways.

Work through this part slowly before you go on to the next parts.

☙ Practice 22:
Entering into Communion with the Earth

Most of us live surrounded by brick and concrete, glass and steel. The humility to attend to the messages of Nature is often lacking in us: we have neither the time nor the patience for any such communication to take place. It is therefore very important that we increase our exposure to the natural world. We tend to let mundane purposes justify our being outdoors: sport, gardening or car maintenance. Actively seeking the natural world begins

121

with placing ourselves in the right relationship with it, by willingly offering it our time and attention. Single people in an urban environment may need a good reason for being outdoors: jogging or walking the dog may grant acceptable 'invisibility' or protection from disturbance.

Try and spend at least an hour a day out of doors. If your circumstances make this difficult, ensure that you get at least two connected hours at the weekend. During this time, sit upon the ground and be present to the earth. As you breathe out, let your breath enter the ground. As you breathe in, let the earth enter you. Let the earth breathe you. This basic practice will reconnect you daily, making a circuit between yourself and the earth. Your mind should rest upon being present to the earth. If you become distracted, gently recall your concentration to your surroundings and the connection between you and them. You are not taking from the earth, but sharing with it.

✋ *Practice 23:*
Finding a Middleworld Journey-centre

In order to learn about a new country, we gradually explore outwards from a central point. It is exactly the same with shamanic travel. Our centre or starting point must therefore be somewhere dear and familiar to us, a place that exists in physical reality in the Middleworld, *not an imagined place.* Your journey-centre is a place you enjoy being; it might be a sacred site that inspires you, a place in a country where you go on holiday, a place of childhood play, somewhere in the country where nature's beauty reigns supreme. The bottom line is: it must be or have once been in physical reality (in the case of childhood venues now built over, for example), it must be a place where *you* have physically been and be located somewhere upon the planet earth.

It is preferable for your journey-centre to be a place where you have been safe and happy, rather than a place reminiscent of stale or unhappy situations. So, if you could return to anywhere in the planet to be inspired, happy and refreshed, where would that place be? Without sourcing, just bring that place to mind now. Do not make subsequent journeys until you know your journey-centre very well. If your journeying founders due to a poor choice, then find another place, and stick to it.

♨ *Practice 24:* Making a Middleworld Journey to Find Your Guardian Animal

Having found your journey-centre, plan to journey to it and meet your guardian animal. Exclude light and any potential distractions or interruptions, be comfortable, prepare your sound-source and state your purpose: 'I am making a Middleworld journey to my journey-centre, to meet my guardian animal.'

1. Start sourcing with an open heart, without prior expectation. Your quest is to find your primary guardian animal who will help you with shamanic work. Listen to the singing resonances of your sound-source (a headset with a drumming CD or tape), lightly holding your goal in awareness. If distractions or mental noise occur, let them fade, and return to your listening and your purpose. You may lie down or sit propped up.

2. Enter your primary gateway (your journey-centre) to the Middleworld. You may arrive at your centre very quickly, or more slowly. When you arrive, be present to it; allow your subtle senses to enjoy being there – feel, smell, see and hear whatever is around you. Be aware of the differences and similarities between the physical and subtle realities. Appreciate the spiritual form and appearance of your journey-centre.

3. Now call out and ask your animal to come and appear. It may be waiting for you; if it is not, go looking, don't sit there and wait for it to turn up. As you search, keep calling out, asking it to please appear.

4. Ask any animal you subsequently meet if it is your guardian animal. If it is not, it will either ignore you or indicate, by speech or body-language, that it is not. If it is your animal, it will indicate this clearly. You may also experience a sense of deep bodily recognition or emotional excitement.

5. During the search for your animal many things may happen. If you are reluctant to accept an animal which offers itself to you, either because it is one of the animals which are unsuitable for a primary helper or because it makes you feel uneasy, then thank it for its kindness but decline to take it and carry on looking.

    If an animal you have rejected or ignored reappears several times in significant ways during your journey, then that is probably your animal, even if it one of the species which doesn't normally offer itself as a primary guardian animal. Accept it.

If your animal runs away from you, go after it and beg it to stop; ask it why, negotiate with it, do a deal with it. It may be avoiding you because of some perceived imbalance or habit which discourages its co-operation: you may have to promise to work on this.

If your animal appears in a flock or herd, single out which one it is or ask it to appear. Bring back only one animal. Very occasionally, a mother animal with young will appear, in which case check whether both animals are intended for you.

If an animal is openly aggressive towards you, avoid it, and keep looking.

6. After identifying your animal and accepting it, perhaps embrace it, talk to it, remain with it, communicate with it. Do whatever you would normally do on meeting a stranger who is a kindred soul. Finally, embrace your animal and when the call-back signal sounds, bring it back with you.

7. At the call-back signal, return from the otherworld by the same route you journeyed through, bringing your animal with you. This return is normally quite fast. Sometimes, instead of you carrying or running with your animal, the animal carries you. Emerge in physical reality and record your experiences, however bizarre or vestigial they may initially appear. Check any problems or difficulties against the lists in Chapters 2 and 7. Dance your animal, as in Practice 25 below.

8. If your first attempt is unsuccessful or inconclusive, don't worry or berate your failure. Try again another day and let your expectations graze peacefully. Before your next attempt, become as relaxed as possible.

Permit yourself to get things wrong and also to find solutions!

☙ Practice 25: Dancing with Animals

Immediately on returning with your guardian animal, you will need to dance with it. Just as your animal will introduce and guide you through the subtle realities of the otherworlds, so it is your turn now to introduce it to your own physical reality world. Dancing your animal expresses your joy at finding such an important friend; it also allows the subtle reality of your animal and the physical reality of your own body to become attuned. For your dance, take up rattle, drum or other instrument and provide your own rhythm. Let your awareness embrace your animal still as you begin to dance, sing, make music. You will find that your body and even your voice take on the characteristics of your animal, as you allow your animal to explore what a human being is like. Let your veneer of adult self-consciousness drop off and have fun. Dance for 5–10 minutes and then resume normal awareness again.

✋ Practice 26: Introducing the Animal to the Everyday World

In the next few days, be aware of your animal near and around you. Let it see through your eyes and experience through your senses what your human life is like. In situations where you feel threatened or frightened, call upon your animal to help you. When you have to deal with difficult people or situations, ask for your animal's wisdom in dealing with these. Thank it for any help given.

You may wish to set up an image of your animal somewhere in your house: a postcard, object or something which you have made, embroidered or painted which need not proclaim your activities to your household, but which acts as a reminder to yourself. We have photos of friends and family in our homes – they do not all have to be physical reality ones! It is not necessary for you to tell others about your spirits if you don't want to. If you do, choose your informant wisely; the early stages of any relationship need gentle encouragement, not the full blast of media attention. Your animal will reveal who is a good soul-friend to share your shamanic side (see Practice 73 in Chapter 8).

✋ Practice 27: Exploring the Middleworld

The following suggestions are useful in consolidating your Middleworld practice. Before you set out on any journey, always have at least one helper with you and focus your intention clearly. For example, 'I am journeying to ask for help with the difficulties surrounding my new job.' Some of these suggestions involve physical reality tasks only, but their effect has its own subtle reality manifestation.

1. In everyday situations, without deep sourcing, practise checking ahead on the way to your destination. You may only receive a few bat-signals (see glossary) from which to intuit response: check these on arrival. Example: 'Does the village shop have any pineapples today?' Proficiency in checking ahead can prevent wasted time and effort.

2. Find an area in which your walking between the worlds can be put to practical use (i.e. not just in subtle reality ways): voluntary social work, environmental guardianship, working for a charity actively and financially.

3. Adopt a sacred site of your choice. Visit it, then return home to journey there and meet its guardian spirit. Ask its needs and whether your human interest or help is appropriate. Some sites need healing if they have been misused recently or in the past: be guided by your allies and the spirit of the site. Obtain or draw a picture of the site and place it on your shrine and try to remain in contact/awareness of the place as regularly as possible. Help maintain your chosen site in practical ways by clearing rubbish, helping any resident wardens, being part of its team support.

4. Communicate or make social contact with another ethnic group. Study the ways of this group and help bridge the divides that separate races.

5. Attune regularly to particular beings in your locality: the spirits of local animals, plants, trees and rocks. Slowly gain familiarity by study, observation, journeying, always asking permission and showing respect. Your journeys will increase your knowledge and understanding.

❦ *Practice 28*: Finding a Middleworld Teacher

Your Middleworld teacher will be a primal ally in any Middleworld shamanic work you do, someone of whom you may ask advice and guidance. S/he often appears as the spirit of your journey-centre, and it is in this form that you will seek to find him or her.

Journey to your centre, as in Practice 24, and look for the spirit of the place. You may become quickly aware of it, or you may find you need a few return visits. Any form you meet here may appear in the shape of any living creature. Ask it, 'Are you the spirit of this place?' When you meet a spirit which confirms this, greet and thank it. Ask it further, 'Are you my Middleworld teacher?' If the spirit of the place affirms this, then greet and acknowledge it. The subsequent journey may unfold variously: you may remain in quiet companionship here, you may learn more about this place, the spirit may ask for your help in maintaining the guardianship in some way (for example, cleaning debris from a stream, seeking help, with others, to preserve the sacred integrity of the site); you may ask the spirit to help you in your walking between the worlds.

If the spirit of your journey-centre is not your Middleworld teacher, ask it where the teacher may be found. Consult your guardian animal also and look for the teacher together. Call out for your Middleworld teacher to appear. Teachers nearly always appear in human-like form, although they may sometimes have a mixture of forms – animal with human, or perhaps human with plant, for example. Ask any living beings that you meet if they are your Middleworld teacher. If you do not succeed, try again another time.

At the call-back signal, thank any helpers and say farewell to the Middleworld teacher, who remains in subtle reality. Return to your body and record your experiences. On subsequent journeys, you will visit your Middleworld teacher to ask about issues such as those in Practice 27.

2. EARTH CYCLES

Those who practice know that there is something more in woods than in books.
Trees and stones will teach you what cannot be heard from a master.
– St Bernard of Clairvaux

All shamanic work is grounded in and illuminated by the patterns of the natural world: they are our primary Middleworld teachers. Whatever we learn or gain from our journeys is manifested in the realm of ordinary reality, where time and space give shape to our lives. Although we are learning how to co-operate with the timelessness and unlimited dimensionality of subtle reality, and how to walk into otherworlds, our aim is not to become subtle reality spirits. We cannot cease relating what we learn to our everyday world. Though we journey to the three worlds, we must also return to our own.

Although some people are born with an innate sense of fitness and time-liness, others lack all sense of occasion. The latter are not properly ground-ed in physical reality, but are always partially off somewhere else. Look at the following signs; if you recognize yourself in them, then you need to work through the practices at the end of this chapter and stop any walking between the worlds for the present:

Failure to note what is said or done near you.
Inability to keep stable relationships.
Inability to sustain any activity for more than a short time.
Lack of interest in the world around you.
Intense self-absorption.
Continual day-dreaming.
Suspicion that everyone is against you.
Feeling of being 'out of sync' with life.
Never living in the present moment, always brooding over the past
    or worrying about the future.
No sense of humour.

These are all symptoms of soul-straying or moderate power-loss which soci-ety normally defines as being anti-social, selfish or mildly paranoid. All of us go through periods when we wander about insufficiently grounded. Worries, disruptions and problems all have the ability to unsettle us, unseating one or more soul-parts.

We are not talking about major soul-loss here, just soul-straying, when one or more soul-parts are dislodged and float off, usually remaining close by and within range, to be consciously recalled. Some people live their whole lives in this slightly out-of-focus way, never really achieving any strong definition in career, relationships or interests. Just when they feel that they are finally grasping what life is about, some slight worry comes along and off floats that soul-part again, like a balloon in the wind. There is no better way to call the soul home than by focusing on the power-cycles of the earth and steering our lives by their currents.

Earth-cycles are the co-ordinates of home. People who experience the kind of soul-straying described above primarily need to define where their home is in physical reality; they need to stress their belonging to the earth, to increase their mundane presence. When they have grasped this defini- tion and have become properly grounded and integrated into daily life, they may wish to start exploring subtle reality, but not before. If you had decid- ed that this world wasn't much use to you and that the otherworlds might be more help, then this advice may sound irritating, but it is a fact that the best walkers between the worlds are people with their feet firmly on the ground, with well-integrated lives and actively taking part in a variety of mundane pursuits.

Grounding in Time

Earth-cycles are the power circuits of which all life-forms in physical reality partake and share. They govern growth and decay and are intimately asso- ciated with the flow of life-energy. The criteria for such cycles are based upon the frameworks of time, space and the quality of matter, upon the three dimensions of earthly life, in effect. When we consider these cycles we begin to apprehend the immensity of the cosmic web from the physical side of the worlds.

TIME CYCLES

The following time-cycles govern the growth patterns of life:

Day-cycle	SUN	Dawn	Midday	Twilight	Midnight
Moon-cycle	MOON	Waxing	Full	Waning	Dark
Year-cycle	STARS	Spring	Summer	Autumn	Winter
Growth-cycle	EARTH	Flowering	Ripening	Harvesting	Seeding

The diurnal cycle of the sun is marked by one revolution of the earth, giv- ing us day and night. Our vitality is affected by the active light of the sun; our energies fluctuate considerably through twenty-four hours, depending on the amount of light we are exposed to. In circumpolar regions the year itself takes on a day and night shape, as several winter months are spent in near darkness and summer months in perpetual sunlight. If we attempt to work at night, we run counter to this cycle and need to concentrate to maintain wakefulness. During sacred ceremonies, the movement of objects or people is normally sunwise in the northern hemisphere: in the southern hemisphere, ritual motion is generally counter-sunwise or widdershins.

The monthly cycle of the moon is marked by approximately twenty-eight revolutions of the earth. Our creativity is triggered by the passive light of the moon which brings hidden potentialities and seeds to germination. Gardeners, farmers, seafarers and women all understand that the moon's power is not 'just moonshine'. The moon illuminates the night and influences the subtle tides of our lives. (For a perpetual moon-calendar as well as a devotional practice for the earth cycles, see my book, *Celtic Devotional*.)

The yearly cycle of the stars is marked by approximately 365 revolutions of the earth. One earth year is the equivalent of one sun day. Our destiny and vocation are reflected by the ever-changing kaleidoscope of constellations, as astrologers of all eras have testified. The larger patterns of our lives, submerged in dream or intuited through vision, sometimes leap into active focus as the seasons succeed each other: we are sometimes given a wider view of our life's panorama.

The growth-cycle of an earth year can be applied to all life-forms which undergo conception, birth, life and death: some insects may go through one cycle in a few days, while the cycle of trees and rocks may be years or aeons. Many traditional peoples reckoned the growth-cycles by comparing that of different life-forms, as in this Gaelic saying:

> Three ages of a dog, the age of a horse.
> Three ages of a horse, the age of a man.
> Three ages of a man, the age of a deer.
> Three ages of a deer, the age of an eagle.
> Three ages of an eagle, the age of an oak tree.[1]

The time-divisions of the year have been variously calculated by different cultures, some favouring moon-cycles more than solar-cycles: all divisions have been defined by stellar observation. The seasonal tides of the year are governed by the subtle influence of the sun and bring marked changes to our lives. In the northern hemisphere, the spring tide changes at the spring equinox; it cleanses outworn ideas and sweeps away the ills of the winter, bringing new ideas and fresh impulses. The summer tide enters with the summer solstice, bringing the confidence to expand and broaden our ideas, encouraging the burgeoning of life. The tide of the autumn equinox is a time of assimilation and gathering in, when we assess projects and monitor results. The tide of the winter solstice brings the completion of long-term projects; in the deep quietness of winter, we may contemplate the year ahead.

If we live our lives attuned to the tides, currents, influences and energies of earth-cycles, we will come into better alignment with our physical existence and have a deeper appreciation of the subtle networks which connect us to the cosmic web.

The passage of time and the continuity of life were clearly understood by medieval peasants who worked the land; only the rich and privileged were exempt from such work and it was for them that the medieval books of hours, devotionals marking the sevenfold monastic daily prayers, were made. These included a yearly calendar of saint's days, with each month commonly illuminated by a depiction of the monthly tasks such as sowing or wood-gathering.

Recently, in both books and training courses, earth-cycles have been similarly codified and ascribed to various frameworks such as the mandala, medicine wheel, tree of life or horoscope. There is no tradition of such a rigidly tabulated method of learning in traditional societies. To a person living through the cycle of the year, such matters would be so obvious as to be hardly worth stating. It is only as we have grown further away from the natural world that these teaching models have taken on far greater significance than was intended.

The correlation of elements, colours, skills, tasks, qualities, and so on, to certain directions or times of year is misleading to those who take such wheels at face value without any personal input or relationship with the part of the earth on which they live. A loose codification of such cycles *can be* of great benefit when they serve as reminders for modern urban people who have lost touch with the seasonal lessons that unfold, as long as these people don't then become hampered by someone else's definitions. It is far better to derive their own.

For one thing, we need to be sensitive to specific power-cycles when we move from country to country, for they change as we move around the globe. National secular calendars rarely have much to tell us about the subtle life of that country; however, local religious and seasonal festivals highlight different aspects of the year and have much to teach us.

Grounding in Space

Our spacial and dimensional relationship with the earth is very important. Ancient wisdom reveals that all peoples regarded their own tribe, village, location as the centre of the universe. This may strike us as either unscientific or presumptuous, but it is a true understanding of subtle cosmology. Wherever we are upon the earth colours our understanding of the universe; wherever we are when we enter into spiritual practice *is* the primal gateway to subtle reality, to the three worlds and to the cosmic web. Wherever spiritual practice has evolved in dynamic ways, there we find the shrines, temples and sacred landscapes of the earth. Such sacred sites are the junctions where physical and subtle reality intersect. Certain sacred sites are in geomantic alignment, and the relationship between them can be dowsed as leylines or energy currents. The manner in which we understand our position on the globe affects how sacred places are identified, how and where houses are constructed, where roads are laid and myriad other factors. The true architect needs to be a geomancer, one sensitive to the art of placement, able to divine the needs of place, time and purpose, able to create a ground plan that will be harmonious.

The directions are not merely compass points which lead off abstractly into infinity. Each direction brings us different information with which we need to relate sensitively, whether we are on land or sea. Geomantically sensitive people can predict movements of animals, changes in weather, the prospects for the growth-cycle. Diviners and dowsers are able to trace the network of energy veins through the earth to find water, minerals or other substances.

The directions may only be understood in relationship to where we stand at this time. The ascription of the classical elements (see opposite) to the cardinal directions is an example: in North America the earth element is sometimes assigned to the west, in Northern Europe to the north, in Tibet to the east. Shamanizing in a different land presents us with opportunities to intuit and co-operate with these power-cycles. The ascription of the elements to the directions is markedly different in the southern hemisphere, as the polar ice-cap is in the south, not the north. But wherever we are upon earth, the association of directions and elements can be determined by the nature of the winds which blow over a particular land-mass.

Grounding in the Elements

As the sun, moon and stars define time and the directions define space, so the four classical elements of air, fire, water and earth define matter. Nearly all peoples recognize the four classical elements in the winds, sunlight, waters and soil of their land as well as perceiving the elemental spirits which typify their subtle reality appearance.

The four elements are everywhere used to cleanse: bodies are cleansed with sand in deserts; fire is used to cauterize wounds and cleanse surgical instruments; smoking herbs are used to cleanse and heal; water is our universal cleanser. Saunas and sweat-baths use mixtures of the elements to cleanse.

The elements are also agents of decay and physical disposal: upon the Zoroastrian Towers of Silence and the Tibetan and North American death platforms, bodies are subjected to the swift disintegration of the winds; in India and other places bodies are cremated in fire or given to the waters; many cultures inhume their dead in consecrated burial grounds.

The elements are used in sacred ceremonies: air is used in smoke offerings to the spirits, as incense, or as bundles of sweet-grass, sage and other herbs; fire is used to bless and increase growth; water is used to bless and anoint; earth is used to make sacred mandalas.

Different cultures have diverse associations with the qualities of the elements: some associate water with vision and creation, others see fire as the regenerative element. The elements of fire and water are often the subject of creation myths. Sacred fire-keeping is a universal tradition, stemming from times when the kindling of fire was an arduous routine; stories of stealing fire from the gods abound.

Our bodies have their own reflection of the elements: in the air which inspirits our lungs, in the heat of the blood which circulates our veins, in the water of which our bodies are composed, in the rock-like framework of our bones and the soft earth of our skins. But it is in the realization of the subtle reality of these associations that we begin to learn about our connection with the earth-cycles. 'In the perennial wisdom traditions, our bodies are the most potent form of spiritual realization,' wrote R.J. Stewart in *Power Within the Land*.

Just as the admixture of time, direction and matter results in weather, so does the admixture of the senses with the three dimensional life-cycles create the mood or weather of people. Medieval medical philosophy understood the human body to be influenced by the qualities of the elements and directions, the combination of which created 'the four humours', which demarked the different kinds of physical and psychic constitutions. These are shown below.

The Four Humours

Cold
Earth
North

COLD + MOIST = PHLEGMATIC	COLD + DRY = MELANCHOLIC
Wet	Dry
Water	Air
West	East
WET + HOT = SANGUINE	HOT + DRY = CHOLERIC

Hot
Fire
South

An excess of one or other humour was believed to lead to illness and to anti-social behaviour. Modern Indian Ayurvedic medicine still operates by similar principles.

We have two sets of senses: five physical and five subtle.

The Physical and Subtle Senses

PHYSICAL SENSES	SUBTLE SENSES
Sight	Inner Vision
Hearing	Resonance
Smell	Instinct
Taste	Discrimination
Touch	Empathy

Our physical sight is complemented by inner vision; our hearing by resonance or the bat-signals of intuition; our physical senses of smell and taste
are strongly inter-related, as are our subtle senses of instinct and discrimination; touch is complemented by our ability to empathize and be moved by
our subtle reality experiences.

If our physical senses are well balanced and we listen to their messages
responsively, we are accordingly well aligned when we walk between the
worlds and utilize our subtle senses. We also use our subtle senses in physical reality: an inability to empathize, feel, discriminate or act instinctively
may indicate that our corresponding physical senses are not well balanced.

The power-cycles of the earth are implicit in our living; by reintegrating
our shamanic training with them, we relearn the rhythms of the earth and
enter more deeply into the Middleworld.

♨ *Practice 29*: Relating to the Time-cycles

Formulate your own daily and monthly cycle by observing the season,
weather and mood of the time. Create your own calendrical cycle of the
year, marking seasonal changes, significant days, specific time-related activities that you celebrate, such as sacred festivals. Before sacred days, journey
to your journey-centre with your animal and ask your Middleworld teacher
what opportunities and lessons are available at these times.

✋ *Practice 30:* Harvesting the Sun, Communing with the Moon, Seeding with the Stars

The sun, moon and stars provide us with the three kinds of life essential for our well-being: physical vitality, psychic health and creative potential. In times of low vitality, try and spend as much time out of doors as possible, especially if the sun is in the sky, even if it's winter. During the summer and autumn, be aware of the sunlight striking your brow and consciously store it within you. During the winter, call upon that store of vitality. This can be helpful to those with seasonal affective disorder – a condition related to insufficient light-stimulus.

In times of low expectation, fluctuating energy and difficult growth, be aware of the moon. Even if you live somewhere where the horizon is crowded by buildings or if the sky is often overcast or dazzled by street-lights, track the moon's journey across the sky by looking up each night. Commune with the moon, receive the patience to be fallow and the ability to increase your understanding. At the end of a moon-cycle, release all your old expectations and frustrations. With the appearance of the new moon, make new resolves.

In times of great change, challenge or creative struggle, be aware of the stars above you, present even when it is day. Make an effort to visit a place from which the stars can be seen at least once a month. Watch the seasonal dance of the stars and begin to understand the progress of your own life with greater confidence.

You may sing your thanks to each luminary for help received, and dedicate your activities, plans and projects with gratitude for the benefit of all beings on the cosmic web.

✋ *Practice 31:* The Hearth Shrine

Find the centre of your home's inspiration: this might be an actual hearth, if you have a fireplace, or it might be the gathering point where you and your guests assemble to rest when the day's work is done. Consider your home's centre by sitting in it. Now, source its subtle reality and, with the help of your Middleworld helpers, ask to be shown the heart of your home. You may become aware of the land-spirits which inhabit your bit of earth (even if you live several floors up!). You may experience the vitality which animates your home in another guise. Ask how you may best honour and maintain this essential vitality or spirit. Return and record. Create a small but potent hearth shrine at your centre. It need not be ostentatious or obviously shamanic to look at: the very minimum is a candle or lamp which can be lit for at least a few minutes a day to bless your home and honour the hearth.

⚇ Practice 32: Purifying the Senses

To experience the proper humility which accompanies shamanic work, we need to undergo a purification of the senses. This may entail fasting from food and drink, fasting from common comforts, fasting from television and wrap-around music, fasting from severe or critical thoughts, fasting from spiritual stimulants. Consider your own imbalances and practise one form of fasting this week.

⚇ Practice 33: The Messages of the Senses

Let one of your senses take you for a walk – in the country or in the town. For example, listen to your physical senses when you go shopping for food: 'Does my body need this?' This is not an exercise in gross self-gratification but an experiment to discover your body's essential needs. Let your subtle senses stop you in front of shelves and assess why you are there. This goes beyond reading the labels! Go into fruit and vegetable shops and let your body choose your food for the week.

⚇ Practice 34: Dancing the Seasons

Just as the stars perform a yearly stellar dance above our heads, so many people have reflected this seasonal progress upon the earth with their feet. Hopi Indians of the North American south-west perform complex cycles of dances which bring rain, growth and integration to the earth. British Morris dancers similarly mark the year with formalized seasonal dances, which communicate sacred awareness of the earth and its seasonal mantle. Such dances usually reflect agricultural and elemental changes and the movement or behaviour of animals, symbolically and shamanically marking the effect that these have upon the round of life.

Dance is most often seen as social and recreative art form, yet it is central to shamanism, an ecstatic way between the worlds. Explore the nature of the year and find your own sacred points of reference: these need not be strictly calendrical with festivals on fixed dates, but may reveal themselves to you through the first spring flowers blooming, the first day of a new moon, the day when you feel summer has really arrived. Using a simple instrument like a rattle, or wearing clothes or ornaments which jingle, clash or rustle, stand and enter into the feeling the season evokes in you. Now begin to move on the spot, rattling or jingling. Your movements need not be balletic or from accepted dance forms. Let your mind be free of self-consciousness, let it roam widely over the season. Here is an example:

> DANCE REPORT: The day of the spring equinox was bright and blustery.
> I danced in the garden with rattle and ankle bells. Facing the sun, I sang
> a little and rattled. Then, closing my eyes, I let my body feel the sun.
> My feet began to lift and stamp. I circled on the spot, stamping in each
> direction. The rattle grew busy in my hand and my arm began to arc and
> circle in the opposite direction to the one my body was circulating in.
> I started to source as I danced. It was a dancing of seeds in the earth and their
> effort to be out into the air. The seeds became bees pollinating flowers. Birds
> began to call and I sang their calls. I saw the migratory birds return to our
> shores. Then the sun flooded everything and there was only a whirling
> goldenness in which I became still and fell to my knees.

✋ Practice 35: Sacred and Power-centres

Many places are considered to have particular power or holiness. Some are marked by extraordinary structures like Stonehenge in England or the Nazca glyphs of South America. Others are natural sites of awe-inspiring beauty like Ayers Rock in Northern Australia or the mountain shrine to the sun-goddess, Amaterasu, at Ise in Japan. Sacred centres are 'burning glasses', where the physical and subtle worlds meet. Visit one with respect. Greet and acknowledge guardians, and learn what there is to know. Rather than taking away a part of that site, leave a gift instead: a strand of hair or a prayer of beneficial intention towards the site guardians. Ensure that your gift is not detrimental to any living thing and does not deface or abuse the site.

Some places on the earth are special to us: places where we feel uplifted and encouraged, places where our energy is renewed. Find a place near where you live that works for you. It does not have to be a formally designated sacred site. When you get spaced out, disoriented or out of true with yourself, when being with other people causes you anguish, go to sit in your power place. Be in your body, not in your head. Let being outdoors help to centre and ground you; feel the paranoia subsiding. Let the elements ground you: be aware of the winds that blow, the sun that warms you, the rain that cleanses your tears, feel the support of the earth. Sit and acknowledge the elements and ask their help: make connection, drain out impurities, draw up fresh energies. Give thanks.

☙ *Practice 36:* Shrining

Once you begin working in a regular way, you can formalize your growing friendship with the spirits by the creation of a shrine. A permanent shrine might be erected in your garden or on a dresser at home to honour the spirits. A temporary shrine might be erected where you go out to work or in a hired hall where you meet with others. My temporary shrine equipment is always packed and ready to go wherever I go: it consists of a stone, a water-bottle, a bowl, a small candle in a tall glass container, a bowl of earth in which to put charcoal and incense, and a cloth. Thus, I always have representatives of the four elements with me; I add whatever is appropriate to my practice that day – a fallen branch, a picture or postcard of an animal or being, a pile of nuts or berries – as an offering. Decorate your shrine according to your needs and taste.

Check periodically to see if your shrine is in need of cleaning or changing. If you experience dissatisfaction with it, take it down and build a new one. All urgings to spring-clean the house should start and finish with the shrine since energy can become stalemated or blocked around it. Incoming seasonal tides and currents can be effectively met in this way. As the seasons change, so different influences arise. Your shrine is a point of contact between this world and the others, which is why you should be sensitive to what it is telling you.

☙ Practice 37: The Seven Directions

Only you can ascribe qualities to the four cardinal directions. Wherever you are living on the planet you can use your physical and subtle senses to source these. Answer these questions to determine which elements and qualities feel best.

1. *From which directions does the wind bring the greatest cold/heat/wetness/dryness?* This will help ascribe the different elements of earth, fire, water and air to the directions.
2. *What qualities do you associate with these directions and elements?* If a direction could appear as an animal, a tree, a plant, a stone – what kind would it be?

Do not let your intellect dictate any fixed and immovable associations. If you can't decide about the quality of any direction, then journey into that direction with your animal and ask your Middleworld teacher to reveal it to you.

The four directions are the physical and subtle co-ordinates of the Middleworld. Three further directions need acknowledgement: above – the Upperworld; below – the Underworld; and within – the centre of the known and unknown where the heart of the cosmic web intersects the centre of your own being.

Before you shamanize, it is a good practice to acknowledge the seven directions. This can be simply done by singing or rattling in the directions in turn; in more complex work you might wish to sing specific welcome songs to each direction and make offerings. First, seek alignment with the cardinal directions and their spirits, concentrating on their subtle reality modes: if you live in the northern hemisphere, start in the east and turn sunwise to south, west and north. If you live in the southern hemisphere, reverse this circuit: start in the east and turn north, west and south. Now, call upon the spirits of the Upperworld and Underworld. Lastly, turn to the silent centre of your own soul within; visualize your soul and the heart of the cosmic web intersecting each other.

When you conclude your shamanizing, reverse this procedure, this time thanking rather than welcoming. When you reverse the cardinal directions, concentrate upon their physical reality modes: earth as soil, water as a river or sea, fire as sunlight, air as wind.

☙ *Practice 38:* Invisibility and Becoming Noticeable

There are times when we wish to be invisible – to avoid meeting time-wasting acquaintances, for instance – or to be noticed – in restaurants when you want to be served or to get your bill and leave, for example. The following practices can be quite useful.

To become invisible: relax, breathe, and source your animal. Ask it to help you become invisible: specify whether to all viewers or to some. Afterwards, don't forget to reverse the procedure and become visible. *Note:* It is difficult to become invisible to psychics or seers, who may see you as your animal!

To become noticeable: relax, breathe, and source your animal to help you become noticeable: specify to whom. Be careful not to extend your range beyond the projected area or you may become depleted. Concentrate on the abilities within yourself you want recognized. Ensure you reverse this and practise grounding afterwards (see Practice 1).

142

• CHAPTER 5 •

The Underworld

From you,
ancestral holy land,
history nourishes itself.
And I continue to walk
in the paths
of the ancient pilgrim.
– Carlos Reyes-Manzo *The Olive Tree and the Mountain*

1. IN THE HOUSE OF MEMORY

News from a forrein Country came,
As if my Treasure and my Wealth lay there:
So much it did my Heart Enflame!
Twas wont to call my Soul into mine Ear.

– Thomas Traherne *On News*

The Underworld is the power-house of the three worlds. Here we draw upon our deep resources, our traditional inheritance, our memory. Look at the diagram on p.49, which shows the three worlds connected by the great centre tree. This illustrates the way that the Underworld can be envisaged as the rich loam into which the tree's roots go down. In addition, all trees have a tap root which searches out the nearest source of water, whose nurture it then channels to the rest of the tree. When we enter the Underworld, we too put down our tap root and draw up nourishment.

The Underworld has a bad press in the West, since in both Classical and Christian cosmology it has been dualistically understood as Hell. In shamanism the three worlds are primal worlds of possibility without such dualistic connotations. The Underworld is a place of foundations and beginnings, of joy and creativity, not a place of fear and terror.

For many religions, the Underworld has become a kind of toxic-waste dumping ground where the spiritual evils of the world are thought to lie ready to recrudesce. Scenarios of unending hell-fire and fantastic terror have been set up in our imagination to guard the gates of the Underworld from unauthorized intrusion. Our communion with the Underworld has been lost or severed by fearful religious dogmas which would prefer us to imagine a region of demons and searing flame, rather than a place of restoration and reconnective joy.

Let us be peaceful and confident in soul before we undertake the Underworld journey or read further:

Permit yourself to disregard the instruction that the Underworld is a kind of spiritual dustbin!

The Underworld is a place of mirror images, reversals and complementarities where we perceive the physical reality of our daily lives thrown into startling subtle reality relief. Imagine the separation of realities as a gauze veil hanging from floor to ceiling; if you push your hand into the gauze, you cause it to push *inwards* away from your side; anyone standing on the other side of the gauze veil will see your hand push the gauze *outwards* towards them. When we move between the worlds, we often experience the same effect. This sense of reversal or mirrored worlds is usually more marked near the thresholds between our physical Middleworld and the subtle realities of Underworld and Upperworld.

If we bear this in mind, we will begin to understand why the Underworld journey has been discouraged by non-shamanic cultures: for here the threshold guardians assume tiny or gigantic size, here we meet the spirits that complement realities we have neglected or ignored. Without strong and willing allies, such encounters can confuse and terrify – many genuine mystics have gone thither without preparation or ally, returning to report strange sights. Without the correct cosmological information and without a non-dual framework to travel from, religions have barred the doors that lead between the worlds.

The wise traditions of the primal earth draw continually upon the Underworld and are fed by it and many people now deeply regret that we have lost communion with these rich indigenous traditions. Although we may feel that such treasures can never be ours, our hearts are still gripped by the many myths and stories of the Underworld journeys of those who seek the treasures of wisdom: the descent of Inanna to take the initiation of mortality and gain wisdom, the descent of Aeneas to meet and consult his dead father, Orpheus' descent to retrieve Eurydice, the initiatory descent of Christian Rosenkreutz into the vault, the descent of Persephone which triggers the coming of agricultural wisdom to earth, the descent of King Arthur to bring home the Cauldron, the prototype of the Grail. All these myths speak of initiation into wisdom and the winning of empowering treasures, gained through endurance, perseverance and courage.

Such heroic descents can be ours through the shamanic Underworld journey. Reconnection with the Underworld restores communication with the voices of our wise ancestors, with traditions which hallow the earth, with the deep empowering teachings and treasures which remain eternally available.

Many of us already access parts of the Underworld when we check back to a distant memory and simultaneously access times, places and people who are no longer present in physical reality, or when we are faced with immense difficulties we often find superhuman strength and power at our disposal. Whenever we instinctively resonate with or react against something, we are assessing its true integrity, its primal Underworldly fitness: situations and people who do not ring true often have no firm foundation. We often experience a superimposition of the Underworld when we tunnel down our creative roots to reach into the beginnings of a project: this may be primarily stimulated through arduous research, but when we stop, feeling that we can go no deeper, pure information bubbles up and synchronous interconnections are effortlessly made. Whenever we draw upon deep memory, primal power and creative joy, we are sending down a soul-part, like a tap root, into the Underworld. Whenever we re-enter the richness of childhood play, we are immediately immersed in its creative power.

The Underworld is associated, though not exclusively, with the past and is a good place to review the roots of something or to heal imbalances that are the result of past cause and effect. It is where we perceive the subtext or mythic resonance of things.

The beings encountered in the Underworld include ancestral teachers, clan totems, deities who initiate and empower, dwarfs, dragons and other subterranean or watery guardians of power. You may encounter ancestral councils or assemblies here. The *genius* of the Underworld often appears as a Lord or King of the Underworld and is sometimes horned or antlered, like the Celtic Cernunnos or the Hindu Pasupati, surrounded by many beasts. Many primal Underworld deities have the horns of power: such beings have been demonized by Christians, but they simply preserve their original non-dual functions as gatekeepers and initiators. The *juno* of the Underworld often appears as an initiatory maiden or elder, or as Queen and Mistress of the Underworld, often in partnership with her lord, like Persephone and Pluto, who are the keepers of the Underworld's treasury.

Each land has its own native Underworld guardians. Awakening and communicating with these native powers is important work. During the early 1980s with other walkers between the worlds, I visited many parts of Britain, specifically to effect such awakenings as part of the worldwide awakening of interest in global native traditions. As a result of our work, certain powers have become more widely available and contactable. This bridging of realities between the Middleworld and the Underworld has been termed 'awakening the Sleepers' by R.J. Stewart.[1]

Not every ancient power and wisdom tradition is appropriate for this time. The work of awakening the sleepers is important, not to evoke atavistic and inappropriate energies, but to 'clear the ways' between our own world and the deep power of the Underworld after so many centuries of neglect and misunderstanding, so that the primal wisdom of the ancestral traditions may once more flow as a corrective to our over-urban and increasingly fragmented lives.

The Underworld activates our remembrance. It precisely locates that part of the brainstem where the deep memories are stored, creating branching pathways which feed our central cerebral cortex. As the place of primal beginnings, of the ancestors and deep memories, the Underworld is where we often find our most enduring allies in this world.

⍟ Practice 39: Finding an Underworld Entrance

In Chapter 4, you found a centre from which to start Middleworld journeying (see Practice 23). In order to reach the Underworld, we need to find an entrance which has an opening going down into the earth. This entrance should exist in physical reality and not be an imagined place: an underground cavern, a spring or well, an animal or tree hole, an ancient chambered burial mound. Natural places are best, although I have clients who readily employ a London Underground tunnel. There is no one right way to the Underworld. If your entrance is near your Middleworld journey-centre, even better, but it doesn't have to be. For journeying in all three worlds I use the same favourite tree, using the hole in its trunk as a way down, its branches as a way up and its actual locus as a place of Middleworld journey. Find an entrance that works for you. If you choose a hole which in physical reality is too small for you, it will be big enough when you come to journey. If you choose to travel down through water, you will be able to breathe.

⍟ Practice 40: The Underworld Journey

Since the Underworld Journey is more complex than the Middleworld one, we will proceed in stages:

1. Your purpose for this first journey is to seek power and reconnection with the Underworld. Exclude light, be comfortable either sitting or lying down, start to source, recalling your purpose, and bringing to mind your entrance.

2. Before going into your entrance, call your guardian animal to come with you. If it does not come fairly quickly, then proceed downwards without it, intending to meet it when you emerge. Allies you have met in one world can appear in

and accompany you to other worlds. But if your Middleworld animal does not appear here, and you do not encounter it in either the tunnel or the Underworld, then you may meet another animal ally in the Underworld.

3. In the tunnel which leads between entrance and Underworld, be aware of your surroundings and keep going downwards. If you meet difficulties or obstacles ask your allies for assistance, even though you may not have one with you at that moment.

4. When you emerge into the Underworld, you may be surprised to see that you are not underground! The landscape into which you emerge may appear as any known geographical zone of the earth – desert, snow-covered, temperate, seascape. It will have landscape and sky. Wherever you emerge, whatever you see, is how the Underworld looks for you. Remember that the cosmic web is not two- or even three-dimensional: it interpenetrates all zones simultaneously. All people access the Underworld through their personal tunnel and may arrive in different parts of it. So how do you know you've hit the Underworld?

There is a kind of 'deepness' to it which cannot be confused with other levels. Some people experience this as a feeling of homecoming or ingathering, of belonging or wondrous remembering. Others do not experience this, but feel the Underworld as a place of awesome power or strength. People with tinges of claustrophobia often feel uncomfortable with Underworld travelling, and feel enclosed. In many senses, going there is like returning to the womb. Within the Underworld, we experience and receive teachings by osmosis, just like a foetus in the womb feeding on the nourishment of the placenta.

5. Meet your animal or go looking for a guardian animal or teacher in the Underworld, following the directions on pp.123 and 126.

6. Having made connection with your guardian animal, make your request for power and reconnection with the underworld.

7. Follow your animal's direction: you may be shown things, taken to places, given advice, encouraged to dance and sing, or many other things: whatever follows is the answer of your request.

8. Continue journeying until your sound-source signals the call-back. If you have met a new animal, bring it back with you the way you came and dance it, after briefly recording your journey. If you have received help from your guardian animal, give it thanks and return alone.

148

☙ *Practice 41:* Exploring the Underworld

The following are suggestions for journeys or work involving the Underworld. We access the subtle reality of the Underworld when we need power, traditional wisdom, memory, when we need to access our authentic creative impulse.

1. Retrieve lost knowledge with the help of your Underworld allies. The more you journey, the more allies you will make. They will make themselves known to you through the issues that you journey upon.
2. Gain solidarity with your ancestors.
3. Go to regain power when you feel at a loss or vitally depleted, when you need reconnection with your deep self.
4. Ask Underworld allies for personal healing.
5. Investigate the deep causes of world problems and ask for healing.

2. IN THE HOUSE OF THE ANCESTORS

She sometimes wished she could make the earth and stones speak and tell her all about the dead people who had trodden upon them.

– Flora Thompson *Lark Rise to Candleford*

Traditionally, the Underworld is the place where we are most likely to meet the ancestors. The ancestors include our blood relatives, as well as the peoples of the past who lived before our time. Without the ancestors, we would not exist. They bequeath us life: we inherit life from them. For this reason, all indigenous societies recognize and revere their ancestors, putting their elders first in all matters, rather than last as in our culture. The Western failure to honour or respect our ancestors has created great problems.

A society which honours its ancestors also honours its descendants; it makes tribal decisions and social changes cautiously, since these will affect not just one, but many generations; it breeds humility and selflessness in leaders; it recognizes the wisdom or futility of past actions and does not repeat them; it nurtures economy of natural resources and a wise use of land. In contrast, our society leaves its descendants a fearful legacy based on a disregard for either past or future: short-term decisions which poison the earth and waste natural resources are made by hasty, ignorant and egotistical leaders.

Traditionally, we have been fearful of the ancestors because they are dead, and the dead have been seen as jealous of our life and likely to steal whatever vitality they can from us. Most indigenous peoples recognize that the affairs of the dead and the living are normally kept separate, but this does not stop them from recognizing and giving thanks at regular intervals for the help, wisdom and guidance of the ancestors. Respect for our ancestors is not given in order to appease the dead, but to acknowledge the gift of life they have given us. This is often celebrated by an annual festival where the dead are honoured: in the West, we remember our dead at Hallow'een, the ancient Celtic festival of Samhain when the ancestors were believed to be abroad.[2]

The Ancestral Bequest

We each have visions of what our ancestors might look or be like. Unfortunately, romantic images of ancestors are found in the same box as dreams about the 'noble savage'. Stark reality tells us that human beings will be human beings in whatever age or nation. Just because a person is old, doesn't necessarily make her also wise.

We are each programmed to fulfil certain ancestral expectations. We may have an unspoken dread of repeating ancestral patterns, aware that many family problems underscore our present lives. Modern therapeutic methods often address current family issues by concentrating on analysis of our upbringing and family relationships: it has been my experience that distant family history also has a bearing on current situations, that significant patterns have already been laid down for generations. Some of these can be dealt with in family therapy, but some problems go beyond counselling, especially when ancestral mediation is needed.

The work of Dr Kenneth McAll, a consultant psychiatrist, to 'heal the family tree' is based on the principle of cutting unhealthy links between a person and their ancestors by prayer and a celebration of the eucharist.[3] Dr McAll works from a strong Christian belief and is sternly discouraging of all

150

non-Christian spiritual practices which he sees as evil, yet he has correctly diagnosed many family problems and illnesses as having their roots in ancestral unfinished business.

We all understand how certain physical and mental illnesses are genetically transmitted from one generation to another: medical research is now attempting to identify and minimize the effect of genetic inheritances of this kind. But it also true that certain habitual patterns set up in past times also resurface in families: incest and child abuse can recur in generation after generation of a family, for example. We need to say 'the buck stops here' and enlist the help of wise ancestors and spiritual teachers; above all, we need to realize that the longer we leave such situations, the greater is the responsibility for seeking solutions, for finding the circuit-breaker.[4]

Carl Jung wrote that 'possession is caused by something that could perhaps most fitly be described as an "ancestral soul"'.[5] The habits, angers and frustrations of human existence all create waves upon the cosmic web unless we recognize and clarify these issues while we are alive, otherwise we are likely to unintentionally bequeath them to our relatives.

The nature of 'the ancestral bequest' varies from family to family, but it can reach quite staggeringly overwhelming proportions if it is not addressed periodically. It can be avoided only by each of us taking responsibility for our own spiritual clarification. The ancestral bequest can be cleared with the help of Underworld and Upperworld teachers working in tandem (see Practice 48). The burden of ancestral business can also be collectively lightened in any family that becomes aware of the nature of its problem and that earnestly desires to redress the balance: by acknowledging, *not blaming*, ancestral failures and their continued influence in the family, by praying for the release of ancestral spirits from their unfinished business, by seeking and offering them forgiveness, by actively addressing the problem so that it is dealt with.

Vengeance, hatred, fear and guilt are the strongest links in the circuit of the ancestral bequest, which is why forgiveness is an important part of relinquishing ancestral patterns, for it is the supreme circuit-breaker. Forgiveness springs from impartial love, which puts the benefit of the cosmic web before any personal benefit. *Forgiveness restores the broken threads of the web: it rebuilds the pathways which allow the ancestral soul finally to go home.*

The National Bequest

Just as families have their ancestral bequest, so too do countries. This has been apparent in the inability of nations to agree on global negotiations under the umbrella of the United Nations. The disunity and squabbling between nations is like that of a huge family, what we can call 'the national bequest'.[6]

Avoidance of or obsession with ancestral issues is often at the root of unhealthy nationalism and racism. Pride in our country and forebears must always be balanced by our awareness of the rest of the cosmic web. Many countries are now harvesting the seeds of colonialism sown in past centuries. Ignoring this legacy will not make it go away; our responsibility is to deal with it now. The conflicts in the Middle East, in Northern Ireland and former Yugoslavia have their roots in unresolved territorial disputes of past ages; religious intolerance is not a cause, just a symptom of a festering ancestral imbalance.

Wars and conflicts are most often rooted in territorial boundary disputes, in the invasion of privilege or custom. Vendettas and mafia activity are the manifestations of whole tribal groups, while terrorism is the result of the unassuaged desires and unfinished business of racial groups and countries who, like the ancestors, are not being acknowledged with respect or justice. But to clear the national bequest of one tribe or country requires a massive collective and co-ordinated effort on behalf of all people in the world and of all their allies in the otherworlds.

We can each work with the national guardians and spirits of our native land and ask their assistance, not seeking to blame or to manipulate any particular outcome, but to ask for ways of healing. Again, we must become aware of our national bequest and the ways in which its accumulated legacy affects our situation now: we must seek and offer forgiveness which is the only possible circuit-breaker for such complex accumulations of anguish.

To truly arrive at a global and international consensus, each country and people must first deal with past issues.

Although we often feel uneasy when family and national problems are discussed, we must pass beyond personal discomfort and any thought that we are raking over old embers or trying to keep old divisions erect; we must go to the heart of the issue and recognize that *we and the ancestors are one*, that we live one collective and continuous life. With this realization in our hearts, we will be able to sing a song of reconciliation that will call home the national soul from acts of defensive outrage and senseless violence.

Encountering the Ancestors

Our first encounter with the ancestors may cause us to be fearful because some personal and family issues will have to be dealt with; but we should not avoid ancestral work, for by so doing we also avoid the deep ancestors – those who have clarified their souls and are at home in the ancestral realms. In dealing with the problems resultant from ancestral legacies, we must not ignore or minimize the gifts and wisdom which we inherit from the ancestors. By releasing memories and knowledge we can reclaim and enrich our over-intellectual world. As walkers in ancestral realms, we can help rebalance our unstable world by bringing the corrective of practical, humorous ancestral wisdom.

For every set of difficult ancestors, there is also an ancestral teacher who will assist us, initiating us slowly and surely into our true treasury of wisdom. It has been my experience that, with the help of such a teacher, we can proceed with confidence and enter more completely into our present life tasks. When we find the deep ancestors, our sense of family is restored, however unparented we feel, however dislocated from our roots.

Working with the ancestors seems a waste of time to many people who want to focus on living in the present. We do well to remember that the cosmic web runs timelessly forwards and backwards without a break. We are the ancestors of children yet unborn, living links between what we regard as the past and future, but which in subtle reality is eternally now. No part of the cosmic web, no spirit that ever was or will be, is absent from the eternal now.

☙ Practice 42: Finding an Ancestral Teacher

When we seek out ancestral allies in shamanism, we are targeting 'the deep ancestors' who are closest to the heart of the cosmic web: these are usually distant ancestors of whose existence we may have had no previous knowledge;

yet recently deceased ancestors who have lived lives of great peace and wisdom may also be in this category. Some ancestors are unsuitable allies simply because they have not sufficiently clarified their souls to be of help: although dead, they are still actively part of our world, still pursuing their unfinished business and have not yet entered into their own realm.

You will recognize your ancestral teacher by his/her practical and impartial demeanour. Manifestations of self-importance, selfishness or inhuman disregard for life are signs of unsuitability. A knowledgeable discarnate human being is often a more valuable teacher than a deity or spirit from the Upperworld because she knows what human life is about, thus enabling her to be a more pragmatic guide in the mazes of life. An ancestral teacher is someone of your bloodline who is a guardian of traditional wisdom. This teacher is one to consult when issues arise that require Underworldly help, perhaps family matters, issues involving land and its use and most matters which directly affect your immediate community; she can also be consulted when something needs protection or there is a desire to know traditional precedents for modern situations, or as a means of accessing ancestral memory or finding 'lost' knowledge.

1. Exclude light, start sourcing and begin your journey to the Underworld in search of an ancestral teacher from the deep ancestors.
2. Go down your Underworld entrance from the Middleworld with your guardian animal, or meet your animal as you emerge into the Underworld. Ask your animal's help to find an ancestral teacher.
3. With your animal, set out looking. Ask any figure that you meet on the way if he is your ancestral teacher. Your animal will also help and direct you, so keep asking and looking until you find her or him. Check your animal's reaction to the proposed teacher: if your animal is calm, shows excited recognition or attentive appreciation in his presence, you have found your ancestral teacher. If your animal shows complete indifference or signals you to go onwards, you have not found him.
4. Your ancestral teacher may be a deceased relative known to you, but is most often a distant ancestor who is not in conscious memory. *He or she will not be a person now living.* You may find your ancestral teacher in a group of ancestors, or at his own abode.

5. Greet and meet your ancestral teacher. Ask for help with clarifying the ancestral bequest that runs in your own family. What follows is the answer to your question.
6. At the call-back, say goodbye and return the way you came. Perform Practice 44 afterwards.

☙ *Practice 43*: Dancing with the Ancestors

Ancestral and traditional memory is retained in a variety of places: not only in the genes and customs of your family and people, but in songs, stories and dances, in non-verbal communication, in places and symbols. Some of the oldest and most potent memories are stirred by dance, where the body itself becomes a receptacle for memory. The rhythms, cadences, intervals of accompanying dance music are as redolent and memory-wakening as odours. Because the whole body is involved, something else happens.

Many societies dance, not for their own enjoyment and recreation, but for the unseen audience of ancestors, spirits and deities. Dance is rarely seen to be revolutionary but the Ghost Dance, spread by the Paiute Indian prophet Wovoka (c.1856–1932) in the 1880s in North America, was indirectly responsible for the last Indian war. A communal trance dance, it was performed to beg the assistance of ancestors to help their descendants in a world that had become increasingly beleaguered by a restrictive US government. Alarmed by the large assembly of Indians taking part in the dance, the government descended upon Wounded Knee, South Dakota, and massacred an entire Sioux encampment. This tragic over-reaction sent many to join their ancestors.

Find some dance music which derives from the folk-culture of your ancestors (rather than the land in which you are now living, if you are a naturalized citizen). Feel the music through your body, absorbing its resonance, harmony and rhythms; let the *music*, rather than your mind, dictate the movement of your body, the steps that you make. When you feel wholly at one with the music, stretch out your hands and feel the hands of your ancestors in your own. Dancing together, feel the continuity of life. In joyful celebration, rejoice in the tapestry of lives. Finish with a prayer for the continued help of your ancestors and bless them.

155

✋ *Practice 44:* Finding an Ancestral or Clan Totem

Each bloodline and family has ancestral helpers which have traditionally aided and strengthened its allies. Some families, especially those which have maintained genealogical records or which have heraldic grants of arms, have a close working knowledge of these helpers. The mythic and armorial beasts which support the family shield in heraldry are the medieval equivalent of the totemic beasts allied to ancient family lines.

We can each discover our own clan totem by making a journey to our ancestral teacher and asking to be introduced to our clan totem. This helper, which is usually animal, but may be a tree, plant or other being, may be consulted in matters requiring crucial family decisions. It is possible, by this method, to source into family strengths and resources.

This practice should not be confused with finding your personal guardian animal. Your totemic ally will often accompany you on Underworld journeys.

✋ *Practice 45:* The Ancestral Shrine

Set up a shrine to the ancestors. This could be a very simple shelf or just a photograph of your relatives, living or dead, or a symbol which represents 'ancestors' to you.

The ancestors are the forerunners of our whole life – where would we be without them? All indigenous traditions honour their ancestors: something we have forgotten to do. Many of our present problems derive from inherited ancestral patterns, so we need to have a good relationship with our forbears and give them their due and pay them respect. This may be especially true if you do not know much about your ancestry because you are adopted, for example. A journey to your ancestral teacher could help reconnect you with your blood kindred. In this case, your shrine will not have photographs of your relatives but may include other items which you associate with your family.

ꙮ *Practice 46*: Learning from the Master/Mistress

By journeying to an eminent master/mistress of a skill we wish to emulate, we can learn from an expert teacher and increase our awareness and obser-vation. Journey to the Underworld with the intention of finding an expert among the ancestors. This is a specific skill-teacher who will use their per-sonal expertise to help us practise our craft. Your skilled teacher may not be the one you were expecting: ask what help is available to hone your skill.

ꙮ *Practice 47*:
Recognizing and Clearing Ancestral Patterns

Some features of this practice can only be undertaken by students who have teachers of both ancestral and spiritual lineage. See Practice 54 for an explanation of spiritual lineage, which you will need for the second phase of this practice.

All new parents at some point utter the deathless words, 'I shall never make *my* child do such-and-such,' in reaction to their own upbringing. However, this often plays straight into the hands of invidious ancestral pat-terns and reinforces them.

Review your family and all the members you know, without judging any of them. Look at maternal and paternal family sides. Taken collectively, which tendencies are a particular feature of your family? In which ways do you reflect and implement these features in your own life?

You may come from a family of impatient people who frequently make unfortunate decisions or relationships; there may be a deep vein of anger or resentment running through your family which also mars your life, or you may be delighted to discover that the ability to handle life situations with a light and humorous touch descends to you. Evaluate the qualities you have discerned in a neutral, not negative, way; also see in which situations these qualities would be useful. Impatience may betoken a frustrated enthusiasm, anger may indicate a strong sense of thwarted justice.

Make a journey to your ancestral teacher and ask, 'How may this fami-ly quality be of use to the universe?' or 'How may this family tendency be transformed in my life?' If you are a 'learner parent' with your first child, you might wish to ask, 'What does my child need from me at this time?' If all parents journeyed during their child's development, they would find considerable help. If you are adopted or do not have any information about your family, journey to discover your blood lineage ancestors in company with your ancestral teacher and allies.

Your journey may reveal that the ancestors require acknowledgement. Proper respect and acknowledgement will lay the beginnings of right relationship. If you hit a particularly unregenerate bunch of ancestors in your journeying, call upon your guardian animals or ancestral teacher for help.

To understand the rest of this practice you need to read Chapter 6, particularly Practice 54.

If you detect a family pattern which needs to be seriously brought to an end, ask your ancestral teacher how this may be done. You may find that this is not currently possible due to the fact that you need other helpers to assist. We have two lineages: the blood lineage of our ancestors and the spiritual lineage of spirit teachers. *We often have to find a teacher of our spiritual lineage in order to help deal with the ancestral bequest of our blood lineage.* All gods and spirits who assume mortality and personally enter the gates of death have this ability, which is why they are regarded as saviours or deliverers. These allies are often the most helpful in ancestral mediation.

This is how esoteric Christian tradition understands Christ's voluntary descent into the ancestral realms, which is called 'the harrowing of hell' in medieval tradition. This act of reaching down to the peoples of the past is believed to neutralize unbalanced ancestral influences for all Christians. Other spiritual traditions have their own saviours and deliverers who perform similar functions.[7] To help clear or transform your ancestral bequest more effectively, meet both your ancestral and spiritual lineage teachers at your Middleworld journey-centre and ask their assistance. Get a plan of campaign by conferring in council with your allies (see Practice 82).

Perform Practice 45 when you have clarified your ancestral bequest. The souls of your ancestors are now free to return to their home and you can extend the hand of love to them and dance in harmony for the first time.

We may feel that our known ancestors are a disgrace and that the less we have to do with them the better. If you feel that you have inherited an ancestral legacy of guilt, shame, anger or whatever, it is still possible to honour your ancestors without repeating their patterns in your life. *Love them for themselves and not their deeds*, which may well, in their turn, be inherited from their ancestors. We are not obliged to carry our ancestors' burdens, but we owe it to our descendants to ensure that these are not passed on.

3. IN THE HOUSE OF SOULS

They're not dead ... they are simply touching earth. All manner of wonderful things will be happening to them. Old spirits are flowing through their bodies; new spirits are whispering in their heads.
– Robert Holdstock *Lavondyss*

Death's inevitability casts a dark shadow in our society. Very few of us have seen a dead person, since death rarely takes place inside the home. Yet the doors of life and death open and close every second, with souls moving in either direction. We have acclimatization classes for trainee parents to learn birth procedures, yet no preparations for the process of dying.

Where once a young person's first experience of death would have been the passing of an elderly relative, it is becoming increasingly likely to be that of a close friend of their own age, by crime, accident or immune-system related illnesses. This is already having the effect of bringing the prospect of death and how to cope with it into much clearer focus, and creating a climate where the procedures around death and the prospect of the soul's continuing life are discussed more openly.

Death holds the greatest fear for people for whom physical reality is the only reality: they cannot share the sense of continuity or homecoming which accompanies the prospect of death among people who accept subtle reality. For many people in our culture, death signals the end of the only life they know about. Yet a majority of cultures hold that death is not the end.

What is Death?

The easiest way of understanding death is to see it as a birth into the fullness of subtle reality; conversely, birth may be seen as dying to our

159

awareness of subtle reality. Soul-life is a circuit which runs without ceasing. Many variant philosophies concur and conflict on what happens when we die. The following sequence is offered as a suggested shamanic rule of thumb:

1. At the point of death, life signs cease in the body.
2. During the next few hours/days, the soul separates from the body and passes into a solely subtle reality existence.
3. Before the body is buried or cremated, the soul may briefly visit the places and people with whom it was associated in life, before passing on to its appointed place.
4. At burial, the soul passes into the Realm of the Ancestors (see below), conducted by its allies, and is greeted by dear souls who have most recently entered there. This journey can sometimes take longer, if the soul has made no prior preparation for it.
5. Various possibilities arise following this reception: the soul may join the assembly of the deep ancestors, or it may work out any unresolved life problems from subtle reality or it may choose to reincarnate again; it may be appointed tasks in some part of the three worlds; it may become a teacher or guide to someone in physical reality.

Beyond Death

How it is possible for a soul to be contactable in some part of the three worlds and yet simultaneously be reincarnated somewhere in physical reality? I can only answer that time and space are different in the three worlds, and that the particular soul-resonance of a person is heard through the cosmic web in much the same way that the light of the stars still shines upon us even though its shining may be hundreds of years old. There are many different philosophies about reincarnation; most of these reinforce the subtle relationships of life upon the cosmic web. Some cultures have a closer kinship with other life-forms, such as animals, trees and plants; others perceive the reincarnation of human souls as a purely human affair.

In the Celtic tradition of the West Highlands of Scotland, the body is called the soul-shrine. At death, the soul leaves its shrine and passes into the house of souls, which is called the Land of the Dead or the Realm of the Ancestors in other cultures.

One of the prime shamanic tasks is to act as psychopomp, leading departed souls from life into death and into this realm. Many indigenous cultures ensure that the living have rehearsed their passage. The Egyptian and Tibetan Books of the Dead are afterworld maps and itineraries, to be learned before death so that the soul's journey is made more easily. Recently, many helpful books have been published to enable modern people to prepare their soul-route.[8]

The Journey Through Death

The Realm of the Ancestors most often appears as a separate enclave within the Underworld, although it has been my experience that different ancestral groups can be encountered in *any* of the three worlds. It is advisable to enter the Realm of the Ancestors only with good purpose and strong allies at your side. If you don't believe me, read the myths and folk-tales of any culture to confirm this: taboos against eating, drinking or sharing everyday transactions with the dead are encountered worldwide. If the shaman has to enter the ancestral realms, then it is usually to restore soul-parts of bereaved relatives or to have converse with one of the dead. Normally she will not even pass within its boundaries but merely travels to the gates from where her Underworld or ancestral allies go within. Just as Aeneas had his silver bough as a passport to the land of the dead, so too we need to discover our own signs and allies who will strengthen our soul on this perilous journey.

Death is viewed differently by those who die and those who are bereaved. In every case, the wishes and needs of the dying one take precedence over the survivors, for it is his journey, not theirs. Many people who die suddenly do not realize that they are dead; they may return to the places they inhabited in life and remain there, causing fright or consternation. Ghosts are usually wandering spirits who are lost; very rarely they are persistent spirits whose unfinished business causes them to remain earthbound. In such cases, these spirits need to pass into their own place. *Ask your allies for help in such cases: they may provide particular strategies for enabling earth-bound spirits to move on.*

When death is expected, due to age or sickness, then more preparation is possible. It is helpful to the dying one to create opportunities for talking about this process and finding out their wishes and expectations, and helping them to conclude unfinished business as discreetly and efficiently as possible. If the dying one is open to a shamanic perspective, it is possible to help prepare the soul-route (see Practice 49).

When we have to make decisions about who shall live or die, our first thought should be for the subject in question, whether it is someone on a life-support machine, a severely handicapped person or a foetus when a pregnancy has to be terminated. Even among people who are unconscious, injured or unborn, the soul is functional in subtle reality and may be consulted. We can avoid being manipulative by asking this soul what its wishes are. Only the dying one can choose to go. Make a journey to your allies and teacher to ask whether your help is appropriate; if it is, ask your helpers to take you to the dying one's helpers and find out what is required. This is especially important for those souls who wish to live but do not know how to get back to their bodies again after an accident and are in deep coma, or who need the reassurance that their relatives, partner or friends will support them in appropriate ways. In such cases, the shaman can help find the stray soul-parts and bring them home through soul-restoration (see Chapter 7). If the decision to abort a foetus or to terminate life-support has to be taken due to other factors, it is still imperative that the soul of the subject is contacted and prepared for this process: if this is impossible, then the soul should still be contacted afterwards to ensure that due honour and respect is paid, and that it has passed on appropriately.

Coping with sudden and accidental death is hard on the survivors who have no time to resolve matters with the deceased or say goodbye. Dealing with bereavement is easier if you can walk between the worlds at will and gain the help of your allies. But the links of need, love and sorrow are not so easily assuaged for others. Writing a letter to the dead and burning the letter so that it goes to the ancestral realms is a good method of saying our goodbyes. This is also useful for someone whose sibling or father died before they were born. A simple and appropriate funeral ritual is essential to announce death, to honour the dead and to aid the mourning process (see Practice 51).

It is always best to disperse the physical remains of the dead by burial or the scattering of ashes not longer than a month after death. Cremation is now common, but the etiquette of what to do with the ashes remains a vexed question for some. Many people fail to disperse the remains through ignorance of what to do, perhaps wanting a ceremony, but not a conventional one; meanwhile the ashes of Aunt Grace remain on the mantelpiece. Sometimes it is grief that prevents dispersal.

Some spirits of the dead purposely remain close to their loved ones to watch over them for a period. The daughter of Clara, one of my clients, died in a tragic accident while on the threshold of adulthood; Clara was aware that her daughter had not passed on and, in the depths of her grieving, took comfort that Nickie was still near, both seeing and talking to her. After a period of several months, Nickie began to appear in the company of other spirits about the house, as though her friends had come to collect her. Shortly afterwards, the presence of the dead girl left the house. Clara still grieves her loss, but is better able to cope as a result of Nickie's loving presence during the initial months of bereavement.

In cases where the body is not recovered, or is buried abroad, or where it is retained by the coroner pending investigation, it is often difficult for the bereaved to comprehend the reality of the death. During the First World War, many relatives of the men who died and were buried abroad consulted mediums in order to be reassured that the dead were at peace, and to reassure the dead that they were still loved and remembered. We can also check that the dead are peacefully passed over, by asking our allies' assistance.

Only a hundred years ago, a proper and recognized period of mourning used to be observed in the West, with the bereaved first wearing deepest black and then changing into purple and violet before assuming ordinary coloured clothing again. This was a helpful practice, signalling to all that the bereaved person needed sensitive treatment over a long period, since the process of mourning usually lasts for a minimum of two years. If we treat the bereaved as though they stand on the borders between life and death, as though looking upon a distant land where their loved ones walk, if we speak to them lovingly and with humour about the dead rather than avoiding the issue, if we weep with them and are available long after the event, we will enable their gradual return to daily life.

Facing Our Own Death

Only by facing and dealing with our own mortality and our certain journey into subtle reality will we be able to improve communication about death. By good preparation and resolving unfinished business, we will be able to pass into the house of souls and join the ancestors.

☙ Practice 48: Unfinished Business

One of the most salient features of death is its untidiness. If you were to die in the next twenty-four hours, what unfinished business in your life would worry you the most? Would it be an unreconciled quarrel, your unresolved plans for someone's well-being, the fact you'd not yet made a will? List the ten most pressing items. Issues like these cause our souls to remain earth-bound, but many can be resolved while we are alive and healthy. Now pick one item from the list and journey on it, asking your ancestral teacher and allies how you may best resolve it.

The regular practice of self-clarification is necessary if we are not to burden our descendants with our own unfinished business – mental baggage and behavioural problems. A periodic journey to our ancestral teacher to ask, 'What unnecessary burdens am I carrying and how can they be laid down?' will often clarify problems which have been slowing us down. Self-clarification keeps our lives healthy.

If you have unfinished business with someone who has died, journey to your ancestral teacher and ask to be taken to meet this person somewhere known to both the deceased and yourself during their lifetime. This may be somewhere in the Middleworld or elsewhere. Remember that the dead person may also have things to say to you.

☙ Practice 49: Preparing the Soul-route

Do not attempt this practice until you have visited all three worlds and gained allies there. This practice is for those who would like to prepare themselves better for their own death. Just as we rehearse the itinerary of our holidays in a far country, so too we can discover our soul-route. Please follow these instructions exactly.

Journey One:

1. Journey first of all to your guardian animal and Middleworld teacher and ask whether discovering your soul-route is appropriate for you at this time. If your allies indicate that it is not, do not go further.

2. If your allies advise this journey, then ask if there are any instructions you must fulfil before setting off. Ask your Middleworld teacher for a symbol to act as your anchor. Return from your journey and *draw this symbol* until it is imprinted on your memory.

Journey Two:

1. Ensure that your sourcing tape has a good recognizable call-back signal. Go with your guardian animal to your Middleworld teacher and ask him or her to be your anchor for the following journey. Your Middleworld teacher will tie a cord around your symbol which you will keep with you as you journey; as you do so your teacher will pay out the cord and so keep in contact with you.

2. Now journey to your ancestral teacher and ask to be shown the soul-route which you will take at death *as a map or diagram. Note:* you are *not* asking how or when you will die.

4. Your teacher will show you – by drawing in the earth or by showing you a map or in some other way – your destined soul-route. *Do not journey into this map.*

5. At the call-back signal, your Middleworld teacher will pull you back. Return and draw your soul-route as a map or diagram.

This journey helps you to chart the route you will follow. If you are on the threshold of death, you can familiarize yourself with your route, and call upon the help of allies, teachers and ancestors to greet and aid you. When the moment of death comes, your itinerary will be known to you, and your soul will not wander without direction.

✋ Practice 50: Scroll of Direction

Following the journey above, you may wish to create your own 'scroll of direction'. Several Orphic initiates of southern Italy and Crete were buried in the fourth to the second centuries BC with precise directions, inscribed on sheets of gold in amulets about their necks:

> Thou shalt find to the left of the House of Hades a spring,
> And by the side thereof standing a white cypress.
> To this spring approach not near.
> But thou shalt find another, from the Lake of Memory,
> Cold water flowing forth, and there are guardians before it.
> Say, 'I am a child of Earth and starry Heaven;
> But my race is of heaven alone. This ye know yourselves.
> But I am parched with thirst and I perish. Give me quickly
> The cold water flowing forth from the Lake of Memory.'[9]

From your own journey, compose your own instructions. You may write down directions, as in the example above, or you may choose to paint yours on paper or cloth as a map or picture. However you choose to do this, roll up your verbal or pictorial map and place it within a suitable container (such as a roll of leather or a small box) and inscribe your death-route symbol upon it. It can be stored in your shamanic bag (see Practice 62) until the time you need to rehearse the route, nearer your death.

🖐 Practice 51: Passage of the Soul

This ceremony is not one that you will ever personally facilitate: it is a ceremony to mark your own passing, to be celebrated by your family and friends. The existence of such a ceremony alongside your legal Will will be of great benefit to your loved ones who may be too stunned by your death to make arrangements that you would approve of. It also avoids any family contention about your actual spirituality: 'He was life-long Presbyterian and that's how he's going to be buried.' Your ceremony need only be short; it doesn't have to conform to the funeral service of conventional religion. If you wish to create a full funeral service, you can do so; any person appointed by you can legally act as the celebrant or facilitator at a crematorium. This ceremony enables you to draw upon your personal spirituality while providing a framework for your family and friends to say goodbye to you. Your ceremony may come together through long contemplation as well as by journeying to your allies for advice and guidance.

As a walker between the worlds, you will inevitably collect items of power which you use. Drums, rattles, feathers, stones and other objects that you habitually use in your shamanizing will become empowered, tuned to the frequency of your work. To ensure that they are bequeathed to other practitioners or decommissioned respectfully, leave clear instructions in your will, appointing a ritual or shamanic executor who will respect your wishes.

168

• CHAPTER 6 •

The Upperworld

For a fortress to be secret, it must be invisible. It must have no boundaries of exclusiveness – it must be an Internal Fortress of Practice rather than an external institution.

– Ngakpa Chögyam

1. THE SONG OF INNER SPACE

Thou shalt be in league with the beings of the future, and the generations to come after shall be at peace with thee.

– Joanna Macy *World as Lover, World as Self*

The Upperworld is the visionary and archetypal realm of the three worlds. Here we access knowledge, information and inspiration; here we gain overviews of things and perceive the blueprints of life. If we recall the image of the great tree, p.49, we will see that its branches pierce the Upperworld; it is here that we discover the fruits of that tree and are enabled to bring home the harvest of our lives. The pristine beauty and primal connection we experience in the Upperworld is immediate and moving. There is no shadow of decay, pollution or spoliation, but a paradisal realm of vision.

This realm has been written about by every major artist, poet and visionary. Visions of the Upperworld haunt our imagination with dreams of paradise. Many shamans speak about the Upperworld as 'the pure country'.

169

Samuel Coleridge's description of his opium-induced vision of Kublai Khan's Xanadu attempts to convey the pristine perfection of the Upperworld. Wordsworth wrote that 'heaven lies about us in our infancy' and, truly, children whose fontanelles are not yet closed do experience deep communion with this realm. The fontanelles, the bones at the top of the skull, remain soft and pliant in childhood to allow for the growth of the head: this area is believed to be a shamanic gateway to otherworlds. Adults find contact more difficult, so they may have recourse to drink or drugs to reach it, rather than seek the Upperworld by simple exposure to nature's beauty.

Distortions of the Upperworld

The Upperworld has been promoted as the goal of many spiritualities: here the gods dwell in unchanging bliss, here the blessed souls of departed heroes or saints are to be found, from here angelic beings descend as divine messengers. We are told that only the good and truthful and perfect are admitted, while all others are shut out. Again, many religions have barred the way to this world, seeking to admit only their own members, 'the chosen', to unending bliss, content in the notion that the remainder of humanity (all other species are not admitted, as they are believed not to have souls!) to the torments of hell. The hubris and exclusivity of fundamentalist claims to heaven have so tainted our view of the Upperworld that many people have declared they would rather burn merrily in the company of the damned than endure a pious eternity in the company of the chosen.

According to this dualist viewpoint, the Underworld is associated with the evils of the past, with the fall from grace in Genesis, while the Upperworld becomes the focus for the millennial and apocalyptic visions depicted in Revelations.[1] If the West has neglected the Underworld, it has also concentrated too strongly upon the Upperworld, vaunting its benefits in an unbalanced way which has led to a great deal of paranoia and illusion. Just as neglect and avoidance of the Underworld create shadowy and fearful projections, so overdependence upon the Upperworld creates gross stereotypes out of primal archetypes, producing people who are intolerant of shadow and who live only for 'the light'. For such people, the Upperworld is a phantasmagoria of illusions which can be as beguiling and misleading as any Christian projection of hell upon the Underworld. From a distorted Upperworld vision we derive our passivity, which expects heavenly beings to do everything for us, with no effort needed from ourselves. Such an obsessional craving for things to be 'of the light' can create a sickly and dishonest view of life, as well as casting a giant shadow behind us in which the problematic and inconvenient aspects of life accumulate. In an attempt to be supra-heavenly, we can incarnate gross imbalances.

The Spirit Quest

Loss of communion with the Upperworld is related in countless myths, involving the withdrawal of the gods and great teachers or the severance of the bridge which links us with wisdom and knowledge. The theft of heaven's fire by Prometheus and the theft of divine substance by Sophia are myths about our reconnection with the Upperworld, with our spiritual quest.[2] We must view these stories about the theft of divine knowledge with the eyes of mystics and shamans: this reveals that the gods guard wisdom which they intend humans to find eventually, that the whole spiritual quest is about this finding and its implementation. The human dilemma is that we may steal knowledge without wisdom: *we want the techniques but not the responsibility.* This is why initiatory threshold guardians are met upon the spiritual quest: angels with fiery swords, mythological beasts with riddles and gods who change into a variety of challenging shapes. Only those initiates who are willing to take on the task of gatekeeper to the mysteries in their turn are entitled to use the wisdom that they find. Only by practice and personal implementation can we become initiates of knowledge.

Yet we can journey, freely and without favour, to the Upperworld and find inspiration and vision that will nurture our lives and refresh our own world. Just as the power of the cosmic web wells up from the Underworld and cannot be kept from flowing into us, so too the love of Spirit flows down from the Upperworld and permeates our whole being. Reconnection with the Upperworld restores to us ways of spiritual understanding, intense ecstasy and vision. When we clearly observe the lines of our creative destiny and the patterns of our soul's questing, we are restored to our authentic spiritual vision, which no-one can take from us.

Through reacquaintance with the shamanic principles of the cosmic web, we realize how some religions have kept us from our true heritage. Our relationship with power and Spirit is primarily experienced in the physical reality of the Middleworld, but when we are denied our natural access to the power of the cosmic web, we are denied entrance to the Underworld; when we are denied our natural access to the Spirit of the cosmic web, we are denied entrance to the Upperworld. Effectively, our souls become trapped in one world.

In our post-religious age, this spiritual strait-jacket is taking a different shape. Because our society accepts only physical reality as real and sees subtle reality as unreal, because it is increasingly influenced by a narrow and blinkered media, we run the risk of being imprisoned in a mediocrity from which creativity, original thought and spiritual passion have been purged.

More than ever we need to pursue our spiritual quest.

Permit yourself to reclaim your own access to power and Spirit!

Recovering Our Own Spiritual Identity

Humankind's territorial greed has extended to the inner space of the three worlds. Many religions have made strong attempts to colonize inner space for themselves and to dictate who may go there and under what conditions. One of the great freedoms of working shamanically is the ability to reclaim inner space. Throughout time, humankind has told stories to explain and understand where inner space is, who inhabits it and what happens within it. Many stories tell how beings came out of inner space, from heaven or a high mountain, to help humankind; there are also many stories of how some humans have travelled into inner space for wisdom, power or a healing gift, like Gilgamesh for the elixir of immortality or like Perceval for the Holy Grail. These are not individual quests for a personal nirvana, but heroic reclamations of the common reservoir of inspiration and healing.

Shamanism today is about the re-discovery of inner space. Although the appropriation of people's personal perceptions of inner space is still rigidly maintained in our post-religious culture, the fact remains that no-one can impose one story upon all people to explain the purpose of our life. This is beginning to be realized as more and more people seek their authentic spiritual identity by other than orthodox means.

But if we abandon 'the one saving story' how will we know our life's purpose? *Authentic spiritual identity can only be discovered by accessing all the appropriate co-ordinates of our life: these are unique to each person.* Certain groups of people will be in closer accord than others, and will associate together to follow broadly one story or myth. All myths and saving stories should be regarded as rules of thumb, working plans and blueprints which have their currency upon the cosmic web. In addition, we will find parts of the story from our own life and experiences: our dreams, visions and journeys will reveal the landscape of our soul.

In all generations and times, Spirit manifests in certain energy frequencies which we can contact. We are currently undergoing a spring-cleaning of many old forms relating to what astrologers call the Piscean Age: these forms are typified by abnegation of sexuality and purgation of the body, and by hierarchical spiritual frameworks. And, just as when we go to throw something away, we are tempted to find another use for it or we discover that it is really most precious to us, so some people are discovering that the old Piscean forms are suddenly most attractive and desirable. Waves of fundamentalism shake our world, as this spring-cleaning current is denied. Fundamentalism arises from fear of change; the threat of the new terrifies it. So people seek order, structure and community frameworks which totally dictate their lives rather than swim alone in the seeming chaos which heralds the incoming current.

The incoming Aquarian current is heralded by a striving for more liberal, equitable, socially conscious and spiritualized structures. Self-empowerment and the search for personal spiritual identity are regarded as dangerous by those of the old mind-set. Just as the Piscean world-view distorted our perception of the three worlds and barred access thither, so the Aquarian world-view tends to go to the opposite extreme and burst open all gates in order to access information, power and Spirit that much quicker.

The walker between the worlds must still heed the milestones, signposts and border checks of the three worlds, without the fear and exclusivity of the Piscean seeker, yet always remembering that she is responsible for her motivations and subsequent actions upon the cosmic web.

Knowledge and Responsibility

Responsibility for knowledge that we receive may seem an alien concept but all shamanic knowledge-keepers realize that *knowledge must be applied with wisdom*. We do not teach three-year-old children how the controls of a car work; only when they are sixteen or so are they sufficiently mature. When the physicists who discovered nuclear power realized to what terrible uses their discovery would be put, it was already too late for them to be responsible: that knowledge cannot now be forgotten, only used wisely.

When we journey to the Upperworld, we discover many things and must live forever with that knowledge. This is why it is important to have a well-balanced life and a good, well-grounded knowledge of the Middleworld and the Underworld before we soar off to the Upperworld. This is especially important if the access to power and Spirit has been barred to us for significant periods of our lives. Indigenous societies rightly fear unscrupulous shamans who seek to appropriate power and knowledge: this is how sorcerers, fanatics and manipulators come into being. They gild their own route on the cosmic web instead of being a part of it. We are familiar with this pattern wherever power and knowledge become the perquisite of any specialist group, whether it be in politics, religion or learning.

Our task is not to manipulate the universe to our vision, but to connect with the cosmic web in a healthy way, allowing the power and knowledge of the universe to flow into and through us for the benefit of all, conscious of the Spirit in all places. As we are brought into closer harmony with the cosmic web, we may become guardians of knowledge and power – not in order to bar the ways of genuine seekers or people in need, but in order to keep the connections wisely. And who guards the guardians? Why, none other than our allies in inner space, at whose behest we are appointed, with whom we keep watch, and who offer correctives when our human weakness or lack of vision threatens the work. This co-operative guardianship keeps us safe.

Accessing the Upperworld

Let us return to our consideration of the Upperworld. Many of us already access the Upperworld in our daily lives, as when we seek to gain an archetypal overview of a situation, when we turn to any creative or spiritual source for inspiration or enlightenment, whenever we seek guidance in a difficult situation, whenever we bounce ideas around in our heads and get an overwhelming hunch that something will work, whenever we envision the prototype or blueprint of something we wish to create.

As the Underworld is associated with the ancestors, with beginnings and the past, so the Upperworld is associated, though not exclusively, with the future, with possibility and outcome. It is a good place to divine information that we will need, to find sources of inspiration and knowledge, to seek solutions to incomplete sequences of events. With the power of the Underworld to help us make Upperworld ideas manifest, the Middleworld comes into true balance.

It is not for nothing that the luminaries of the Upperworld, the star-spirits, are associated with the patterns of our destiny. Modern astrology associates our birth date with a sign of the zodiac, which is comprised of the twelve constellations visible to the classical Mediterranean world. Each constellation has a planetary ruler who is considered to be a salient influence. Although modern systems of astrology have been adopted to cover the whole globe, it is clear that indigenous peoples each have different planetary foci, based upon the constellations visible in *their own* night sky. They regard the stars and constellations as powerful teachers, and many peoples derive their tribal genesis and protection from ancestral star-beings.

The influence of the stars upon the Middleworld and the harnessing of the gifts they revealed was the concern of the hermetic way, which essentially sought to reveal the divine likeness in humanity and in nature by alchemical transformation and spiritual realization. In Neo-Platonic and medieval hermeneutics each planet corresponded to terrestrial substances, qualities, metals. This system perceived the underlying and superimposing similarities by which the worlds mirror each other and this was expressed in the hermetic dictum: 'That which is above is like that which is below, and that which is below is like that which is above.' Hermes was the tutelary deity of this magical way of perception. The arts of healing, change and transmutation were in the hands of magicians who travelled between these worlds in more sophisticated ways than the primal shamans.[3]

It has been suggested that the symbols painted on the drums of Saami shamans may indicate star horizons visible from the earth.[4] Across the world are many terrestrial patterns that can only be appreciated from the air, yet they were inscribed upon the land by earth-bound human beings – the Nazca lines and images, the chalk hill figures of Britain and the configuration of many sacred landscapes, for example. How did they come to be there? Some of these designs have stellar relationships, like the Egyptian necropolis of the Great Pyramid and its surrounding monuments which are reflections of the Milky Way. Perhaps the designers of these sacred patterns placed them there not only as a result of celestial observation but also through Upperworld journeying.

Our Upperworld journeys restore us to a similar sense of perspective: when the jigsaw of our lives seems to be coming together but we cannot see quite how, an Upperworld journey will give us the piece that we lack and reveal a clearer picture. Just like the Navajo *hatali*, the sand-painting shaman, we are able to restore the *hozho*, the harmony, balance and beauty of our lives by looking upon the shapes of our earth.[5]

Beings encountered in the Upperworld include great birds, large sea beasts, spiders, starry spirits or seraphic angels, deities of spinning, weaving, fabrication and creation, companies of ancestors who teach certain skills and schools of spiritual teachers. The *genius* of the Upperworld often appears as a creative and solar god, while the *juno* of the Upperworld frequently appears as a spinning, stellar goddess like Ariadne: these may appear in partnership as the guardians of a celestial court, as Logos and Sophia.

The Upperworld stimulates the frontal lobes of our cerebrum, connecting the two hemispheres and drawing upon the deep memories of the brain stem to create brilliant fruits of revelation. As the place of beauty, harmony and vision, of spiritual help and guidance, the Upperworld is where we find the allies who are able to give us answers and solutions.

ॐ *Practice 52*: Finding an Upperworld Ascent

In order to reach the Upperworld, we need to journey upwards. Find a place from which to ascend that exists in physical reality, not an imagined place: a tall tree, a high mountain or cliff, a waterfall, a rainbow, the smoke of a fire. This ascent might be near your journey-centre, but it doesn't have to be.

In the northern hemisphere, the Upperworld is often typified by the Milky Way and the circumpolar stars, especially the Great Bear which points to Polaris – the nail of the heavens, around which the circumpolar stars revolve. The Milky Way is a trail which has become associated with many terrestrial pilgrimage routes – including the English way to Our Lady of Walsingham and the Spanish route to St James of Compostella. It still makes a good route to the Upperworld.

The Celtic Otherworld, which relates to the Upperworld, has many related islands which correspond to the stars of the firmament in classic shamanic cosmology: it is reached by a shamanic overseas voyage in a boat without oars or rudder, piloted by otherworldly allies.[6] Such a boat is another possibility.

If to make your ascent, you use a medium which would not lend itself to climbing in physical reality, such as water or smoke; it will become amenable to your climbing in subtle reality.

✋ Practice 53: The Upperworld Journey

The Upperworld journey unfolds in the following way:

1. Your purpose for the first journey is to seek access to the Upperworld and reconnection with the sources of your inspiration. Exclude light, be comfortable, start to source, recalling your purpose and bringing to mind your Upperworld ascent.

2. Call upon your guardian animal to meet you at the foot of your ascent. Do not ascend without it. It is possible that, as you climb or when you emerge into the Upperworld, another animal may appear as an auxiliary helper. Follow the procedures for accepting an animal as on p.123.

3. Your initial Upperworld journey may be more difficult than either the Underworld or Middleworld ones. You may start to tire, it may feel as though it's going on too long, you may feel like giving up. Stiffen your resolve and ask for your animal to encourage you. As you reach the heights of your ascent – the top of the rainbow, tree, mountain – you may experience other difficulties: a mistiness may obscure your way or you may encounter some kind of physical resistance to your journeying further. This is usually experienced as a kind

of skin or membrane, or a zone of confusion or obscurity, a narrow or guarded place. Some people get to the top of their ascent and feel there is nowhere else to go except to jump off.

To gain the Upperworld, you must pass beyond this critical point. Check that your animal is with you and keep on going through the mist; press forwards into the skin as if your whole body were a pin going to prick a balloon, go through the obscure door, jump off your mountain top: you will be able to fly. Note that, though on subsequent journeys your animal will sometimes fly or ride you up with great velocity, *it will not usually precede you on your first entrance to the Upperworld.* Your own efforts must win a way through. Ask for your animal's encouragement and help.

4. Your successful entrance into the Upperworld may be accompanied by a feeling of being sucked through an hourglass or the kind of inside-out feeling that sometimes accompanies fairground rides. This is not generally repeated on subsequent journeys. Check that your animal is with you and look around. You may have been expecting clouds or featureless space, but on emerging through the difficulty of the doorway you will find a world with ground, landscape and sky. Because the Upperworld is associated with the gods and originating blueprints of life, you may see great cities or edifices of extreme complexity, but it may equally appear as a broad and beautiful landscape of any kind of geographical zone.

What does the Upperworld feel like? Unlike the often womb-like enclosure of the Underworld, where we draw upon power by a process of osmosis, in the Upperworld we often feel that all our faculties have been given the clarity of crystal. The archetypal brightness and clarity of this place nearly always strikes us as very beautiful and harmonious. You may also experience a complete sense of blessedness.

5. Now ask your guardian animal, or any new animal you have accepted on the way up or when you emerged here, to be led to the sources of your inspiration. Your animals may work in tandem. Follow its/their direction.

6. Your journey may unfold in a number of ways here. You may be led to a place or series of places where you may meet inspirers and reconnect with them; you may be shown or may engage in skills, crafts or actions which inspire you. Follow your animal's direction; do not try to appreciate intellectually what you experience during the journey: there is time for interpretation afterwards.

178

7. At the call-back, give thanks for any experience or gift, return the way you came, bringing any new animal with you, record your journey and perform Practice 55, simultaneously also dancing any new animal you have met.

Note: People who are not well grounded have a tendency to drift off slightly in the Upperworld. Counteract this by concentrating on what is happening, minute by minute, and what it feels like: be aware of your body walking, climbing and acting in the journey. Ask your animal to keep you well anchored.

This is a good point to discuss what lies beyond the Upperworld. Many traditions speak of the area surrounding the three worlds as 'the void' and see it as a trackless and unformulated emptiness. I have visited the void during shamanic healing sessions and indeed found it to be a place of great vastness. However, to allay any fear of 'falling off the edge of the universe', I must say that, even in the void, the filaments of the cosmic web still run. My experience of the void suggests to me that the threads and intersections of the web are here so widely spaced that it is difficult for us to perceive them, but they *are* present.

We do not generally journey into the void except in order to rescue stray soul-parts or for some other good purpose, and then only at the behest of and accompanied by our strongest allies. In many ways it feels like the space-walk of an astronaut: attached by a slim life-support line and totally dependent upon a vast back-up team. The ability to remain calm and directed when travelling through the void is dependent upon the help of our allies, in whom we must have great trust, but they will not direct us thither unless there is important work to do.

☙ *Practice 54:* Finding an Upperworld Teacher of Your Spiritual Lineage

In the last chapter, we found an Underworld teacher of our blood lineage, drawn from near or deep ancestral kindred. But we actually have two kinds of lineage: that of blood and that of spirit. Our physical relations are our blood kindred, but our spiritual relations are our spiritual kindred. Our spiritual kindred can include our otherworldly allies and teachers, as well as other living beings with whom we share a particular resonance or kinship of heart, mind and spirit. We each have several human friendships of this nature of which we are aware, as well as certain unspoken and unacknowledged affinities with other species in physical reality.

Our spiritual lineage often has little to do with formalized religion. We are each attracted to certain kinds of activities, ways of thinking and believing, and will gravitate towards others of our kind and towards teachers in whom we discern the authentic current of our life's motivation. If we trace these influences and correlations beyond these like-minded people and resonant teachers, we come to the broad strands of the cosmic web which lead through the Upperworld into our own world. Like the spectrum of the rainbow, through the range of academic subjects or practical skills, we will find that we arrive at the strong motivating energies which weave the web: justice, compassion, truth, love, healing, guardianship of the mysteries, creation, recycling, vision – we instinctively seek to enter the stream which sings to us the song of our motivating genius.

Our spiritual lineage receives inspiration from our upbringing, culture, teachers, education and many other factors. Spiritual inspiration is found in many traditions. *Shamanism does not ask you to give them up or gainsay their help or guidance.* The pressure of our spiritual lineage is forever seeking new river beds. This is especially true at this time when orthodox spiritualities themselves are under demolition and restructuring.

This time you are going to journey to find an Upperworld teacher of your spiritual lineage: that is, a teacher with whom you are in total sympathy of heart, mind and spirit, *not a spiritual guru or guide.* Your Upperworld teacher will advise, grant wisdom and knowledge, and give overviews: he will not dictate the order of your life or give advice on trivial matters. A teacher is a companion, not a nanny. He or she will usually be humanoid in appearance, though not always a discarnate human; he or she will never be a person now currently incarnate.

1. Prepare an issue about which you need help or information. Exclude light, be comfortable, begin sourcing and journey to the Upperworld in company with your animal, in search of an Upperworld teacher of your spiritual lineage.

2. Emerge into the Upperworld and go looking for your teacher, asking your animal's assistance. Ask any figure you meet if she is your Upperworld teacher.

3. When you have found your teacher and mutually accepted each other, ask about your current issue. Follow directions or listen.

4. At the call-back, conclude your business together, say goodbye and return the way you came, remembering the co-ordinates of your teacher's abode. You do not bring your teacher back with you.

♉ Practice 55: Dancing with Our Inspirers

The spaciousness of the Upperworld can become our dancing floor where we dance with the stars, with our inspirers and spiritual guardians, where we enter into a non-dual and ecstatic dance of unity. Find some music which inspires and uplifts you. Feel it lifting your spirits and move with the music. As you begin to source, stretch out your hands and reach for the hands of your inspirers and spiritual teachers. Dance in a circuit of blissful elation, feeling your steps and movements rippling out upon the cosmic web in joyful inspiration. Rejoice in the wisdom of your inspirers and feel yourself becoming part of the chain dance. Finish by acknowledging the seven directions (see Practice 37) in slow, formal motions, so that you and the dance are grounded and reflected in the Middleworld.

♉ Practice 56: Exploring the Upperworld

The Upperworld is where we find the archetypal patterns of our lives. Journeys to the Upperworld are often ecstatically moving, and we often find ourselves dancing, singing or chanting here. Knowledge of the divine mysteries of Spirit is imparted here and the blueprints of the universe are often found stored in the Upperworld. In the hermetic tradition, the akashic records are also discoverable in the Upperworld, although these days you may as easily find a microchip library as a conventional book-filled one. You may see 'viewing screens', or windows which access different parts of the cosmic web. The Upperworld is not only attuned to future possibilities and developments, but is important for discovering the potentialities of our present situation.

181

The following are suggestions for increasing our proficiency in Upperworld work.

1. Which deities/archetypes/heroes/heroines attract you most? What functions/ skills/qualities do they have? How are these present within yourself? Travel to the Upperworld and meet with one figure with whom you feel a strong connection.

2. Check out your known spiritual lineage by asking yourself, 'Who are my spiritual kindred? Who are my spiritual ancestors?' Poets, philosophers, practitioners, artists, musicians, spiritual teachers alive and dead may be included on your list. Give thanks for their lives, inspiration and teachings by writing them on a scroll. This can live on your shrine or be carried in your shamanic bag. Look at it periodically and burn a candle or some incense to honour and celebrate their influence.

3. Journey to your inspirers when you begin or conceive a creative project, to assist your making.

4. Journey to your spiritual lineage teacher to ask, 'What is the purpose of my life?' or 'What is my spiritual vocation?'

5. Journey to your spiritual lineage teacher to ask what needs restoration and renewal in your life, and how this may be accomplished.

6. Ask your teacher what you may restore to the Upperworld.

✋ *Practice 57*: Creating Spaciousness

The West has attempted to fill its spiritual vacuum by accumulations of consumer durables. 'To a great extent, our culture emphasizes accumulation, enrichment, storing up; other cultures have elevated emptying to the ultimate goal,' writes Holger Kalweit.[7] This principle encompasses all spiritual work: the greater the space, the greater the capacity. To give away is to make space, to create potential.

Many cultures practise almsgiving, tribal sharing of goods as in the north-west American *potlatch* ceremony, or the voluntary abnegation of possessions prior to an important initiation. The West's attitude to giving things or resources is rooted within a mistaken application of Christian sacrifice: as a painful rather than a meritorious action. We are all too happy to give away our second-best efforts or our outworn things to benefit

someone, but we generally avoid giving of our best. Giving of our possessions, resources, service, time and expertise, space and power, helps unseat
the consumer-mindedness of our society, reconnecting pathways, creating
spaciousness and better distribution of energy upon the cosmic web.

This week make a journey to one of your Upperworld allies and your
teacher, asking, 'What can I give away to create spaciousness on the cosmic
web?' This is often a very difficult journey for Westerners to take and to
implement, but it is also a very revealing and clarifying one. Don't be surprised if your giveaway is not a material one. It might be your sense of self-
importance or your anxiety about losing weight.

2. THE SONG THAT SOUNDS IN THE SILENCE
Silence is the general consecration of the universe.
– Herman Melville

The lessons of the Upperworld are about discovering peace and harmony,
about becoming resonant with our destiny. Too often we attempt only the
mundane correlatives of this quest in the Middleworld – a quiet life, an
orderly regimen and a satisfactory collusion with circumstance; these content most people. But when we travel to the Upperworld we begin to suffer
'divine discontent' with such mundane ambitions, realizing that we need to
feed our souls, not just our bodies.

The Song of the Universe

We discover peace, harmony and resonance with our destiny only by entering into the spaciousness of the Upperworld and allowing that space into
our lives. It is then that the overlay of the Upperworld can open up new
dimensions in our lives. The first essential is to enter into the silence of
space, to still the internal dialogue, to separate our song from its entangle-
ment with other songs, to create an internal fortress from which we can
review our lives. This is achieved by simple meditation: closing our eyes,
breathing and reviewing things with neutrality in the space of silence. Some
people fear that to separate ourselves in meditation, for however short a

time, is somehow selfish or exclusive. The priestess, Felicity Wombwell, writes tellingly of this fear, reminding us that:

> '... freedom is space: boundaries represent love. Boundaries and space need to be properly maintained so they are not constantly infringed by society and others ... if we have our own space where we can go to find the true self ... we can remember who and what we are ... This is why meditation is so useful and powerful.'[8]

The quietness in which to be ourselves is extremely rare. It is often only in situations of enforced waiting that we have the leisure to enter that silence, when the circumstances or surroundings are usually inappropriate. For many, the spaciousness of silence is intolerable, to be speedily dissipated by radio, TV or music. In a world saturated with visual stimuli and the written word, we may also need 'the silence of the eyes', and rest in the darkness. Unused to the desert wastes of silence, we never enter the boundaries of our souls to find that spacious freedom in which peace dwells. For those who have not ventured into their own internal fortress in love and freedom, this peace is unimaginable – a blank, static emptiness in which nothing happens.

It is only in the intentioned silence of vigil and meditation, or in the quiet places of nature, that we encounter the song of the universe. Like the wind through telegraph wires, this song echoes along the pathways of the cosmic web: it includes the celestial spinning of the planets, as well as the hum of insects and the dancing song of the grass, it includes the song of all the ancestors and spirits as well as the beating of our own hearts. The song of the universe is the voice of Spirit.

Most primal myths speak of the world coming into being through the utterance of sound. The ineffable power of sound with intention is immeasurable; the use of the sacred word causes divinity to be present, as in the Gospel of St John, where the Word becomes flesh, God incarnate in the person of Christ. When Hindus utter the sacred Sanskrit word *aum*, they recreate the world by sounding the original creative word, for each letter manifests the Hindu *trimurti*, the threefold deities who bound the universe: 'a' evokes the changelessness of Brahma, 'u' evokes the endurance of Vishnu, 'm' evokes the transmutation of Shiva, so that existence, consciousness and experience are comprehended in the one syllable. 'The past, present and the future are all included in this one sound, and all that exists beyond the three forms of time is also implied in it.'[9] Classical tradition similarly speaks of the celestial 'Song of the Spheres', the harmony of notes issued by each planet in the solar system.

It is in the silence of inner space that we become aware of the harmony of Spirit, of the song that Spirit is always singing in the silence. This is the secret of meditation: not an empty silence or a hollow peace, but a living pulse, a shapely song which becomes the music of our soul.

Since I was a baby, I've always maintained a 'humming brief', unconsciously tuning into the song of whatever space I was in. This got me into trouble at school where successive teachers hissed or shouted at me: 'Stop that irritating noise!' I have never stopped singing. When I began to take up my shamanic work in earnest I found that this practice of singing the song of the universe was important in helping people. In most soul-work, I sing the healing song that comes from the soul of my clients. Since it is rare in our society to be sung to, this experience usually wakens the soul and speaks to the heart, helping that person to hear and sing their own song.

'The voice is an instrument that echoes the soul and it is the soul's energy that makes every sound unique,' writes voice expert, Patsy Rodenburg.[10] We only arrive at harmony when we ourselves are in harmony.

Finding Our True Destiny

We think of destiny as being pre-determined, laid down ages ago, unchanging and inflexibly related to time. Time bludgeons us into conformity, dissecting the eternal moment and fragmenting the creative hour. The tyranny of time can only be broken by perceiving eternity. It is not in the stop-gap solution or in the sound-bite that we live but in the spaciousness of eternity. Continuity is timeless upon the cosmic web, where 'then' and 'when' have no currency. The healer, Barbara Ann Brennan, reminds us that:

'... what occurs in Great Time has sequence, but it cannot be dated ... As we live our life *now*, it becomes more likely that we are rewriting our personal history, both past and future.'[11]

185

To be at peace with ourselves, we need to know ourselves. Each person's incarnational cord – the connected linkage of life after life – has its own unique twist: this metaphor derives from the spinning of yarn where the thread is teased out of a hank of wool and spun on a drop spindle. We may imagine our lives as such a thread, the wool teased from our ancestral blood lineage and the colour provided by our spiritual lineage; but the twist of the spinning is something we personally provide.

In seeking our destiny in this life, shamanism works with the present incarnation. Whatever our purpose in life, whatever lessons we may be learning, we can discover these from looking at our own life in relation to the cosmic web. Although many people have found regression to past incarnations helpful, seeking after past lives can be an escape from committing fully to the present life, as well as a means of abrogating responsibility for dealing with issues now. Whichever lifetime of our incarnational thread we examine, we will find a unique twist and coloration which bespeaks our motive and purpose.

In the eternal now of subtle reality, each walker between the worlds must clarify the ancestral bequest and seek out the spiritual pathways which are most appropriate to her. Our incarnational thread is stretched between these two directions; in between these we can examine the nature of our thread, the ways it behaves when we weave with it, the kinds of patterns and blocks of colour it creates. The call signature of our destiny comes to us from our spiritual lineage, just as our physical appearance derives from our ancestral lineage. The behaviour of our own thread is determined by the way we name and ensoul our desires.

When our desires and motivations are hidden from us because we have lost direction or been lured into inappropriate lines or because we have just failed to provide ourselves access to good soul-food, our incarnational thread enters a meaningless phase of meandering which it will be necessary to unpick before long.

The Upperworld challenges us to seek our spiritual pathway for the benefit of all beings on the cosmic web: this call has caused many to scale the heights of altruistic effort, but it has been frequently ill-applied by those who have not as yet unpicked the muddle of their incarnational thread. Conventional religious sentiment has confounded with selfishness any such

spiritual preparation. It is very important that we all understand this principle before we go further on the shamanic path: for without vocational
impulse, incarnational clarification and spiritual preparation, any shamanic
work that we propose will become entangled with our own muddle. Any
tendencies and imbalances within us will be mercilessly illuminated by the
light of the Upperworld. (See Chapter 7, Part 2.)

Permit yourself to untangle your incarnational thread!

The Upperworld encourages us to take a whole overview of our lives so that
we may know ourselves through self-discovery and so be able to release the
energy which is seeded within us, just as the Underworld encourages us to
dive deeply into our heritage and tradition, to realize our resources, to
remember our capabilities and to take up the power that flows through the
universe, so that our roots are nourished.

But the Middleworld is our mother place, our home, where we work out
what we have learned, to which we mediate the advice and healing which we
gain from the otherworlds. It is now time to return to this realm and start
putting what we have learned into practice.

☙ *Practice 58:* Soul-food

The issue of soul malnutrition rarely enters the agendas of governments, yet
people are dying of it all around us and we don't even notice. We need
soul-food to the same extent as we need ordinary food. Our soul feeds on
beauty and harmony, needing times of recreation, of creativity and of
ecstatic uplift. There are no rules about soul-food: you eat when you are
hungry, wherever the food is offered. Dancing, painting, reading, walking,
contemplating, making things – any of these may be soul-food. Communion
with the Upperworld necessitates that we seek out the soul-food that we
need for life as a primal responsibility.

Journey to your inspirers and spiritual lineage teacher and ask, 'What
nurtures my soul? What soul-food do I lack? Where can it be found?' The
response to these questions may entail pursuing your vision and creative
quest with continual commitment, realizing that receptivity and rest must

be balanced by practice and activity. For our creative processes must follow their own seasonal or natural growth patterns: we cannot always be creative or always fallow, there will be the between times when practice brings only meagre results.

Permit yourself to make space for soul nourishment!

✋ *Practice 59*: Creating the Inner Fortress of Silence

Sacred space generally has meant one thing in our society: a temple or church which has been blessed for sacred practice. In shamanism, all space is sacred. This space can be as narrow as the amount of room your body displaces in physical reality or as limitless as inner space. We all have our own access to inner space where our creative spirit can have reconnection with the universe, an inner fortress of silent space which comes with you wherever you are.

The tantric shaman, Ngakpa Chögyam, writes:

'For a fortress to be secret, it must be invisible. It must have no boundaries of exclusiveness – it must be an Internal Fortress of Practice rather than an external institution.'[12]

Your fortress is a strong place of refuge where you can retreat in order to clarify your daily life, where you still the inner dialogue and find the creative silence. In this silence, your shamanic hearing will develop.

If you are irritated, hassled and fraught, the chances are you've not entered your inner fortress for a long time. Practise this once a day: sit outside, if possible, or inside in a quiet place where you can see some part of the natural world. Release any tensions and worries that you are holding in your body. Still your breathing and enter the rhythm, laying aside all distracting thoughts. If distractions arise in your mind, don't hold them but let them become like clouds that float away. Feel your own body space around you – this is your own space which cannot be taken from you. If you have been hard-pressed recently and your body space feels flattened, inflate it now with your breath.

Now, become aware of the space surrounding the place where you sit/stand. Feel this as a distinct space at first, then allow your space and this space to merge. Experience how your space is also part of the larger universal space. Now turn your thoughts to the abode of your spiritual lineage teacher in the Upperworld and, without straining to retain this image, allow this abode to descend about you as your own internal fortress of practice. Make no attempt to source or journey, but remain in light meditation. Reverse the procedure until you are aware of your own body space again.

Practise this whenever moments of natural introspection come upon you. Use these precious moments of insight to see into the heart of things. At night, enter your secret fortress of stillness to unprocess the day's events; without self-blame, guilt or anger, but with neutrality, mark how your actions, words and thoughts have moved the cosmic web today.

✋ Practice 60: Voice as the Soul's Pathway

As you have begun to source and journey, you will have discovered how many parts of your body become vehicles for power, especially the voice. The songs that come to us when shamanizing are not recreational songs. They may come with yelps, animal cries and syllabic vocalizations that are not words, in spirit language, ignoring the accepted musical structures of our culture. Such songs are sacred songs of great power.

Many people are alienated from their own voices and reluctant to use them, but no vocal expertise is required for shamanic singing. Learn to enjoy your own voice and not be estranged by it. One way is to allow your animal or teacher to sing through your own vocal cords: then it can't possibly be your problem! Any kind of drone around which your voice can weave is a good way of overcoming your personal vocal resistance: try practising when you next drive your car, vacuum the carpet or just sing along with the refrigerator! Self-consciousness about our voices is not helped by thin walls, but you don't have to sing very loudly. However, do try to vocalize in your comfortable middle register so that your breath supports your voice to be free and without strain.

The secret of shamanic voice is to follow the experiences which we are having as we begin the source, to let the song emerge as the images and

189

feelings unfold. This way, you are using your shamanic voice as a soul-path: a song which goes straight through to the cosmic web and which can provide a strong pathway for straying souls.

Next time you journey, instead of lying still, sit up and sing what you experience into a tape or mini disk recorder. This will only work if your sound-source is on a head-set and you have something else to record onto.

When you next dance with your spirits, lend them your voice, so that the song that is always singing in the silence can be heard and given.

Permit yourself to sing this silent book alive!

👋 Practice 61: The Song of the Star Watchers

Some people find the stars dwarf them or overwhelm them with interspatial agoraphobia, but the next time you have a multitude of small personal worries snapping at you like dogs, go out and look up to the stars to gain a sense of proportion. Study the constellations which are visible, year round, from where you live on the globe. Regularly watch their progress through the heavens, periodically selecting particularly significant ones as places to journey to. Go first to your Upperworld teacher and ask for guidance and permission to journey to particular stars or constellations. Ensure you have at least one ally with you at all times. Ask for a song from each star or constellation that you visit. *Note:* star work is very powerful and should be performed only occasionally; as star-spirits are concerned with the germination of seeds throughout the cosmic web, it is especially important that women scrutinize their own fertility cycle very carefully if they don't want an addition to the family! For those who wish to conceive, asking help of the stars and dancing their pattern upon the earth is one of the best methods.

👋 Practice 62: Gathering Your Powers

As you go deeper into this work, you will gradually draw together your powers. On journeys you will encounter new teachers and helpers. You may be given objects in subtle reality to use in your work. The interesting thing about these gifts is the way they manifest in physical reality as shamanic objects. Gifts acquired in journeys are often subsequently given to you in the Middleworld by friends who say vaguely, 'Oh, I saw this object and thought you might like it.' These gifts represent the gathering together of your powers and are the basis for a collection of objects that will help you in your work. They should be kept securely in a shamanic bag and not given away, unless your spirits tell you otherwise.

Medicine bundles or shamanic bags are not readily available. You will find your own ways of making a container for your power objects. Each object may need to be individually wrapped so that it does not break or injure any of the others. Needless to say, your shamanic bag is not for showing to all and sundry. I review the contents of mine seasonally to ensure that objects are still willing to remain in my keeping. If they are not, I return them to nature or else decommission them in a ritual way that returns them appropriately to the universe.

We do not own or command the power of any object, it chooses to co-operate with us as an ally. The power objects which you use can be dedicated in a short ceremony of consecration.

This may be a good place to discuss shamanic regalia in general. Many firms specialize in making power objects so that it is possible for the beginner to arrive at a shamanic course professionally equipped with custom-made objects of all kinds from drum to clothing. By all means find your own shamanic style, but let the objects come to you in the course of your life, or make them yourself if you can. They will mean more to you if the spirits who have contacted you in journey are able to help you create them and imbue them with their power.

Create your own short ceremony for consecrating power objects in your shamanic work. Different objects may need specific dedication; the use of a crystal for cleansing or healing may need a different dedication to an eye-fringe or a rattle. A simple method is to ask the spirits of the cosmic web to bless your power object, or you might symbolically pass your object through the four elements or the three worlds.

192

Divination

Everything can serve prophecy. You only have to pay attention. The universe is full of signs. When you have learnt to look at things the right way, you will understand what I'm trying to say. The shape of clouds, the way birds fly, the sounds of nature, an unexpected meeting – all these transmit a message that expresses the will of the gods.

– Maria-José, a Brazilian Macumba priestess

1: MAPPING THE THREE WORLDS

Whoever departs from this world without having realized his own inner world, to him life has been of no service: it remains unlived, like an undone deed.

– Brhad-aranyaka Upanishad

Divination is literally the art of 'asking the gods or spirits'. It is a prime shamanic task whereby we turn away from our own intellectual processes to unzip the universe and perceive the answer which is often staring us in the face. We turn to divination when we don't have the answers. This process involves recognizing the patterns which are constellated around any issue under scrutiny.

We all remember playing 's/he loves me, s/he loves me not' with a petalled flower. As children we all watched raindrops falling down windows and betting which one would reach the windowsill first. We have all

193

touched posts, jumped cracks in pavements, played counting out games all in order to determine whether an action shall happen or not. Children know more about divination than most adults.

Divination has been more recently associated with divination systems, but commercial cards or symbols are not needed for you to ask the universe your question. Anything in this universe can and has been used for divination: the flight of birds and the behaviour of animals; the sequence of cards, stones and twigs; lines on hands and bumps on heads; tea leaves and coffee grounds; and many other bizarre methods. We are using journeying in this book to discern the subtle patterns of the cosmic web.

The Purpose of Divination

We need spiritual understanding about the sacred nature of divination or it can soon deteriorate into a superstitious and meaningless practice. To ask Spirit for answers, to question the Creator is regarded as ultimately blasphemous in many religions. This is why they have always relegated the practice of divination to experts or forbidden it entirely so that blind faith might be safe-guarded. However, looking for signs and wonders in every small and insignificant event can become a bad habit, if unchecked.

Passive fatalism or innate superstition have no part in shamanism. Trust in the spirits of the universe, good oracy and alignment with it are better friends. We divine only for issues that are beyond our human capability to solve; the use of divination, whether by cards, stones, twigs or by journeying to determine everyday affairs is a misuse of spiritual help. It reveals sloppy alignment to attribute some minor ailment or occurrence to some totally unrelated cause: for example, 'I must have missed that train because I was meant to/because of Mercury going retrograde.' This may make us feel better about missing a connection, but the real reason is more likely due to our unpunctuality rather than to any mystical influence.

The fortune-telling element of divination has unfortunately become a dominant feature in all prognostication: a virtual obsession with the outcome or final result. Divination is really a two-way process of alignment which may be likened to stretching a musical string between an issue in physical reality and its correlative in subtle reality: we stretch our string and then pluck it to see what kind of resonance it has. A resonant note tells us that the issue is well aligned and connected; a buzzing or totally unresonant string tells us that the issue lacks alignment and purpose. This process merely tell us *what adjustments are necessary*, not what will come to pass. The implementation of divinatory advice remains in our hands.

All divination turns about the way we frame our question. If we ask our question badly, we will receive evasive answers or none at all. Our spiritual direction is based on the questions we ask in life: *if we ask the right question, we will achieve our quest* (see p.198).

Understanding the Oracle

But when we ask the spirits, the answer comes by way of oracle, which is 'the language of the spirits': an answer is rarely conveyed in words but rather by means of metaphor, which is our original language. Sometimes the oracle does come in verbal form, with a person acting as the god's voice. We call such people mediums, though this term is often narrowly associated with spiritualist mediums who act solely as oracles for the departed. Many countries have state oracles. Before the Chinese invasion, Tibet's state oracle was the prophetic voice of his people: this is still practised in Ladakh. The oracle of Delphi was the sibyl who acted as the voice of Apollo. Such oracles do not speak in mundane language, but in the heightened speech of seers and poets. Irish vision poets used a poetic form of prophecy called *teinm laegda*, where cumulative phrases created a full answer to problems.[1]

The interpretation of this advice is of course the critical feature of divination. We all want to know what things mean, and rush to experts or to divinatory manuals to be enlightened. Divination is really about discerning the deeper patterns of life from a perceived series of different criteria which are clear to the individual diviner. As walkers between the worlds, we are gradually amassing a series of criteria from our own journeying, and this will eventually form a divinatory database. Each person's database is different: some areas may be commonly held, others will be distinctly personal.

Every time we journey, we are divining. But as we have not been trained as diviners, making sense of our journeys is an art in which we will become more practised when we have more experience. You will not always understand everything. The authenticity of your own practice will come from trusting your helpers and the experiences you have on journeys. The more you practise, the more journeys you log, the greater your oracy and alignment. This is why it helps to have good records of your journeys for, as you accumulate 'flying hours', so will you begin have begun to navigate and map areas of inner space which are currently unfamiliar (see Practice 63).

Over the last hundred and fifty years, our society has made great strides with literacy: this has also meant the erosion of our symbolic literacy. We no longer respond to symbols and images in an immediate way. Our oracy has been sacrificed to literacy. More recently, metaphor and symbol have been jettisoned and the descent from literacy to literality has begun. When we journey or divine in other ways, we have to relearn our own symbolic language.

We need to trust the symbols and images that appear to us in journeys and to break our reliance on encyclopedias of symbolism. It is true that many symbols are shared by the collective understanding of world culture, but each also has a localized significance to a part of the globe and a core meaning to each person. We each have power-bearing images in our oral pool, images that bear banners, symbols that are mysterious yet charged with meaning. The gift of a white feather in a journey may signify cowardice to one person or the power of inner flight to another. We cannot seek arbitrary meanings, only personal ones; we must contextualize our own findings and trust our own personal nuances.

Above all, we need context. Whatever the intention, question or issue in your journey, that is the frame of reference against which to set the information that you retrieve. If you don't understand something you experience, ask how it relates to the issue. Between the intention and the journey evidence lies an answer.

Making sense of our journeys requires us to pay close attention to what we experience and to cross-relate it to all the factors. Beginners often want to pigeonhole their journeys into a known frame of reference, such as that of conventional psychology, but shamanic experience is too broad to be confined like this. The stream of information to be synthesized and understood cannot be submitted to analytic or scientific categorization, or catalogued on file cards. You might as well try to catalogue poetry or dance!

196

Having looked at the symbolism and metaphors of our journey, we have to look at the different scenes or episodes into which it falls: what story is emerging? Finally, we must look at the journey as a whole, for we can fail to see the wood for the trees if we concentrate too much upon one or other factor.

Notes for Interpreting Your Journey

The following questions and thoughts will help you crack open your journey if the answer is not clearly obvious. Beware of interpreting your experience by means of conventional psychological methodology. Journeys usually have a sequence; some have many scenarios. Break these down and deal with them in turn, as they unfolded, before looking at the whole journey.

1. *What was the object of this journey?* Always relate what you experienced to your original issue, quest or motivation.
2. *Which part of the journey held most power for me?* Recall which parts evoked strong emotion in particular.
3. *Which part was most difficult?* Recall any blockage of emotion.
4. *How did my allies help me?*
5. *What did they tell me, verbally or non-verbally, about my issue?*
6. *Did they ask/advise me to do anything during the journey? How did I react?*
7. *What power/gift was I offered on this journey?*
8. *What did my journey show me? How will I implement this? What next step is suggested by this journey?*
9. *How was Spirit present on this journey?*

With particularly obscure journeys it is helpful to write it down as if it were a story. Write in the third person if this helps you unlock it: 'Once upon a time a woman climbed a high cliff and met a jaguar who took her to a far country ...' Distancing ourselves from our experience will sometimes help give perspective to the answer which stares us in the face.

Useful Question Formats

The way we frame our question is very important. Having helped hundreds of clients to frame their issue into question form, I have discovered that issues have many layers and that we have to dig to get the ultimate core. Beneath a presenting issue may lurk a far more important question, and it may take a few sessions to discover what it is. Also, for some unfathomable reason not unconnected with our innate curiosity, human beings always want to *know* rather than to *receive* the help that they need. With shamanic work you don't have to be reticent: if you are ready to deal with an issue, then you really can ask about what deeply concerns you in plain language.

Before you journey with an issue, spend more time on deciding the intention and on framing the question and you will get much better results. Before you start, repeat the question or request out loud several times so that it is fixed in memory. When you meet your allies to ask for their help or advice, ask this question, *in the same words that you originally decided upon,* within the journey. Asking questions opens up ways that have been blocked or neglected and keeps clean the spirit pathways that you walk.

Here are some questions formats that have proved useful. As you will see, they are very concise.

1. Please give me help with … (*your issue*).
2. Please show me how to deal with … (*your issue*).
3. Please tell me what help is available for … (*your issue*) and how it can be manifested.
4. Please give me a teaching on … (*your issue*).
5. Please heal me.
6. Please give me power and help to deal with … (*your issue*).
7. Please reconnect me with … (*your gift or other quality that is mislaid*).
8. Please help transform my … (*quality that is troublesome*).
9. Please show me how to nourish … (*a new project/friendship*).
10. Please show me how to conclude … (*an old project/relationship*).
11. Please give me the rules for the road ahead. (*When periods of change or disruption upset your life.*)
12. Please show me the unnecessary burdens I'm carrying and help me to lay them down.

Advanced Troubleshooting for Your Journey

We all encounter difficulties and problems in our practice. Some of the following are commonly experienced. All of them are about trusting the process of shamanic information retrieval.

Is it all right to move from one world to another during a journey?
Yes. Sometimes your quest cannot be accomplished in just one world; allies normally initiate this movement to another place. Ensure that your guardian animal remains with you when you move swiftly. You will soon recognize the corridors, doors and windows which connect the three worlds for you, apart from your central routes up and down.

How can I trust that what I experience is right?
This worry can still recur in the more experienced. You retain your free will and are under no obligation to accept any advice or instructions. Check journey content against your subtle senses – does it feel instinctively beneficial to you? Act 'as if'. (See 'None of it seems real', p.201.) Interpret the symbolism and metaphor of your journey carefully: some things will reveal both their physical and subtle reality simultaneously and you will instinctively know which these are. If you have a hunch about a possible meaning but can't verify this, wait a few days and see what your daily life and dream life bring up. Some validations follow journeys almost immediately. It is often a matter of understanding the way you and your spirits talk to each other: expect humour, outrageous puns and sudden spotlights as you go through life.

My journeys are very different to my friend's – is one of us doing it wrong?
There is no 'right' way to perceive shamanically. You are a unique person with your own connective pathways to the otherworlds. Your journeying will unfold an inner map *from your own point of departure*. The things you see and experience will appear in your own symbology: only you can interpret them. I have witnessed hundreds of clients' journey experiences and have concluded that, like the findings of the Six Blind Sages of Hindustan who examined an elephant and came up with a variety of interpretations as to what kind of beast it might be, journey information often reveals a high level

of similarity of landscape and experience, but that we each have our personal viewpoint. Beware of interpreting other people's journeys, dreams and visions: only the person who has actually experienced these can hold the keys. You can help a friend arrive at their own interpretation by asking some of the questions from p.198, always referring back to the context of their quest.

How can I implement the advice I receive as it involves others?
The advice we receive results from the question or purpose we have journeyed with. We cannot expect to be able to implement journey advice for others if we have journeyed without consulting or asking permission of them in the first place. We cannot give enlightenment to another, nor can we manipulate the cosmic web in order to help someone accept something.

Why did my teacher lop off my head on my journey?
A common and disconcerting experience of journeying to one's teacher for healing, change and initiation into knowledge is that of dismemberment. The stripping away of flesh and the reorganization of the body into its constituent parts, the treatment of organs, removal and rejigging of body parts may all take place within a journey. The reconstitution of the body is the final experience before returning. What does this mean?

Terrifying though this may sound, a dismemberment or physical readjustment journey happens periodically to most shamans. It is an initiatory and healing experience in which spaciousness and nothingness are critically present. The Dzog Chen school of Tibetan Buddhism actively meditates upon this process, and many Tibetan and South American depictions of the process are extant. To experience this is to be reconstituted so that the whole universe is simultaneously re-membered within you.

Journeys involving issues about healing and change often have violent or shocking imagery: trust your helpers to know what is best for you and allow that change to come about.

What should I do if I encounter something frightening or become blocked by some obstacle?
If you encounter something you can't deal with on journeys, don't try. Ask

200

your allies for help, or, if they have no strategies, such as to take you on another route, get out of there. If this keeps on happening, consult a shamanic practitioner and get help.

Is it all right to fly or swim on journeys?
The ways in which we travel through the worlds varies tremendously, and is often influenced by the nature of the ally we travel with. You may fly, crawl, leap, swim or slither to your destination if you shapeshift! Within one journey you may traverse several of the worlds. Facility to travel in all the elements is a skill which can be acquired. You might also try shapeshifting into the form of your animal/s and see how that feels when you journey. Always travel with one ally.

None of it seems real.
When you are learning to perceive subtle reality, it takes a lot of practice for journeying to seem normal. The adage, 'act as if it were real', is a useful one to adopt: when you perceive that the answers and advice do work when you implement them, you can move with more confidence.

I'm still having difficulty seeing anything.
Not everyone has a strong gift for visualization. I am one such: my chief organs of perception are sound and touch, giving me a kind of bat sentience when I journey. Rather than 'seeing' my journeys, I experience them with other senses. The result is the same: I receive impressions. When you journey, try moving your hands or smelling where you are, listen more acutely.

Nothing happens when I journey.
People who have good mental control find sourcing difficult, because they find it hard to let go. Journeying is about releasing that control, not dictating what you experience. Trick the mind to get results from the body – relax and release the 'watchdog mind' by story, song or monotony. Experiment by spending at least three hours with no possible distractions – you can do this indoors at night by switching off the lights; you can go out into nature and sit perfectly still; you can stare at a brick wall. Record what happens when you do this. Removal of stimuli and mental chatter results in a new

kind of perception. Journeying is like learning to float – the universe will hold you up!

Now when you next journey, allow what is happening to you to unfold, just as in dreams. Don't edit or fight to control the experience: just let it occur naturally. Use all your senses.

I keep seeing irrelevant things when I journey.

Ask yourself, 'Is this *really* irrelevant?' We all experience distractions and mind-wandering, when we find ourselves rehearsing our shopping lists or social calendar, but we're not talking here about lack of concentration. Don't automatically dismiss what you experience as irrelevant. I recall a client who realized halfway through his journey that the scenario he was in was identical to a film he had once seen; his disgust was immense, but he pressed on with his animal, complaining heartily. His issue was about how to survive in his chosen profession: the film-scenario of his journey was about the sole survivor of a plane-crash in a deserted region, and his return to civilization. He realized that this journey may have borrowed from a film, but that it was indeed relevant to his situation and eventually enabled him to cut through immense difficulties to achieve a real breakthrough in his career.

How long should I journey for?

Normally the length of your journey will be determined by the length of journey-tape you are using: fifteen to thirty minutes is an average time. Sometimes you will experience the whole universe in two minutes, at others, twenty-five minutes may pass slowly and uneventfully. You will also have your off days when nothing seems to work. If someone is drumming for you, you can signal when you have concluded by a prearranged gesture. If you are drumming for someone who shows no signs of coming back after a reasonable time, then you may need to sound the call-back and go on sounding it.

I shared my journey with my partner and now he's convinced I'm deranged.

Journeys can seldom be shared with non-practitioners because there is no common conceptual vocabulary, no shared cosmology and an unequal perception of reality. If you want to talk about your practice, seek out a soul-friend on whose support and discretion you can rely (see Practice 73). If you want to share some part of your practice with a relative or partner, if only in order to allay their fears, then choose your words wisely, use non-specialist vocabulary and speak in that person's conceptual framework.

My journey was inconclusive.
Sometimes the call-back sounds before you have finished: try to briefly conclude any action or exchange before returning, but do not hang about hoping to continue. Sometimes, the journey itself may require another journey to explain it or to sort out a prior problem. But even enigmatic journeys which conclude abruptly can reveal important clues, however episodic they may seem; try applying the interpretation questions above. Aimless journeys often result when we have failed to pose our question to our allies. If your journey was inconclusive as a result of any of these factors, it is often better to journey again the next day. As with all divining, repeated consecutive efforts on the same day often result in non-responsive journeys or a stern instruction from one's allies to leave matters alone for that time. If you asked for help in your journey, then trust that the help will be brought: your allies will do their best for you and will continue to work on the issue outside the journey session.

I feel that I'm answering myself.
When conversing with your allies, especially when you pose your question or request, allow the response to come naturally. We frequently have a response that seems 'obvious'. The answer that comes back may indeed resonate with your own instinctive response: trust your instincts more.

My experiences are very different from the ones outlined in this book.
Do not be afraid to accept that your route to the worlds may vary from ones you have been taught or read about. Do not worry if you find different animals come to help you in different worlds. Accept that your inner teachers will assume different guises at different times. No book or teacher can possibly prepare you for the variety of experiences that you have; your own life and background provide the most important framework.

Ways of Improving Your Journeying

1. Avoid journeying when you are rushed.

2. Consciously leave your burden of worries behind when you journey, unless you are focusing on one of them as your journey issue.

3. Ensure that more than half of your journeying is not on personal issues: journey to benefit the cosmic web in some way.

4. Ask allies what you can do for them.

5. Maintain neutral expectation and maximum receptivity.

6. Simplify the way you frame your issue: repeat it to yourself several times before sourcing.

7. Do not analyse your experiences as you journey, but allow them to unfold like a story.

8. Always check with your allies when decisions are required on journeys. They will not think you are stupid; they will show you or tell you what to do.

9. When making a series of journeys about an issue, ensure you cross-reference your previous record: have things been clarified since the last journey?

10. Ask allies to explain or repeat things you don't understand.

11. Record your journeys aloud on tape and listen to the play-back. Listen to the quality of your voice at significant moments: does your voice achieve release or become stressed – cross-refer the significance of these moments carefully to your quest.

12. Upgrade your journey record into a real navigator's log and look for connections and cross-referrals in your daily life.

♕ Practice 63: Mapping the Worlds

We each have our own maps of the cosmic web which teach us about the otherworlds. These explorations are analogous to the rediscovery of lands once frequently visited. Only you can understand how all the worlds fit together for you.

Start first with the appearance of the three worlds. You may find that the mood of each of the three worlds brings a different coloration to your journeys. Underworld journeys are frequently calm, strong and empowering: many people feel that nothing much has happened, because the Underworld is a place where the body receives deep and moving changes, but these changes are nevertheless profound. Upperworld journeys tend to be ecstatic, moving and enlightening; there is a greater sense of definition, and archetypal perception. The Middleworld journey is generally busy and practical, bringing clarification and order.

Moving between the worlds comes with practice. The unity of the three worlds is much more apparent when you have journeyed over a long period. We must remember that they are not three distinct and separated zones, but worlds which interconnect.

Regions that you visit may become increasingly familiar, but exasperatingly unconnected. You may know only that on your last journey you visited 'the ivy-covered house where the broken piano waits' – a place familiar to you from recurrent dreams. The mapping of your inner landscape can be likened to living in a town with an underground railway which connects everything. If you travel by it regularly, you will theoretically know which regions link up, but you will seldom know what the ground level looks like and how regions really join on to others.

Try to collate the information gained on your journeys and see if you can work out a map of how it all relates. Do you have specific pathways between the worlds? Check out which scenarios, teachers, animals appear in the three worlds, what kinds of help/information/healing are given in these places by these spirits? What gifts have you obtained in these realms, and what uses do they have?

You may find it helpful to draw your journeys; artistic ability is unimportant – as a glance at any shaman's sketch of the spiritual worlds will show. The important thing is to understand how *you personally* relate to the spiritual worlds.

Take a large sheet of paper and begin to sketch a map of your findings; as you proceed, this map will also change and come into greater clarity. Saami shamans put their own cosmological map on their drums in a symbolic manner. There are many variables in shamanic work which require spontaneity and creative response. No living human being has ever totally mapped the cosmic web; we can only have our own sketch-map where we know help will be found. Keep on exploring and discovering, watch the map change and develop.

✋ *Practice 64:* Stone Divination

Create your own divination method by bringing together a series of stones. Each can be assigned a particular quality or you may wish to source each stone and discover its own gift.

Play with these stones until you know them by their distinctive features, colours and shapes. Fill a tray or box with silver sand and practise throwing the stones. See what shapes you come up with. Or you might create a cloth marked with areas of activity, such as health, relationships, work. You might wish to create a cloth which has the co-ordinates of your own otherworldly map marked upon it in symbolic and oblique fashion.

In this way you may be able to help people answer specific questions: they might throw the stones and listen to your interpretation, or else they might be invited to place stones according to their intuition. This form of divination can be beneficial for helping non-practitioners divine their own question.

2. EVERYDAY MYTHOLOGY

You don't have anything if you don't have the stories.
— Leslie Marmon Silko *Ceremony*

Shamanic divination has two aspects: the walker between the worlds both looks at the signs of personal life-patterns and dreams, and also accesses the otherworlds for help in gaining a broader or more precise overview. By reading these in concert, not in separation from each other, we receive a lively oracle. With this broad view, it is possible to live in a more balanced and insightful way, for we will have gained true oracy — the capacity to hear, remember and relate.

Our journeys provide important episodes from our own unwritten, ongoing story, revealing ways in which it inter-relates with the rest of the cosmic web. In these storylines, we discern patterns, sequences and archetypes which we call myth: stories by which to live, empowering and ensouling pathways which align us with the cosmic web. Our culture frequently misunderstands myth as an untrue, fantastic or imagined story, but we can see myth as a subtle reality story which is mediated to physical reality by shamans, artists and visionaries.

There are four kinds of human myth. These explore :

1. The relationship of people with nature and their environment.
2. The personal quest.
3. The family, tribal or national preoccupation.
4. The relationship of people and the greater universe.

The codification of such stories and their admixture have frequently provided us with religions, some of which have subsequently been compulsorily enjoined upon our belief. In each case, these mythic schemas have been responsible for the evocation and manifestation of subtle reality spirits whom we call gods, heroes, animal spirits and so on. In their original social format, these myths have power and Spirit, but myths often lose their currency as time goes on.

Divining Our Own Myths

We each have a personal myth or 'story to live by'. This may manifest as adherence to a religious belief system and a close following of a specific spiritual leader's story, superimposed upon personal lives as a spiritual template to be imitated. Today fewer people wish to constrain their lives in such a way, but have sought out other ways of living. However, whoever we are or wherever we live, we each do abide by some written or unwritten personal myth, whether it is a political ideology, an ideal of social commonwealth, a mystical set of values or an identification with a hero, heroine or other figure who inspires us. Our 'story to live by' can comprise one or many of these aspects in combination: these become the constants and frameworks which dictate our behaviour, direct our attitudes and moral judgements and fuel our lives, the bottom line beyond which we will not willingly pass.

In their original format, these stories to live by have power and Spirit, but myths often lose their currency as time goes on because human beings change. It has been my experience that if a story doesn't move you to tears or laughter, to exaltation or profound personal change, then it is not a story you need to worry about. It is certainly not one you should be steering your life by.

Stories lose their power when we are no longer personally walking their pathways. When we begin to question the authenticity of our current myth or discard it as outworn, our soul goes forth in search of a myth which aligns us with the cosmic web once again. At this time, even deeply mystical people, faithful to their own tradition, are seeking the reinspiration and refreshment of their own traditions by a study of other traditions. As the third millennium unfolds, more and more people are redefining their shared spiritual and social myth by a closer examination of their personal myth and their universal mythic awareness.

Nothing stays unchanging in the universe; everything has its own rhythm. Re-divining our shared myth or personal story is something we must do periodically if it is not to become powerless and disensouled by habit and familiarity. Check where you are being challenged to move beyond its confines.

The mythic pathways we need to find are those which align us with our spiritual and ancestral lineages but which allow our personal story to be strengthened and encouraged at the same time. In the great collective redefinition of myth which is currently shaking the cosmic web, it is often hard to perceive the pathways which have greatest resonance for us, and many people are thrown into a consideration of their own story without regard for the greater mythic resonance. Our own story is part of the universal story: this should be remembered both as an encouragement to maintain our story with courage and as a humble reminder that our story is not the only one.

There are many story-paths transecting the cosmic web: some of these have greater resonance than others, some leave broad tracks into which our personal story-path sometimes merges. The biologist, Rupert Sheldrake, defines his notion of 'morphic resonance' as 'the influence of previous structures of activity on subsequent similar structures of activity' by any unit, whether it be a single cell or culture or galaxy; morphic resonance transects time and space, leaving discernible pathways.[2] Myth is nothing less than the morphic resonance of life on the cosmic web: its patterns are held in our memory and, if they are steadfastly followed, will result in increasingly habitual pathways.

Oracy

The morphic resonance of our story becomes apparent if we review our lives and become aware of our oracy. Oracy is the horse's mouth; it is our capacity to hear, remember and relate. Oracy is not dependent upon the written word but gives primacy to the oral traditions that maintain our connections with the ancient wisdom whose lines transect the cosmic web. It has no authority except itself. To write of oracy in a book which is visually presented and which asks you to make written notes of experiences may seem ironic, but your shamanic experience is leading you into the heart of your own oracy.

Oracy has been well respected by shamans of all cultures. The druids did not allow their teachings to be written down, fearing that this would erode the capacity of memory. Certain chants and teachings are transmitted only 'from mouth to ear'. This transmission is often thought of as some fixed transfer of data, but I have not found it so. My experience of teaching many groups of people leads me to suppose that any such group always has certain needs and expectations: they come to learn a particular subject, but within its broad criteria I will find myself speaking and teaching in such a way as to address their needs in ways I had not intended. As one who also learns from others, I have also noticed that certain seemingly 'off the cuff' remarks or personal anecdotes of a teacher will spark exciting realizations within me, this new knowledge re-constellating information and experiences already available to me. The nature of knowledge-transmission is therefore happening at a much more creative and uncodifiable level than we imagine. We maintain the oracy of our lives by allowing power and Spirit to enter them freely and spontaneously, without a script.

Oracy gives us immediacy of understanding which comes from being shown a technique rather than working it out alone from an instruction manual. The hand-holds and connections of any practice are always best imparted by a practitioner at first hand. This book allows me to speak to you and has been written to be as helpful as possible, but it is no substitute for first-hand transmission. Oracy has its own spaciousness which allows the unspoken and incommunicable to become spoken and transmitted. Written words often constrict and confine, creating passivity among those who read them, preventing the spirit from flowing.

Our way of life becomes our morphic field: a pattern of oracy which actually speaks to others through our actions, words, thoughts and intentions. We tend towards stories which nurture the morphic field of our oracy. The stories that we read, the televisual stories that we watch, reflect how we seek nourishment for our own habitual story: we use all kinds of stories to keep us going from the snack (short-story, anecdote, magazine article) to the banquet (myth, novel, biography).

Permit yourself to contemplate the possibility of your life-journey as myth and story!

The stories which we learn in childhood are remembered more clearly by us because we have *heard* rather than read them. Such stories have power. Sarah Grays, a Cree elder, recalls her uncle Otiokmuskoo telling a story about two hunters lost in the snowy wastes.

> 'I remember I sat under a quilt because his story was about getting very cold
> ... we all got lost with them in his story ... some other elders who saw that
> us children were really worried and afraid began to talk about what to do if
> you get lost. We learned quite a bit ... Those elders had all been lost
> themselves at least once ... After that, Otiokmuskoo's wife sewed me a quilt
> with a map of our region on it. Lakes, some trees, some birds. Also she sewed
> on it a lot of paths. It was a good quilt to sleep under.'[3]

Sarah Grays had the supreme fortune of being part of a story whose boundaries overlapped with her own. The quilted map gave her a sense of belonging in her story so that she no longer worried about the blurred edges, of becoming lost. Sarah *enters* the story and shares its wisdom.

This is the truth at the heart of divination: we discover meaning by becoming aware of, by entering, our story. If we remain detached from our story, if we stand to one side of ourselves always analysing, we lose our oracy along with power and Spirit. Neither shamanism nor any form of divination is an end in itself: when we have learned where the filaments of the cosmic web run, we must get on with our lives and engage with them.

Preserving the power-bearing and soul-nurturing aspects of our story will help us deal with the areas where our power and soul are under threat. In our story, certain events recur, creating a series of seemingly set patterns which then become self-perpetuating or by which subsequent life is judged or restricted. These patterns of disempowerment have great influence upon us and make us susceptible to their recurrence. They become our story. You may have picked up the signatures of these stories in yourself and others: be attentive when you hear the words 'I'm always … tired, late, unable to cope with money' or 'I never … win, hold down relationships, get to sit in the front seat.' These are unhelpful recurrent patterns which cause our story to get stuck. Going beyond these patterns takes great determination and encouragement.

Recognizing and changing them will help us untangle our incarnational thread. We do not need to follow old, repetitive stories, which may stem from patterns established in this life or as a result of past incarnations. In shamanism we avoid past problems and entanglements by relating them to our present life and time-frame: we only need to review our present incarnation and list the related and recurrent difficulties which we continually encounter.

Often the most important strands of our unfolding story happen in the spaces between: the little sendings, thoughts and realizations that we have throughout the day but are often too busy to notice or note down. When these happen, try and pay attention: these are the voices of your instinct, your spirit allies speaking wisdom to you. In our noisy and busy world, their voices seem very small, but these are often the most important messages that we ever receive. Do not disreagard them as being of no importance: by ignoring the small messages, we may become deaf to the really important ones.

By finding, living and telling stories which have power and Spirit, we become authentic guardians of oracy, the true currency of the cosmic web: it is an open story which has no ending.

Dreams

But sometimes our story is unclear to us and we are unaware of the patterns which lay down morphic resonance on the cosmic web. This submerged part of our personal story can be divined through our dreams, revealed to us by the spirits who fly by night. Dreams have been used for divining since the world began: they are everyone's door to subtle reality, practitioners or not. Dreams speak to us at night of things we haven't given time for during the day, they utter direct or encoded messages about our life's direction, they offer us opportunities to experience the otherworlds directly.

For people who lack confidence about their ability to journey I often liken journeying to dreaming. In dreams, we follow the story that is spun out of our sleep, observing or interacting with it; there are few people who can manipulate their dreaming sufficiently to change the story, and we conclude that dreaming is a largely involuntary function which all people engage in. Journeying, however, requires us to follow the story that is spun out of our sound-source, observing and interacting with it. Although many worry that they might attempt to change the story, very few are actually able to do so. Although both dreaming and journeying are means of accessing subtle reality, we should remember that while dreaming is involuntary, journeying happens in *voluntary* shamanic awareness.

During dreaming, part of our soul is journeying, which is why it is considered unwise to roughly awaken a sleeper. Many cultures recite protective prayers for the soul before sleeping, so that the soul's helpers accompany it during the night. Such blessings before sleep are the common prayers of children, providing soul-protection while they are out of their bodies.

Dreams are food and nourishment for us in our sleep. We leave our bodies and journey to those realms which give us what we need. The dreams of those who are deprived of home, loved ones and food, such as prisoners of war, are usually richly nurturing. The dreams of those who are confused or worried often follow labyrinthine contortions which irritatingly mirror the disturbed mental pattern. In such cases, we visit the Middleworld to derive comfort or to pace over our problems. Yet sometimes we have a dream which grants great clarity and direction, giving effective solutions or cessation of panic. The really great and memorable dreams of our lives are those which take us to the Upperworld and the Underworld.

Among some indigenous people, dreaming becomes not only a personal but a tribal activity, where the dreamer's vision, like the shaman's vision, provides the myth of a whole people. This vision is not fixed, but inter-relates with the dreams of the ancestors and with the dreams of descendants – a group alignment of great importance takes place, allowing power and Spirit to flow into the lives of all beings in that place. In a consideration of the aboriginal dreamtime, the writer and traveller, Bruce Chatwin, wrote about the continuity of myth and story:

> 'I have a vision of the Songlines stretching across the continents and ages;
> that wherever men have trodden they have left a trail of song of which we,
> now and then, catch an echo.'[4]

Those song, story and myth lines are everywhere to be found, if we will only look into the oracy of our lives.

Permit yourself to become a nomadic story-finder!

☙ Practice 65: The Oral Pool

It is all too easy to lose touch with our oracy unless we occasionally freshen our oral pool and review its contents. Our oral pool is our living memory of teachings, stories and songs of nurture that we remember without the aid of book or tape. Each people or group also has its own oral pool which draws upon group memories. If you were the only survivor of your planet/country, what could you relate from your personal oral pool? If all written and recorded media retrieval were to cease, which items of your collective oral pool would you most wish to save in oral memory? Journey to your Underworld teacher and ask to be shown your own oral pool: you may be shown things you need to remember. We source our ancestral oral pool when we seek forgotten wisdom: here it is possible to recover rituals and find strategies for our community from the council of the deep ancestors.

☙ Practice 66: Exploring Our Myths

Memory shows us the handholds of our life's patterns, it reveals the places that our soul has touched. The signposts, markers, boundaries, restricted areas of our lives form an inner landscape. Every being living has a different set of handholds, signposts, memories, although we do share some. These memories create patterns, songlines, subtle pathways that weave us into the universe.

What myths do you inherit from your ancestral, educational and cultural background? Which still work for you, and why? Which do you discard, and why?

What present story is unfolding in your life? Who are the major actors in your story? Who are the challengers, helpers, lovers, inspirers? What patterns are you laying down for the future? Look for the repetitive images, figures and feelings which crop up. Look over your journeys and dreams, underlining or highlighting significant features which strike you. Tell your life-story to date as a myth, drawing on these major protagonists and patterns, but going further than you have now lived, bringing it to a satisfactory resolution in the next life-phase.

How does your story relate to the shared myth of your age and people? How does it relate to nature and to the earth? How does it relate to the story of the cosmic web?

✋ *Practice 67*: Dream Diary

Begin to keep a dream diary. A notebook and pen beneath your pillow or close at hand is essential for this. Dreams often take wing on waking, and even minimal movement can cause them to flee.

Write down the sequence of your dream and, most importantly, how it made you feel. For example, 'reminiscent of holiday in Holland', or 'sense of foreboding and tension throughout', or 'smell of geraniums reminded me of Gran'. At the end of each week, review your dreams and entitle them like stories, such as 'Flying With Pink Birds' or 'The Cliff's Edge' or 'In Glasgow with my Sister'. What gift/quality/focus did each dream give you?

Our dream experiences often seem surreal and strange: impossible things like flying or breathing underwater are common: people; things and events appear in bizarre juxtaposition. Some dream sequences are remarkably like journeys and we can interpret them by the same criteria. Among pre-literate peoples, symbol and metaphor are rich sources of exchange. Literacy has the effect of damping our imaginative faculties, of promoting

214

our intellectual comprehension at the expense of our soul's comprehension. Symbol causes reaction in the soul, stimulating physiological, emotional and mental response. You must always interpret the symbols and images you experience *from your own symbology*, not from a dictionary of symbols. 'Metaphor is the foodstuff and substance of dreams, which are, themselves, pictographic metaphors, only of the unconscious dimension.'[5] We do well to remember this when we attempt to understand and interpret dreams or journeys. The symbolic language of dreams is *metaphoric*, not literal. If you dream of beheading pigs or of sleeping with your aunt, this may be disturbing but it does not mean you have or will do either of these acts. Crosscorrelate your journeys and your dreams.

❦ *Practice 68:* Calling the Dream-spirits

Dion Fortune called dream 'the door which has no key', regarding it as an initiatory way to deeper knowledge.[6] This may seem a very good definition for those people who find it difficult to remember dreams or may have no awareness of ever having dreamt. Make a journey to your Upperworld teacher for some help or ask for directions to find dream-spirit allies who will reconnect you with your dreams.

Dreams as well as journeys can enable us to find solutions to worrying problems. If journeying does not work for you, try incubating a situation or decision that seems unresolvable in this way. First formulate your dilemma as a question to your dream-allies: for example, 'Please help me perceive the hidden aspects of this new job,' or 'Please reveal healing pathways towards my reconciliation with X.' Before bed, light a candle, bring the question to the attention of your helpers and spend at least five minutes holding the question in your awareness without emotion, urgency or analysis. During this time, you may wish to hum or sing quietly. Now lie down to sleep, saying your own incubation prayer or song, something like this:

> On my right side I lie:
> May my dreams be crystal clear.
> In the morning as I wake,
> Let me know which way to take.

215

Do not repeat this practice more than three times in one week unless you have a very unstressed life-style. Nights are intended for sleep and refreshment of our being, not for work.

You might also open up your dream-life as a form of community service, to divine by dreaming the problems or dilemmas of your people. Before sleeping, call upon your dream-spirit allies and make your own petition in your own words or like this:

> I offer my dreams for the life of the people:
> I seek to know all about … (*the issue*).
> May my mind be clear,
> May my heart be pure,
> May my recollection be complete.

✋ *Practice 69:* Navigational Shrine

One of the easiest ways to keep your directional focus in this work and acknowledging the allies, influences and concerns of your earth-journey is to make a navigational shrine: one which reflects the issues that are currently predominant in your life right now. This could be in the service part of your home – the kitchen, the study, a niche on the stairs – somewhere you are occupied in daily activity. The shrine contains whatever you wish and is subject to frequent changes as your earth-journey continues. Here your own mythology rules. A navigational shrine might contain the following: photos of family and absent friends; flowers, fruits and items of the season; pleasingly shaped stones; an object, picture or poem which represents your present spiritual direction. If you are out of space in your small home, you might create a mobile to hang from the ceiling. At least once a month spend some time adjusting this shrine to the latest focus on your story.

· CHAPTER 8 ·

Healing

Healing is remembering what has been forgotten about connection, and unity and interdependence among all things living and non-living.
— Jeanne Achterberg *Woman as Healer*

1. SINGING THE SOUL BACK HOME

Soul loss is regarded as the gravest diagnosis [in shamanism], being seen as a cause of illness and death. Yet it is not referred to at all in modern Western medical books. It is becoming increasingly clear that what the shaman refers to as soul loss – that is injury to the inviolate core that is the essence of the person's being – does manifest in despair, immunological damage, cancer, and a host of other very serious disorders. It seems to follow the demise of relationships with loved ones, career, or other significant attachments.
— Jeanne Achterberg *The Wounded Healer*

Health is the continuum of alignment we enjoy with power and Spirit: when either is disrupted, illness or imbalance result. Our society has associated illness almost exclusively with physical ailments, but illness and imbalance occur on all levels of life. Shamanism has been preserved down the ages because of its ability to provide healing by reconnection with sources of power and removal of power-blockages. Indigenous societies usually have a variety of healers: herbalists and bone-setters who doctor bodily ailments, as well as shamans who interact with the spirits to diagnose imbalances of power and Spirit. Sometimes the shaman will assist healing with the help of a herbalist; sometimes she will effect the healing with the aid of her spirits alone. Minor ailments are generally treated in non-shamanic practical ways among indigenous peoples. A shaman is called in to diagnose the spiritual cause of an illness or imbalance and to bring appropriate healing.

With the improvement in health-care throughout the world, the primary function of shamans today is to look after the spiritual and subtle reality aspects of healing. But in indigenous societies which do not have Western medical care, they also cure physical ailments by using 'the most ancient system of marshalling the emotional and visual triggers in the brain to mobilize the body's natural immune system to cure illness'.[1]

We must be clear that, although shamanism may have a therapeutic effect, it is not therapy, nor can it be treated in a comparable way with therapies. By rectifying one imbalance, shamanism brings healing to the whole cosmic web, so that universal, not personal, healing is accomplished. Therapy does not address subtle reality in this way. In addition, shamanic healing is normally accomplished at one time, or over very few sessions: therapy may take many sessions over many months. However, therapy may sometimes be required after shamanic healing in the case of long-established dysfunctions or addictive imbalances.

Conventional medicine and psychotherapy have brought many benefits, but they have ignored the subtle reality side of healing, which has been presumed to be a superstitious irrelevance. With the massive imbalances resultant from urban life and a growing impatience with the neglect of the health of their soul, people have turned to complementary medicine where the spiritual wisdom of healing is acknowledged. The return to complementary medicine helps us discover more organic and wholesome methods of healing which draw directly on the spiritual qualities of plants, stones and many other beings. The chief principles of healing involve:

1. A shared world view that makes the diagnosis and naming process possible.
2. Positive personal qualities of the healer that facilitate the client's recovery.
3. Client expectations of recovery that assist the healing process.
4. Specific techniques, material and healing procedures that are appropriate to the illness and conducive to recovery.[2]

Shamanically, it is very important that any person assisting or being present at the healing is at least open to the possibility of the client's recovery by shamanic means. Disbelief may act as a barrier to the help of the spirits since disbelief and healing cannot exist in the same plane. Shamans access the cosmic web, so it is imperative that client and helpers should not block any help so accessed: a general willingness to allow power and Spirit to flow are all that is needed. This is why shamans will always use *the client's own spiritual connections* as primary pathways of healing.

Due to the way that it is practised, and the doctor/patient relationship, conventional medicine has reinforced a passivity in the patient, who is not expected to contribute anything to the healing process: 'take this medicine and see what happens'. Indigenous peoples do not understand this passivity and often ask Western doctors what prayers or rituals should accompany the medicine.

It is not surprising that, with the resurgent return of complementary medicine, many people should reject the passivity of the patient and seek to have an active part in the healing process. Self-healing is a misnomer in shamanism, since we are always in contact with the spirits. Now, while we can provide the intention to be well and to co-operate with healing factors, *we* do not heal ourselves. Those who do think that they have healed themselves of a malady have actually used the help of herbs, minerals, the inspiration or teachings of those who have themselves received spiritual help, not to mention the help and support of other people. Instead of giving due thanks to the spirits who have helped them, 'self-healers' mistakenly take credit for their own recovery.

Our part in the healing process is primarily a wish to be well and a willing co-operation with our allies to effect such healing. It is important that we do not forget that healing can only take place if the subject wishes it. Surprisingly, some people actively retain illness and energy blockages, usually because it is more convenient or familiar to live this way; illness can be worn as a badge bringing care or recognition; energy blockage can be a way of maintaining a selfish dictatorial regime whereby family and friends are subtly manipulated to provide the easiest life-style. Imbalance can be so habitual that any healing would be regarded as a threatening change to be sternly resisted.

How Do Shamans Heal?

Many shamans and medicine people will abstain from conjugal relations for some days prior to any healing, and often fast as well, in order to prepare themselves. This is nothing to do with any perceived 'sinfulness' in sexual relations or food, but in order to keep relationships and personal needs quite separate: the shaman is thus prepared to mediate whatever healing is given by his allies. The first process is diagnosis. Some shamans use their acute shamanic vision to look into the subtle reality ambience of the patient's body; Shoshone medicine men can see right through the body with 'x-ray' vision.[3] It was said of the Ultonian healer, Fingen, that he could tell by the vapours arising from a house just how many were sick and of what illness.[4] The diagnosis may be assisted by the shaman singing his medicine song; sometimes well-wishers or apprentices surround the bed and sing healing prayer-songs as well. The shaman enters into strong sourcing to ask assistance of his healing spirits to discern the cause of the trouble, before journeying for help.

If the disease is to be dealt with shamanically, without recourse to herbs, then one of many different methods of curing is employed, such as the laying on of hands, the stroking or blowing away of illness, the restoration of power or soul by shamanic journey or the extraction of a spiritual intrusion or diseased part.

The extraction of spiritual intrusions is practised worldwide, from the drawing out of subtle reality spirits to the actual removal of very real tumours by 'psychic surgery' practised by many *curanderos* of Central America. European history is full of accounts of people receiving elf-shot, magical arrows shot by spirits or sorcerers, which must be removed before health can return. Shamans who extract intrusions by sucking must exercise extreme care not to swallow them: usually a bowl with water, earth or meat is provided for the shaman to dry-vomit these intrusions forth.[5] One of my clients, Penelope, had a ball of glutinous, bloody matter sucked out of her back by a Nepalese shaman as part of a healing ritual. Afterwards, the old woman instructed her to take the bowl of offal onto which the intrusion had been vomited forth to a crossroads and leave it there to be dispersed. Such techniques can only be learned first-hand from an experienced teacher and do not appear in this book.

For all their scientific advances, conventional medicine and psychotherapy cannot cure all ills: they tend to treat only the *symptoms* of a disease, rarely its cause. Shamanism is concerned with the discovery and treatment of *the spiritual cause* of illness.

What Causes Illness and Imbalance?

Health is wholeness: whatever is separated, divided or fragmented is unhealthy. The following factors are all considered to be causes of illness in shamanism. All concern imbalances of power, our vital life-energy:

Lack of order or cleanliness.
Neglect of proper boundaries.
Unethical or manipulative behaviour.
Neglect of appropriate nourishment.
Loss, theft or relinquishing of vital power.

We may conceive of power as the scaffolding of the soul, with its own appropriate frameworks and connections: if these are well-aligned, we remain in good health; if they are fractured, then power-loss results. Power does not flow if there are blockages: dirt needs purification; disorder requires reorganization; unethical and selfish behaviour create imbalances in our power; if we neglect physical, mental or social nourishment we grow weak; in addition, we may lose or relinquish power due to different factors, or it may be stolen from us. When power is severely under threat in these ways, power-loss takes place; if too much power-loss is experienced, the scaffolding which supports the house of the soul begins to fall, resulting in soul-loss.

The following factors concern imbalances of Spirit, affecting our soul:

Lack of self-respect.
Neglect of spiritual duties.
Addictive behaviour.
Neglect of soul-food.
Loss, theft or relinquishing of soul-gifts.

223

As the soul begins to fragment, we experience a growing lack of self-respect and may indulge in addictive behaviour to make good the power-loss we are experiencing; these are symptoms, not causes of soul-loss. Soul-loss is ultimately caused by disconnection with power and Spirit, the chief cause of which is neglect of our spiritual duties and failure to nourish our soul; further to this, we may lose or relinquish soul-parts or they may be stolen.

Power-loss and Retrieval

Power-loss is universally experienced to some degree. The minor power-loss which results from lack of food or sleep is easily made good in normal circumstances, but prolonged starvation leads to malnutrition and swift death just as severe sleep-deprivation has been used as a means of torture, to obtain information and gain power over prisoners. Confrontations, examinations, gruelling sequences of events, illness, family circumstances, manipulative relationships can all cause power-loss. Without our innate vitality, without connection to the power of the cosmic web which is always flowing, we become disempowered, depressed and dispirited.

To some degree, we all co-operate in our own power-loss. Instead of noticing the signs and being alert to the potentialities of each moment, we have all taken wrong decisions which have led to power-loss. Unfortunately, our society encourages us to 'give away power' nearly every day; we are programmed not to resist giving up our rights, our boundaries, our integrity and spiritual authenticity in a variety of ways. When we fall into recurrent cycles of unfortunate situations, we need power-retrieval. Solutions to power-loss often involve returning to the sources of our power and re-acknowledging them; removing ourselves from situations and people who cause power-loss to occur, finding and listening to our guardian animal and allies (see Practice 72).

In cases of serious power-loss, whether through debilitating illness, prolonged erosion of self-esteem or any other cause, the shamanic solution is to restore power by retrieving the client's guardian animal. This is done by the shaman going on a journey, with the client lying beside him. Following his allies' advice, the shaman usually searches the Underworld – the place of power – to find the lost guardian animal. When the animal is found, the shaman brings it back and blows the animal into the client's body – through the fontanelles at the top of the head, or through one of the many shamanic doorways to the worlds which exist in the human body, such as the heart, navel or palm.

Following a power-retrieval of this kind, the client's vitality returns, and she is able to take up the reins of daily life with more confidence. This method should be practically learned from a shamanic teacher as there are a number of subtle aspects to be considered. Those who receive power-retrieval may find that the changes and improved confidence that it brings may be delightful to loved ones or sometimes distressful to those who have enjoyed dining out on the power they have formerly stolen. Such manipulative power-drainers suddenly discover that their supply is cut off.

In our society, those with good power-alignment are perceived as powerful and effective in their lives. Acknowledging our power does not entail throwing it about or manipulating others as a result of it. It means keeping clear boundaries, having clarity of purpose and being responsible in our community. Manipulators of power live by appropriating someone else's power: this causes them mental paranoia and massive personality distortion, while leaving the victim powerless and unable to act. Power-theft can occur to both individuals and countries who suffer from manipulative governments and repressive regimes; solutions may involve exile or revolution.

Soul-loss and Retrieval

When we become isolated, separate and unconnected, we are likely to lose power and become susceptible to illness. If disempowerment becomes overwhelming, some people suffer soul-loss and may eventually give up the will to live. It is becoming increasingly difficult to find anyone who is truly at home in their soul; everywhere we encounter women who feel unworthy to even breathe, men who undervalue their contribution to their families, children crushed by cruel abuse. The soul needs lots of help and encouragement to keep going. I call this work 'midwifing the soul', whereby we can help restore self-worth and encourage each other when times are difficult. Each person is an individual with a living soul and deserves to be treated as such, but our society relegates disadvantaged individuals and groups to a

225

kind of limbo, labelling them as 'losers', excluding them from the community. Whatever our circumstances, self-worth and a sense of the indwelling soul are important factors for living.

Permit yourself to encourage and show love to those undergoing trials!

World shamanism supports the notion of a soul of multiple parts which is why soul-loss, or more strictly soul-fragmentation, can occur. It can be brought about by a variety of causes: illness, accident, surgery, being in an abusive relationship, bereavement, redundancy, rape, incest, burglary and violent assault are but a few.

We each suffer soul-part straying on a regular basis. For example, when we are angry: 'I was beside myself with rage'; or disoriented: 'I just feel lost/spaced out'. Most of these losses are not serious and the stray soul-part soon wings home when we are able to co-ordinate ourselves. We have already spoken about soul-straying and the ways in which it can be remedied (see Chapter 5). But serious soul-loss is another matter: it can range in intensity from having a minor accident in which a soul-part is ejected through the shock of impact, right through to having a major accident which leaves the subject in a coma. Death is the ultimate soul-loss, since all life-power leaves the body.

With minor soul-fragmentation, people can still function to some degree, but with serious soul-fragmentation people have great difficulty looking after themselves: a car with one faulty light can still drive relatively safely at night, but a car with virtually no lights working is a positive hazard to its occupants as a well as to others.

One of the problematic aspects of soul-loss is that when human beings lose a vital part of themselves they resort to other substitutes to 'fill the gap'. This is often the underlying cause of addictions. Soul-loss compounds emotional and physical diseases and is often at the heart of many long-term problems that have been submitted to various therapies which have been unable to bring anything more than slight alleviation. The reason for this failure becomes obvious if we understand the concept of soul-loss, since it is impossible to heal something which is not present! Many beneficial therapeutic treatments are wasted as the subject doesn't have the appropriate soul-part to be healed. Most serious soul-loss is seldom curable by therapeutic means, since these nearly always access only the psychological levels and leave the spiritual cause untouched. The concept of soul-loss clearly defines feelings and intuitions about ourselves which we've been hitherto unable to grasp in a concrete way; it is a great relief to be able to put a name to our trouble. Soul-retrieval restores the vital energy or 'will to live' without which therapeutic healing is useless.

Soul-theft usually occurs unconsciously when the client has been in a dependent or abusive relationship. It is *very rarely* consciously malicious. Examples of situations where soul-theft might occur include: when relationships break down and one partner announces 'I'll never let her/him go!'; when a child's vitality or spontaneity is sapped by a dominating adult; at death, when the dying one has unwittingly become dependent upon the survivor and still clings on. Such cases require the shaman to 'steal', cajole or entice the soul-part/s back. We have all, at some time, perpetrated subtle forms of manipulation on those with whom we live. Sandra Ingerman, in her remarkable book, *Soul Retrieval*,[6] urges us to have compassion for the soul-thief, since he is probably a victim of soul-theft himself.

A soul-retrieval is effected by the shaman making an initial diagnostic journey to check the story-lines of the client's soul-loss. Her allies will indicate whether help is appropriate, which soul-parts are missing, where they may be located and whatever special instructions are important for her to know before attempting the soul-retrieval. With the client lying beside her, the shaman then journeys forth into the three worlds to seek the soul-parts, as instructed, always following her allies' advice. The soul-part or parts may be difficult to locate, there may be dangers to avoid, especially if it involves malicious soul-theft, some parts may not wish to return or indeed understand that they belong elsewhere. Through negotiation and the exact instructions of her allies, the shaman will bring home the soul-part and blow it into the client's body, as in a power-retrieval.

The shaman relates her journey and any messages or information that she has received at this point: these are often validated immediately by the client who recognizes their truth or resonance. This work cannot be learned from a book; it involves hands-on tuition and a great deal of shamanic experience. Soul-loss invariably entails the need for extraction of spiritual intrusions that have colonized the vacuum left by soul-fragmentation. (See Resources, p.263, for teachers and shamanic practitioners.)

When a significant or key soul-part is returned and assimilated, the subject often finds that other minor soul-parts come home naturally, since the whole being is fortified and enriched by this return; it also makes future soul-loss less likely. Soul-loss is unlikely to recur, although future situations may arise when soul-retrieval is required again.

Soul-restoration often brings the return of honesty and awareness, of a sense of self-responsibility. Abusive relationships and addictive patterns must now be treated in a radical way: this is the time for addicts to seek formal therapy and for women suffering domestic violence to seek professional assistance, for example. A distaste for old habits and addictive patterns may be experienced. Soul-restoration enables us to be the person we really are, and that will mean *change*. Soul-integration sometimes takes a few weeks, but its strongest validation is when other people begin to notice how much improved we are.

Collective soul-loss occurs during war, famine, disaster, defeat, foreign occupation, disease or loss of a national figure. A group-soul and identity arises when any group gathers – a family, tribe, association or nation. If the self-esteem or integrity of that group is injured then group soul-loss can occur. The world community must always remember to treat such peoples and countries as sensitively as we would treat someone who had been bereaved, enabling the group-soul to mend and reintegrate. Such countries need not only physical resources but experienced soul-workers.

Abuse and manipulation have existed since time began; it is only now that we are recognizing the signs of power and soul-loss. The resultant over-sensitivity to abuse among us has led to a paranoiac recognition of it everywhere. Even some forms of therapy set up to deal with abuse have themselves become forms of abuse, creating 'recovered-memory' syndrome where images and events triggered by therapy have been interpreted as true personal memories rather than memories of the group or collective remembrance. We have to exercise great discrimination in interpreting our own dreams and journeys, remembering that impressions revealed by symbol and metaphor do not denote physical reality events: that our imagery and experience are often radically different from another's. To interpret another's experiences according to our own personal beliefs or symbol system is to be a manipulator of power. The excerpting of subtle reality from our society has resulted in a very literal mentality, which relates everything to a narrow set of correlatives.

We live in a society that is showing grossly archetypal symptoms of soul-fragmentation: disregard for life, neglect of the old, lack of communion with nature and other species of life, forgetfulness of spiritual sources, disregard of subtle reality and neglect of cause and effect. The stories and songs are being forgotten and the wholeness of community is disappearing in many places. But all is not lost: many people are now emerging as midwives of the soul, willing and able to co-operate with their spiritual helpers to lead the soul back to its home.

Note on Shamanizing for Others

Most of the practices in this book have been written for the support of those who are learning how to make and sustain shamanic journeying by themselves. From time to time, people may ask you to help them. Walking the worlds takes on a whole different perspective when people actively ask for your shamanic help. This is advanced and specialist work which cannot be adequately covered by any book. The following notes are offered as guidelines in such cases; *they are not instructions qualifying the walker between the worlds to set up in professional shamanic practice.* You cannot qualify as a shaman with certificates or educational endorsements. This is a vocational call. Your allies are your primary teachers, but they will be the first to suggest when you should seek the help of an experienced shamanic teacher.

Rules of thumb in shamanizing for others:

1. Have you been asked by someone to shamanize for them? If you haven't, don't.
2. Always journey first to your spirits to ask if work is possible and necessary, and to receive instructions if appropriate.
3. Follow these instructions carefully, or refuse the work.
4. Prepare to provide reasonable follow-up or support to your work.

5. If you don't know what you are doing and the consequences of any action, do not work for others.

6. Ensure that you and your space are purified before work and properly cleansed afterwards. Physically clean your room and prepare yourself by fasting from food and distracting influences for a short period before helping anyone. After helping a client, cleanse your room and any tools you have used (rattle, drum) with incense. Wash your hands in salt water.

7. Do not work for severely unstable people, people who have difficulty in distinguishing realities, or children; even if you are professionally qualified in one of the caring skills and suitably insured, this won't cover shamanic work.

8. Lastly and most importantly, it is not your duty or responsibility to work for everyone and everything. Do not be manipulated into working for others at their insistence when all your instincts are screaming, 'No!' Be responsible for your own path in life, aided and guided by your spirits.

Let compassion and humility be the basis of all your dealings with others. Just as none of us can heal ourselves, neither do shamans heal people – that happens by co-operation with the spirits.

When You Need Shamanic Help Yourself

With the help of your allies and spirits, you can attend to many of life's problems. However, do not be so self-sufficient that you do not seek help from a shamanic practitioner if necessary. This year, I have sought shamanic help twice for difficulties that lay beyond my power. I did not have the perspective on the problems, nor could I affect healing without the help of a sister practitioner. That help now makes sense to me, whereas, at the time, I was too disoriented to understand or perceive it. If you are getting little help or sense from your journeying, if you are unable to journey or are beginning to go round and round in circles, then you need some help for yourself.

✋ Practice 70: Checking Power-alignment

The following questions can help you establish your current power-alignment and help you recognize danger signs. Some questions concern not only your own power but the ways in which you may be manipulating that of others.

1. Do you continually push yourself beyond your physical limits into exhaustion or collapse? Are you making similar unreasonable demands upon others?
2. Do you maintain your personal standards of behaviour in the face of opposition or peer pressure? Do you infringe or cause the infringement of others' standards?
3. Do you maintain your basic rights, needs and desires or abrogate them at the behest or need of others? Are you trespassing on the rights of others?
4. When did you last check on the motivations which fuel your life, work, relationships, hobbies and so on? Are these power-connections between you and your gifts still operative?
5. How does your personal presentation and home environment reflect your present power alignment? Does outer disorder reflect inner disorientation?
6. Are you allowing others to encroach on your environment, time or resources without conscious permission? How are you encroaching upon that of others?
7. Do you have recurrent illnesses? Of what nature? How do they relate to your power? What kinds of things do they prevent you doing?

☝ Practice 71: Checking Soul-alignment

The following questions will help you check your current soul-alignment and recognize danger signs. Again, some questions are two-edged in that they impinge upon your own behaviour as well as on that of others.

1. Are you always depreciating yourself as a worthless person? Are you always running down others to boost your power?
2. When did you last commune with your spiritual source? What opportunities do you provide to let Spirit come into your life?
3. What patterns of habitual or addictive behaviour do you discern in your life? What soul-void do these patterns fill? How does your habitual behaviour affect others?
4. Do you ensure adequate soul-nurture for yourself? Are you preventing others from finding theirs?

5. Have you allowed others to encroach upon your emotional, psychic or spiritual space without conscious permission? Are you encroaching upon that of others?

6. Do you have difficulty in being physically present and attentive? What are you unconsciously looking for?

7. Do you feel emotionally muffled, apathetic or indifferent to life? Around which activities are these symptoms most apparent? How do they reflect your lack of soul-alignment?

♨ *Practice 72:* Power Dance

When you are low in vitality and needing to restore your power, get out your rattle or drum and get on your feet. Call your allies to help show how power may be restored to you and begin sourcing while you dance. As you source, follow your allies. If you dance into deeper journeying, your body will naturally want to stop: sit or lie down and continue journeying.

♨ *Practice 73:* Finding a Soul-friend

It is difficult to be a solitary walker between the worlds. Otherworldly allies may be great companions, but we are human beings who need soul-friends with whom to share our journey. A soul-friend (Irish *anam-chara*) is one who is wise and practical: one who can encourage us when depressed and who can bring us down to earth when we lose touch with everyday life. Your soul-friend can also act as a reality or bullshit detector to ensure that you are well aligned and not getting too full of yourself. If you have no such friend living near you, journey to your Middleworld allies and ask them to help you send out a general call for a soul-friend.

♨ *Practice 74:* Finding Healing Spirits

Healing is able to enter the house of our soul when we unlock the door and invite it in: this means acknowledging that we need healing. One of the greatest healing powers of the world is the Grail which regenerates whatever it touches or whoever finds it; it can only be activated by the right questions: What is imbalanced? How may healing come? Consider what is imbalanced, unaligned, in need of healing in your life, whether physical, psychic, mental or spiritual. The quest and question must be worthwhile in order for healing to come. Journey to whichever of your allies or teachers seems best suited to give you healing. You may receive important advice to put you on the healing path, or you may receive healing during the journey.

It may be that we also have a particular healing teacher or spirit, especially if our vocation is rooted in healing or soul-work. Journey to your centre in the Middleworld and ask your guardian animal to bring you to your healing teacher, following its guidance. When you have found the healing teacher, ask 'What healing ways do you have to teach?' Your initiation into healing methods will proceed via this teacher or through one of your already designated allies.

♨ *Practice 75*: Prayer-songs to the Spirits

When your help is inappropriate or unwanted, the safest way of dealing with seemingly insuperable problems in others is to pray to the spirits, which is a method of healing that all people can employ. Prayer is a wider prospect than our religious upbringing has taught us. Prayer and intercession, pleading with the spirits for help and healing, is a common pursuit of shamans, usually in partnership with healing techniques.

Prayer doesn't involve set, written invocations, although traditional prayers are indeed strong pathways of help. The uttering aloud of our need is something we often avoid; we often allow our need to turn within and bore into our being where it becomes a path of sickness. Prayer is thus a primary pathway of health which can not only prevent illness but can also heal. Prayer is a shamanic ladder of help, extending to the otherworlds.

In the case of people who do not wish for or who have not requested your help, *it is essential that your prayer should be of general benefit and not invoke a particular outcome.* The spirits of these people know what is best for them, so merely ask that appropriate help may be brought to the object of your prayer. It is not our place to manipulate people's lives. Although the temptation to wish for the speedy demise of a tyrant or the victory of one side in a conflict may be great, we do better if we ask the spirits to bring a given situation to a harmonious conclusion for the good of the whole cosmic web: then we cannot be responsible for warping any of its filaments.

With your rattle or other instrument, begin to source, calling upon your allies for an all-purpose healing song. For specific issues or problems, source your allies for particular people or needs.

☙ *Practice 76*: Singing the Soul Back Home

We all have some hidden grief, shock or fear which causes parts of our soul to hide away. Some soul-fragmentation is not serious: the soul-part/s linger near and can be coaxed back. Others are buried deeper and, like crabs under rocks, refuse to emerge. This method is intended for lone use in cases of minor soul-loss only. If you suffer from major trauma which has disrupted your life so that you are unable to work or relate to others, you need the help of a qualified soul-seeker (see Resources, p.263). People frequently ask why they cannot do their own soul-retrieval. I suppose that it would be theoretically possible for us to perform surgery upon our selves, but I don't imagine that many of us would practically wish to do so! If you have a major soul-part missing, the last thing that you want to do is to send out more soul-parts after it. (See 'When You Need Shamanic Help Yourself', p.230.)

We can assist soul-restoration by a sincere desire to be whole again, by an intelligent and loving acceptance of the retrieved soul-parts and by a willingness to retain them. It is important to realize that newly returned soul-parts often evoke difficult memories, feelings and physical sensations for a while, and that integration can sometimes take a little while or may require radical life changes. You can prepare yourself to receive any missing or stray soul-parts by actively courting them in the following ways:

1. With rattle or other instrument, start sourcing for a soul-song that will encourage your soul-part to come home. Spend ten minutes each day singing for and to any of your missing soul-parts and think of them returning and how this will complete your life – this will send out a clear signal that you want them back.
2. Journey to your allies and teachers and ask them to show you if you have any missing soul-parts, where they might be and how to coax them home.
3. Formally break any ties between yourself and anyone who has been responsible

for curtailing your freedom; remove yourself from situations where soul-loss is a daily danger.

4. Before sleeping, ask your guardian animal to fetch any stray soul-parts and bring them home to you as you sleep.

Spontaneous soul-retrieval is also common. An insightful book, an ecstatic uplifting of spirit, a minor accident sometimes clears a pathway between ourselves and the missing part and we are able to receive soul back with grace and love.

👋 Practice 77: Power and Soul Blessings

Preventive measures may help us avoid power and spirit imbalances. Psychic hygiene is a major precaution of indigenous peoples, a method which we can also practise. Since our society has dualistic notions of good and evil, tending to see everything in terms of black and white, we should regard these methods as soul-strengthening or empowering blessings rather than 'spiritual protections', in order to stress their positive rather than their negative benefits. Vigilance and attentiveness to our responsibilities will help.

We all encounter situations in which we feel especially vulnerable to power- or soul-loss: some of these cannot be easily avoided in our daily lives, but we can be better prepared to meet them. Journey to your allies and ask for a blessing or song that will prevent specific kinds of power- or soul-loss to which you are liable. You may also be given talismanic objects, shamanic symbols or rituals as remembrances of inner strengths. The following is a breastplate blessing which calls on the spirits of the directions, to be sung when feeling especially vulnerable:

Power of eagle have I – power of air,
Power of serpent have I – power of fire,
Power of dolphin have I – power of water,
Power of mole have I – power of earth,
Power of lineage have I – power of the ancestors,
Power of spirits have I – power of the gods.
Power of truth have I – power of the inmost soul.

Seven powers about me to veil and support me,
On my journey without fear go I.

Sensible attitudes about power and soul-strengthening procedures can be maintained by good intention and trust in our spirits. The paranoia of 'being under psychic attack' reflects an ungrounded attitude to walking the worlds, pointing to sloppy spiritual hygiene, a failure to close doors or observe boundaries, and hazy intentions. Go back and look at Chapter 5.

2: THE CIRCLE OF LIFE

We can have all the knowledge in the universe, and it comes down to one thing: practice. It comes down to going home and step-by-step implementing what we know.

– Clarissa Pinkola Estés *Women Who Run with Wolves*

All our shamanic practice is a means of creating the capacity for reconnection. If walking between the worlds does not reconnect us with our universe then our shamanic knowledge becomes a defunct currency which we can never spend.

The shamanic vocation is the reverse of what is commonly understood as 'the spiritual quest', whereby a person acquires spiritual merit in order to attain personal salvation or enlightenment. The Japanese actor and director, Yosio Oida, speaks of this:

'When people see that society is difficult and stupid, they think that they should distance themselves and withdraw from the world ... People meditate, it makes them feel good and they think they have seen the light. But what is this light, if it is not connected to action in this world? The most important thing in meditation is to find what the right action for you is.'[7]

Finding out what action is appropriate for ourselves is often a long and puzzling business. We may be a little like the French poet, Rimbaud, who ruefully wrote that, 'for a long time I prided myself I would possess every possible country'. At the beginning of our work we enthusiastically want to be and do everything, to thoroughly immerse ourselves and become experts in all knowledge. But shamanic knowledge is not a commodity to be acquired in this way: it can only flow into the channels which we provide. These may be less broad or broader than we supposed, and we may have to discover what specialist areas are best for us.

When we first encounter shamanism we may want to share this wonder with the rest of the world. Our history is riddled with spiritual chauvinism and the missionizing colonialism that results from convert fervour: shamanism needs no proselytizers. It has existed since the dawn of time and it will go on being needed because it works.

Many people currently seek to understand their vocation through various forms of self-growth. This is an important corrective to numerous forms of spiritual self-neglect and soul malnutrition which are the heritage of our post-religious society. But self-growth must include self-clarification, self-nurture and self-assimilation, as well as self-forgetting, if self-respect is to result. If self-growth excludes these factors, then it fosters an introverted self-focus which separates itself from the universe. True self-respect is not selfishness, but our duty to the soul and its soul-shrine: it includes caring for our body, mind, soul and spirit, enabling us to relate to those who give us love and support, as well as those who challenge and stretch us.

Shamanism is not a one-way street, with all the knowledge flowing from the three worlds into ours, nor are all our efforts solely directed towards the cosmic web. Service to the universe balances self-respect. If we dedicate ourselves to the restoration of power and Spirit in our world, then power and Spirit will come into it via the bridge of our dedication.

In the final analysis, all we have to do is be available for this purpose, not to worry about how and where and with whom we shall eventually implement our work. By virtue of our humanity and our living soul, we are connected with the cosmic web: Spirit and power will support us and bring us into connection in ways which we may not dream. The stoic philosopher Epictetus wrote:

'Whoso seeth the sun and the moon and the stars and rejoiceth in the earth and the sea, he is no more solitary than he is helpless.'[8]

And yet, 'rejoicing in the Earth' has become one of the hardest tasks of our age. As we look upon the beauty that has been soiled by our species and realize the unkindness of our kind, a complexity of emotions overwhelms us. Self-blame, shame, guilt erupt within us, to be followed by a desire to rectify, heal and restore. But some things can never be restored: species have gone, habitats have been destroyed, ways of life and people have vanished. This is not a new story.

Only a short while ago science generally regarded concern about erosion of world resources and the effects of acid rain and global warming as the paranoia of a minority of ill-informed people: now it takes them seriously. Many indigenous peoples have always known that how we live affects the world; others have had to learn it through hard experience. The effects of deforestation and intensive agriculture are not new problems: the people of early Mesopotamian civilizations turned their land into desert, the Neolithic peoples of Europe hacked and burned down forests in order to obtain farming land. Not all ancient peoples were wise.

The same problems lie at our doorstep today. Poor stop-gap solutions are still promoted by self-serving governments determined to see out their term of office without rocking the boat. A few international gatherings like the Rio Earth Summit of 1991 or the Kyoto Summit on Restricting Industrial Emissions in 2000 attempt to create awareness of the need for long-term measures which have to be followed up by successive world governments, but such decisions are regarded as optional and are rarely implemented because governments are seldom run by politicians of spiritual vision.

Spiritual leaders and mediators have always had the important task of reminding the people when balance is being lost and how to return to alignment. Fundamental greed and short-sightedness underlie our current ecological predicament. Whatever we sow today, our children will reap tomorrow. The West has the most complex economic and political frameworks, but it has lost many of the doorways which connect it with the cosmic web. It is time for our people to turn to the rediscovery of inner space, not as conquerors but as humble explorers and soul-seekers. Regarding the universe with intention is the work not only of a shaman, but of all people. Maintaining spiritual pathways is critical in a time when many assume that the material world is the only reality. When that is the case, then only a narrow environmental response is possible, one which expresses empathy, but rarely compassion and never love.

The self doesn't end at the skin, it continues. Arne Naess, the Norwegian philosopher who coined the term 'deep ecology', wrote of the dichotomy experienced by people who associated ecological responsibility with sacrifice and who found moral exhortations to altruism alienating:

'… all of that would flow naturally and easily if the self were widened and deepened so that the protection of nature was felt and perceived as protection of our very selves.'[9]

The true collegiality between ourselves and nature must be experienced as self-identification. The seemingly finite and discrete nature of human existence is an illusion. We need a house of representatives drawn from the many species of life to remind us of our true place in the scheme of life (see Practice 79). Instead of excerpting ourselves as a species from the universe, we need to find our sense of self within the continuum of the cosmic web.

'Healing the earth' has become a supreme cliché in the last few years, all too often meaning, 'I want to save/perpetuate myself/my species.' Our planet has survived many millions of years of changes. As the latest species, humankind has perhaps made significant changes, but we are indeed very much late-comers with no notion of how many more species may supersede ours. Earth will undoubtedly survive, and with it the stubbornly entrenched DNA of the life spiral, but *human* life may be just one of many further evolutionary developements. To live shamanically and creatively means to accept this at a deep level, if only as a spur to humility. Only by our dedicated reconnection with the power and Spirit of our earth can we offer adequate restitution and open channels of healing.

And what of those people who do not share our vision? Convert fervour often urges us to share our spiritual realization with everyone we meet, in an attempt to influence what we see as unproductive lives. This is not only tiresome to others but highly manipulative. For some people 'the lost places are in this world and belong to the people in it and are all that they have to call home', and there is nothing we can do about this.[10] We cannot give our revelation to another being unless they desire to share it, and even then we may only be the way-showers, not the revealers of mysteries.

Only by our equanimity and living example, by our impartial compassion to all that is can we become guardians of the ways who help restore the harmony and balance of our universal relationship. To invite beauty back to our world, we must allow the world-soul to return home in its own way. We can be resourceful in the ways in which we do this, as long as we are not manipulative. If we create pathways of connection ourselves, these will in turn provide channels for beauty to return.

We bring the fruits of our shamanic perceptions to the world by focusing our hearts upon the return of the deep song, by remembering the subtle pathways, the resonance of memory and the oracy of living our lives from that centre. The effect of each person's individual commitment resounds throughout the universe, creating resonant pathways, sounding reverberant notes, restoring the web of connection.

☝ Practice 78: Restoring the Balance

Our thoughts and intentions have power. Without this intention prayer becomes a form of meaningless words; prayer with heart becomes full of *kavannah* or 'intentioned transformation'. We can work with this kind of intentioned transformation on behalf of the universe if we do it in accordance with Spirit. We live complex lives which provide plenty of opportunities to forget. Thoughtless acts can destroy the world; intentioned ones help build it up. We can adjust the balance by living at a slower pace, and resisting the urge to speed up all the time, allowing the spaciousness of the otherworlds to be realized here. Those who live in the fast lane have little leisure to perceive clearly; those who live in the slow lane can both perceive and acknowledge.

To become aware of what ails us, we must ask the Grail question. This is given variously in different texts as, 'Why is the land waste?' or 'Why are things like this?' or 'Whom does the Grail serve?' If we seek with humility, bearing in mind past mistakes and areas of neglect, we find an answer through one of the otherworldly doors which accesses the cosmic web. We can rebalance the energy of the cosmic web and make restitution by asking our own Grail question. Journey to your Middleworld allies and ask 'What can I restore to the cosmic web?'

✋ Practice 79: The House of Representatives

Only by entering into identification with other life-forms can we keep true awareness of the variety and wonder of life. You have already experienced the close identification between yourself and your spiritual helpers. If your animal is a blackbird, you will feel warmly about any blackbirds you encounter in physical reality. We can also stretch our skin to encompass other beings. Commune with a species near where you live – animal, plant, tree, stone – and be with it in nature. Our dedication to the earth begins locally, but feeds into a larger understanding of planetary wholeness. Returning home, source one representative of this species and ask its permission to briefly enter into its shape and consciousness, to fuse your two souls together. Experience what it is to be this species. Ask what gift it mediates to the cosmic web. What do you learn from this practice? Thank your subject and return, recording your experience. Repeat this practice to include a variety of different species. These will form your 'house of representatives', your own council of different species, whose voices will be attuned to yours in your daily life, as well as being advisers in local or ecological issues.

Permit yourself to learn from all life-forms!

✋ Practice 80: Legacy of Wisdom

Our kinship with all forms of life is very close:

> 'Every cell in our body is descended in an unbroken chain four billion years old, through fish that learned to walk the land, reptiles whose scales turned to fur and became mammals, evolving through to the present.[11]

The loss of one species in our physical reality is not just a loss of an animal or plant. It is a tearing of the cosmic web, the destruction of a viable bridge to a form of wisdom which keeps our world harmonious. When species

241

revert to subtle reality through extinction they and the wisdom that they bear are still contactable, but only by shamans and seers.

In the next few decades you will die. Before that, many plant and animal species may become totally extinct. You at least have the opportunity to have relatives and descendants: they will be lost forever. Create a record of the wisdom, wonder and beauty of any threatened species which you have experienced, based on your own sourcing, which you can leave to your family as an important record after your death. Joanna Macy reminds us that time does not run on the cosmic web, that the eternal now gives us opportunities for change:

> 'The dimension of simultaneity, where we stand shoulder to shoulder with our ancestors and descendants, is appealing to me, it gives context and momentum to work for social change.'[12]

This practice can be repeated for as many species as you wish, in order to create pathways of connection between your everyday world and that of subtle reality.

1. Choose your species.
2. Meet and experience it in physical reality, if possible.
3. Accompanied by one ally, journey in the Middleworld to meet one representative of that species.
4. Offer it what help and love you can give, ask it what wisdom it represents and whether it is willing to share that with you. If wisdom is offered, remember that you share responsibility of that wisdom, that you are obliged to manifest this in your life and must pass it on.
5. Return from sourcing and record your experience.
6. Create a record – verbal, pictorial, written – by which this wisdom can be transferred to another generation of your family or community.

This method often results in the creation of a story, poem or artwork which encapsulates the wisdom in ways that can be easily remembered and shared. Manifest your work by actively supporting campaigns to safeguard the survival and habitat of species under threat.

3. A SACRED TRUST
'Tis the gift to be simple, 'Tis the gift to be free.
'Tis the gift to come down where we ought to be.
And when we find ourselves in the place just right,
'Twill be in the valley of love and delight.'

– Shaker song

The practice of shamanism has its own ethics based primarily on the fact that the shaman is accountable, not only to the spirits, but to his clients. Their pain is his pain, their loss is his loss. This is the sacred trust of shamanism: to be part and empowered by the universe, to be vulnerable to Spirit. Ego-centric gratification is not part of this work.

A shamanic vocation is not relegated to far-off times and peoples, but is strongly relevant now when it is needed so much. My belief is that everywhere the spirits are waking up many people and asking their co-operation. Whether we follow their call, fully dedicating our life to them and the service of the universe, or whether we decide to live shamanically in our own sphere of influence, we are nevertheless helping to reconnect the world.

Commitment and Initiation

Before we commit ourselves to the shamanic path, let us understand that the spirits *request* our co-operation: we do not have to respond. It is also as well to take stock and realize now that this path has to be walked daily, not just in our spare time or when we feel like it. This is an all-embracing way, into which all that we know and are must be synthesized. All shamanic experience has the effect of showing us the next part of our path and how to arrive there. Sometimes we will glimpse the totality of our destiny, while at other times we will see only the next stepping stone. As we make spiritual progress, we instinctively seek out the next avenue that will lead us on.

Shamanic initiation happens by a variety of means. Initiation is often narrowly taken to mean 'entry, by means of a ritual, into an arcane or closed group'. Shamanic initiation is the complete reverse of this: instead of acquiring status or knowledge which excludes us from others, shamans enter more fully into the widest possible framework of the universe in a way that includes everyone and everything.

Traditional shamanism maintains that a candidate is called primarily by the spirits. Initiation may happen spontaneously at the hands of the spirits or it may also involve training with a practising shaman; in either instance, the candidate must find acceptance in her community.

We do not undergo the complex and painful ordeals which shamans might undergo in traditional societies, such as being coated with red ants, fasting for long periods or suffering total exclusion from daylight. Instead, life itself brings many trials and ordeals which initiate us into new areas. Each challenge and dilemma we encounter is teaching us something new; our shamanic response is to increase our trust in our spirits and to learn from these experiences. For those with a shamanic vocation, Western civilization is a very complex environment in which to live. Our ordeals will include a radical change in our life-style and the effects that this will have on our friends and family; it may involve putting up with ridicule from our peers: less glamorous than a dramatic vision-quest in splendid isolation, less dangerous than being pushed off a cliff with our feet attached to vine-ropes, perhaps, but no less effective in strengthening or weakening resolve.

Shamanic ordeals come in many guises and may be regarded as tests which stretch our gifts into alignment. They do not come to those who are not ready and willing. It is very important that we realize the cause and effect of our shamanic alignment. When we work with a concept, we become its mediator. Our exploration of inner space creates new pathways and keeps old ones open for others to walk. All that we have experienced validates the tradition we uphold. Consent comes from deep abiding. If you never step further down the road of the shamanic vocation, however, you will always have the companionship of spirits and allies whom you have met through journeying. They are your teachers. For your final authority to follow a shamanic vocation, though, something more is required.

Our Own Native Tradition

This book has been purposely written in a non-cultural light, so that anyone may work with it wherever they live on earth. It has been primarily addressed to Westernized, urban readers. As you reach its end, you are invited to consider the cultural tradition in which you were raised and in which you live. Your shamanic work must have its home on the earth. Work undertaken within a primal tradition has a direction and strength that is not found if you work outside your cultural traditions. You may live in a land that seems divorced or distanced from its primal tradition, but that tradition is still available through shamanic work.

In the search for shamanic authenticity, many people have been drawn to other cultural traditions, notably the North American Indian ones. Often in a deeply respectful way, they have tried to become part of that tradition and to learn what they can from it. This has caused a great furore in many circles. Many indigenous people find such adoptions insulting, akin to cultural colonization, whereas others have been more reservedly supportive.

The West has been quick to take colour and originality from indigenous and tribal cultures worldwide. A walk down any high street confirms this as we see for sale colourful ethnic clothing from all countries, bath-unguents and soaps made from exotic perfumes of far-off lands, jewellery from South-East Asia and even bubble-gum with fabulous Amazonian rainforest properties! Each product seems to throw into relief our Western inability to find our own original colour or native power. I sometimes wonder, rather frivolously, whether Amazonian tribes and others buy 'Dull, Grey, Boring Urban Splash Lotion' or wear '9–5 Office Deodorant'! The concept of all races of humanity coming together as 'the rainbow people' is persuasive, but there are many national bequests (see p.152) to address before we may rejoice in this reality. We must give honour and apology where it is due. The best way of proceeding is to discover *our own* ancestral tradition, the ways of our living land.

A word of warning: ethnicity can become a potent weapon for national possessiveness, a cloak for colonial invasion or an instrument of re-empowerment and cultural self-esteem, among other things. It can be manipulated to prove and disprove many things. Shamanism, like everything else, can also slide into its own brand of political wrangling: 'My tradition is more venerable/more authentic than thine.'

The appropriateness of your adopting a spiritual tradition that is not your own can only be judged by yourself. The level of commitment and respect you can provide must always include a very hard look at the way you actually live in the everyday world. If your life-style supports your core spiritual practice, then no-one on earth can gainsay your adoption. If, however, your spiritual practice merely apes the cultural tradition of another land, you may find it less workable.

If we seek to take fire from another's hearth without due respect for the hearth-keeper or the fire, then we are thieves. It behoves us as Westerners to approach indigenous traditions with respect, as humble students, to say, 'I cannot hear my ancestors, I have mislaid the teachings but I want to belong once again to the human family: please teach me, please share your fire with me that I may be warm again.' However, once we have borrowed fire, we then have the daily task of finding the fuel to keep the fire burning. That fuel must be harvested locally, from our own land and culture, from the traditions, strengths and gifts of our own time and place.

The problem of naturalized citizens crops up here. As a Briton with Irish ancestry, I find no conflict in working with the ancestral and Celtic traditions of my land and culture. However, if I moved to Australia or America, this might be quite different. I hear from many who are attempting to reconcile their ancestral traditions with their national citizenship: should they follow their native heritage or borrow from the spiritual traditions of the land they now inhabit? Before you can expect someone from a tribal culture to share their ancestral teachings with you, it is only fair for them to ask you to represent your own tribe first.

In the West, we do not, have not lived in a tribal culture for many hundreds or thousands of years; a few of us still live from the land in an agricultural way, but most of us are fully urbanized. This dislocation and fragmentation from tribal life is often at the basis of our shamanic search, for the filaments of our own indigenous tradition has been either broken or interwoven with other elements. Most seekers find their spiritual family among practitioners like themselves who can meet up at weekends, on courses, through internet chat-lines, but shamanic practice can become a very ghetto-like existence without a social framework where it can be used.

Without the support of tribe or the motivation of a group or community need, the search for our own ancestral teachings can be long and hard, as

I can testify. Such a search leads through diverse territories where we can pick up the rags and tatters of past belief and practice.

These may serve as a makeshift cloak while we search, but eventually we must leave off searching and live now, today. This problem is not just a contemporary one: knowledge has been mislaid before and has been rediscovered. Many myths, including that of the Egyptian goddess, Isis, confirm this. Isis searches for the scattered remains of her husband Osiris' body, which has been cut up by his brother, Set. Having reconstituted all she can, Isis finds that his phallus is missing. Undeterred, she creates a phallus and lies one last time with her husband to engender the child Horus. Plutarch writes of this event in more universal terms:

> 'Set ... tears to pieces and scatters to the winds the sacred writings, which the Goddess collects and puts together and gives into the keeping of those that are initiated.'[13]

No knowledge is ever totally lost, only mislaid or forgotten. It can be found in the otherworlds. If we journey there with trust and an open heart, we will receive teaching from ancestral wisdom holders. If we walk our own lands, we will find the knowledge in the sacred places as well as in the book of nature. Sacred traditions cannot die, as long as there is one living person who needs them.

Speaking of the difficulties of native peoples who have mislaid their traditions in the recent centuries of colonization, Dr Pamela Colorado, an Oneida Indian, suggests ways of recovery:

> 'As native people, we learn to train our minds from the time we are children, to be centred where we are, grounded in reality, and see all the signs that are around us ... In addition, you have to have the ability to project yourself out, "to see what it's not possible to see". I'm just learning this myself, but I know that it is an ability that our people have known for thousands of years and still practice ... the wayfinding mindset, the ability to project ourselves out, is the knowledge that is necessary if we are to create a healthy relationship with the earth.'[14]

This 'projecting ourselves out' is achieved both by journeying and by using our shamanic sight, by being sensitive on a daily and pragmatic level to the spirits who alert us to the hidden signs scattered about us. The ancient wisdom which our own ancestors treasured is still contactable and recoverable, if we seek it out with true hearts. The spirits of our ancestors, the spirits of our land are still here: they will re-inspire us if we call upon them to help us now. This does not involve reactivating atavistic and inappropriate ways or stimulating ethnic hatred and conflict: rather we mend the broken filaments of our cultural tradition with love and honour. I believe that, wherever we live upon the earth, however mixed and confused our ancestral and spiritual heritage, we will find spirits and allies who will reconnect us with the inner light which illuminates the cosmic web.

Spiritual Illumination

Mystics of many cultures have spoken of the human experience of spiritual illumination as of a person travelling through the darkest night which is lit by sudden flashes of lightning: most people have only the memory or retinal image of their spiritual landscape or direction, and some of the lightning flashes are few and far between. This experience of bright illumination in the midst of doubt and uncertainty has been called the 'sun at midnight'. Many shamans report this brightness: Aua, an Iglulik man interviewed by Knud Rasmussen, relates his solitary shamanic initiation:

> 'In the midst of such a fit of mysterious and overwhelming delight I became a shaman ... I could see and hear in a totally different way. I had gained by *quamanEq*, my enlightenment, the shaman-light of brain and body, and this in such a manner that it was not only I who could see through the darkness of life, but the same bright light also shone out from me, imperceptible to human beings, but visible to all the spirits of earth and sky and sea, and those now came to me and became my helping spirits.'[15]

This experience of inner light is common to all initiates of mystical traditions. It cannot be learned as a technique: it comes only when we are truly aligned with the cosmic web. This inner glow spreads its light a long way:

you will know it is beginning to kindle in you when people begin to be drawn to you for help, as ships to a beacon. The further and more extensively you explore the web and gain allies in the three worlds, the more help will become available to you.

The validation of your walking between the worlds is not conferred by ceremony or academic credentials, but by the combination of your practise and experience. It is then that the sun shines at midnight: and it shines out on all parts of the web so that your living and journeying illuminates both physical and subtle reality. Even though your mind has no conscious knowledge, even though you may feel fraudulant or untrained, yet the wisdom that is seeded inside of you comes alive and sends forth its own beacon of light to which others will be drawn. This way you will meet your spiritual kin, like-minded others who are walking between the worlds in their own way; this way, those drawn to the healing skill of your gifts will be able to find you.

The ecstasy that comes from an experience of shamanic non-duality is profoundly moving and humbling. Our identification with the universe is briefly transcendent and manifests in us simultaneously. The sense of omniscience that accompanies some journeying is truly beyond words, though these might begin to approach some part of that understanding:

> 'It's like looking out into time or space or infinity. It's like seeing everything at once. It's like getting out of a train that's going along and seeing it go along, and being independent and part of it at the same time. It's like looking at everywhere at once from everywhere at once.'[16]

Such experiences are often so overwhelming that individuals are profoundly changed by them; isolated people move nearer to the caring social hub of the world, while those who have lived unthinkingly hedonistic lives are jolted into new awareness that needs a desert solitariness.

Thankfulness is part of our reciprocity to the universe. It is the ultimate honesty in shamanism. If we fail to express thankfulness, we are in danger of claiming the power of the universe as our own. In the non-duality of ecstatic communion with the otherworlds, love of the universe brings thankfulness welling to the surface of our heart.

The way we live our lives – in lightness and equanimity – is our gift to the universe: that it may not be scarred by our passing and so that we may continue to be a part of its ongoing chorus of the cosmic web, whose music becomes our song, whose rhythm becomes our dancing.

Most indigenous peoples regard sacred wisdom as holy regalia, to be guarded and tended, to be passed into the keeping of responsible people. In walking between the worlds, we will inevitably learn much wisdom. That wisdom is not our possession, though we may have its guardianship for a short while. If, in our thankful hearts, we acknowledge that it is only lent to us, we will avoid the problem of spiritual rigidity which always indicates that wisdom has become a millstone round our necks and not a liberation of spirit.

We give thanks for what we have learned by sharing it with others. The way we transmit shamanic teaching matters: it is not 'just a technique'. Unless we are able to put ourselves in the shoes of any living being in the universe, we cannot give or receive such transmission. By our oracy are we measured.

Shamanism is both profoundly mystical and very ordinary. It isn't necessary to live in isolation or dress in feathers to practise it. We can practise the shamanic awareness of a walker between the worlds wherever we live. Our connection with the universe and our trust in the spirits will bring its own humility but not a series of certificates – there is no final attainment, no great goal beyond the continuing balance of the inner and outer worlds. Shamanism is the stillness in the dancing: it is the soul within the song.

☙ Practice 81: The Primal Tradition

We owe it to our ancestors and descendants to find out about our culture and traditions and bring them into our lives, to become a bridge for living knowledge.

What primal tradition existed in your land before the coming of orthodox religion? What remains? Which spiritual presences informed it? Which tradition holders are still accessible?

Read all that you can and make a few well-chosen, motivated journeys to research your native tradition: ask your allies and ancestral teacher to show you what is relevant to your own time. Find folk-songs and stories which contain encoded teachings. Research seasonal customs.

When you have done this and with the aid of other like-minded walkers between the worlds, you may perhaps begin to address your national or tribal bequest – the unfinished business of your people or country. Ask your ancestral teacher and allies, as well as the deep ancestors, to help you in a collective effort. Find the deep themes and stories that bring wisdom to the descendants today.

☀ *Practice 82:* Council of Allies

Our spiritual lineage and native tradition already have many teachers and practitioners: some may be alive and practising, others may have joined the deep ancestors or become traditional teachers in subtle reality. We can meet with these in a council of allies. Go to your journey-centre and call your ancestral and spiritual teachers to meet you there, and any other allies or animals who wish to help you. At this gathering, ask to be put in contact with friends and helpers in both physical and subtle reality who will enable your deeper integration into your own tradition: you may be introduced to new allies and teachers, you may be instructed on where or with whom you may find tuition and companionship in physical reality.

☀ *Practice 83:* The Gift

Without thankfulness we give no gift. The deep gift is sometimes hard to find within us because we have unconsciously become separate. When situations reach stalemate or breaking point, move energy by giving: the act of giving empowers the giver, and reweaves the broken filaments of the cosmic web.

When love fails in your heart and you are unable to reciprocate or make an appropriate response, it is time to call upon your companions for help. Sing, call, dance, implore: 'I am losing love, it is slipping from my fingers, the dance is losing momentum, the song is losing its joy – come and fill my heart!' Travel from the heart of the loss to the web of connectedness and make a journey for help, empowerment or inspiration.

Don't let your soul grow dull and unreflective because you have blocked off all spiritual pathways to your heart. This is sometimes hard advice to take, particularly when any action you might take seems worthless to you. However despairing or disconnected you feel, get up and make an offering of thanks in whatever way seems good to you. Even if you feel nothing, act 'as if' this were beneficial. Lift your heart and mind and spirit, attuning them with the universe. Step outside your barricades for a moment and experience the timelessness of the gift of life. Ask your allies for a ritual of thanks for your gift, then perform it wholeheartedly.

✋ Practice 84: Spirit Offerings

We always conclude all shamanic practice with an act of thanks to the spirits who have assisted us; without this important practice, it is easy to become inflated with self-importance. Thanking the spirits is an essential courtesy which helps us retain humility. Praying is one method of thanking. We do not need to take the stance or language of any faith in order to pray: we just speak from the heart of need, joy or thankfulness, addressing Spirit or the spirits of the universe.

Make a journey or series of journeys to enquire which offerings your spirits appreciate best. Maybe your bear may like to be offered a plate of berries, while your eagle prefers a smoke mixture of aromatic herbs.

If you receive the help of a shaman, it is good to take gifts for her spirits: these need not be of great monetary value. My spirits were given some very appropriate gifts by Helen, one of my clients; she journeyed to ask what would be suitable and brought them an empty ant's egg, a bell and a skein of golden thread, all of which were delightfully appreciated by my spirits. The bell is still used to call my spirits when I work for others.

Journey to your spirits and ask what you can do for them, to show gratitude for all that they do for you. Create a short personal ceremony of thanks in their honour, using the information they have given you and relating this to the nature of their help.

✋ *Practice 85*: Shamanic Dedication

When you have read, practised and assimilated the practices in this book, you may well feel that you wish to formally commit yourself in some deeper way to the shamanic path. The only initiators in this business are your spirits. Before making any journey, keep a shamanic vigil of dedication, for 'to learn to take the universe seriously there is no quicker way than to watch'.[17]

Spend at least one night awake in a secluded place, pondering the dedication that you are contemplating. If you choose a remote spot, ensure that your soul-friend knows where and when you are making your vigil, and is ready to offer support. Such a vigil clarifies your intentions remarkably. The next day, journey and call together your allies and teachers and ask them how you may dedicate yourself to this work, if you still feel it's your path.

May You Journey Well

This book has been made up of many separate chapters and practices which you have come to work with over a period of time. Your own experience will begin to find pathways between the scattered realizations you have gained here. New realizations will merge with old ones, abysses of separated understanding will be bridged. Treat your notebook as a friend to remind you of experiences and practices. Don't get so hung up on the minutiae of information recorded in it, or too proud of your own testimony that you can't accept anyone else's experience. Keep in touch with your soul-friend, compare notes and be adaptable.

Finally, I would like to share a few realizations that I have made over the years. They constitute my personal golden rules about shamanism, but you may substitute your own for these, or find others. They are not terminally binding on anyone. Consider them as the eight legs of the spider by which you walk the cosmic web.

1. Everything is connected: we are not alone.
2. Help is always near: trust the power, help and advice offered by your allies.
3. Keep your quest or purpose simple.

4. Only attempt healing with those who believe benefit may come.
5. Respect all ways of being.
6. Behave ethically and teach by example.
7. Be thankful and you will become part of the gift.
8. Be detached from results.

Permit yourself to connect with what you have learned from your practice!

May you journey well!

Notes

FOREWORD
1. Ripinsky-Naxon 1993
2. Matthews, C. & J. 1994
3. Matthews, C. 1990

CHAPTER 1
1. Ginzberg 1990
2. Hoppal 1989
3. Skafte 1988
4. Siikala 1987
5. Colorado 1991
6. Hoppal 1989
7. Amado 1993, Vega 2000, Gallembo 1998
8. Suzuki & Knutdson 1992
9. ibid

CHAPTER 2
1. Kaplan 1978
2. Ereira 1990
3. Harner 1980
4. Ripinsky-Naxon 1993
5. Ahlbäck & Bergman 1991
6. Ingerman 1991
7. Ahlbäck & Bergman 1991
8. Funk & Wagnall 1972
9. Ahlbäck & Bergman 1991
10. Rodenburg 1992
11. Backman & Hultkrantz 1984
12. Siikala 1987
13. Ripinsky-Naxon 1993
14. Ereira 1990

CHAPTER 3
1. Suzuki & Knutdson 1992

2. Ripinsky-Naxon 1993
3. Sams 1998, Gray 1994, Matthews, J 1994, Matthews, J. 2002
4. Tompkins & Bird 1991
5. Tompkins & Bird 1992
6. ibid
7. Macy 1993
8. Matthews, C. 2001
9. Guss 1985
10. Lovelock 1988
11. Nachman nd
12. Gould 1993
13. Lindsay 1970
14. Huxley 1956
15. Gould 1993
16. Ywahoo 1987
17. Ripinsky-Naxon 1993

CHAPTER 4
1. Matthews, C. 2002

CHAPTER 5
1. Stewart 1992
2. Matthews, C. Mabon 2002
3. McAll 1984
4. Matthews, C. Ancestral Bequest, 2001
5. McAll
6. Matthews, C. Ancestral Bequest, 2001
7. Matthews, C. Rosicrucian Vault, 2002
8. Rinpoche 1992, Matthews, C. 1991
9. Fix 1979

CHAPTER 6
1. Matthews, C. 1998 Blessing Seed

2. Matthews, C. 2000
3. Matthews, C. & J. 1994
4. Ahlbäck & Bergman 1991
5. Ripinsky-Naxon 1993
6. Matthews, C. 1992
7. Kalweit 1992
8. Wombwell 1991
9. Daniélou 1985
10. Rodenburg
11. Brennan 1988
12. Chögyam 1988

CHAPTER 7
1. Matthews, C. & J. 1994
2. Sheldrake 1988
3. Guss 1985
4. Chatwin 1987
5. Ripinsky-Naxon 1993
6. Fortune 1972

CHAPTER 8
1. Harner 1992
2. Villoldo & Krippner 1986
3. Hultzkrantz 1992
4. Matthews, C. & J. 1994
5. Harner 1992
6. Ingerman 1991
7. Oida 1991
8. Powys 1974
9. Naess 1989
10. Mayne 1966
11. Seed & Macy 1988
12. ibid
13. Matthews, C. Sophia 2000
14. Colorado 1991
15. Rasmussen 1929
16. Mayne 1966
17. Hardy 1974

Glossary of Terms used in this Book

Certain words used in this book have specific definitions not usually given in standard dictionaries.

Alignment The poise and balance which the shaman has with the universe.

Allies Spirit helpers who are allied or associated with us.

Ancestors Not only our near, personal relatives who are no longer living but also the deep ancestors of our common bloodlines and genetic memories who maintain guardianship of skills and wisdom traditions and who teach us.

Ancestral bequest The accumulation of unfinished business which each human being inherits from ancestors of her blood lineage.

Bat-signals The almost imperceptible messages which are picked up by your subtle senses.

Blood lineage Our physical genetic relationship with certain ancestral teachers provides our blood lineage helpers.

Centre In this book, your journey-centre or starting place for Middleworld journeying.

Client Any person or being who seeks the aid of a shaman.

Core shamanism Term coined by Michael Harner to denote applicable, contemporary, non-cultural usage of shamanic methods by non-traditional peoples.

Cosmic web The universal alignment of all that is; the interconnecting network of spirit pathways and power resonances of all beings now alive, dead or only existent in subtle reality.

Deep ancestors The regenerate ancestors who have entered the ancestral realms and are available as teachers.

Genius The male *genius loci* or spirit of place.

Gift A particular alignment, comprising our unique skills and abilities, enabling us to serve the universe.

Helper Subtle reality allies or companions who accompany, guide and help us in the otherworlds.

Inner space This is totality of the otherworlds. The use of 'inner' here does not imply any psychological quality but refers to the subtle realities to which we travel in shamanic journey.

Journey A shamanic journey or spirit-flight during which soul-parts of a shaman leave the body to travel into the otherworlds.

Juno The female *genius loci* or spirit of place.

256

Oracy This is our oral capacity to hear, remember and relate. Oracy is not dependent upon the written word but gives primacy to the oral traditions that maintain our connections with ancient wisdom. It has no authority except itself.

Oral pool The pool of our memory, constituted by whatever can be remembered or recalled without the aid of book or tape.

Otherworlds All levels of subtle reality in the shamanic cosmos.

Permission In the context of this book, an encouragement and self-allowance to permit liberation of the soul and its faculties.

Personal myth The belief system or 'story' by which we live.

Physical reality The material substance of the ordinary world we inhabit, perceived through our physical senses.

Power The energy, vitality and alignment which are our true gifts.

Reality The unified vision of the universe, comprising of two sides or natures: physical reality and subtle reality – both of which are real.

Realm of the ancestors Sometimes also called 'the land of the dead', this region is usually located as a separate enclave within the Underworld, although it is possible to find it in any of the three worlds.

Re-sourcing Rediscovering the source of our universal belonging to the cosmic web after shock or distress.

Shaman From the Siberian Tungus language, the term 'shaman' is the universally accepted term for a person who is able to journey between this world and the others in order to find healing, information, knowledge or help. Many different lands have their own word for this function.

Shamanize To practise as a shaman, through sourcing, journeying, healing.

Shamanism The practice of reconnecting, healing or restoring the unity of the cosmic web by means of walking between the worlds.

Sourcing The state of consciousness that a shaman enters when beginning to access the otherworlds, prior to and maintained during journeying.

Soul-flight The shamanic journey which is made by the shaman's soul-part/s travelling into the otherworlds.

Soul-friend A close friend with whom you can share your inner and mystical life, who can give counsel, advice or support; derived from the Irish *anam-chara*.

Soul-loss and Retrieval When soul-parts are accidentally ejected from the being through trauma, illness or assault, then soul-loss is said to have taken place; this requires the services of a shaman to retrieve the soul-parts by taking a shamanic journey to find them and restore them to the client; see next entry also.

Soul-parts Worldwide shamanic traditions recognize that the soul has many composite parts, some of which we use to operate in skilful ways, some of which may be accidentally ejected through shock, necessitating soul-retrieval.

Spirit Spirit is the indwelling sacredness, pervading all things, animate and inanimate. Spirit is without form, yet can manifest in any form.

Spirits The many refractions of Spirit which animate all that is and give each thing or being its distinctive nature.

Spiritual lineage helpers Any teachers in subtle reality with whom we are in soul-resonance, providing help and teaching; a spiritual lineage teacher is not a spirit guide or guru who directs aspects of your life.

Subtle reality The unseen reality which exists and interpenetrates physical reality, appreciable by our subtle senses.

Teacher A shamanic teacher can be a living person, an ancestor, an animal, tree, plant, stone or a totality of these. Certain situations and events are also teachers.

Traditional shamanism The practice of shamanism among indigenous peoples who maintain ancient traditions today, as opposed to core shamanism.

Tradition This is always used here in its original sense of a core of wisdom and lore to which new information is continually being added, so that ancient lore is thus refreshed and made applicable to contemporary life.

Walker between the worlds In the context of this book, one who can move skilfully between the worlds of physical and subtle reality and back again, with the ability to learn, co-operate and commune, but not necessarily a fully-operative shaman; the term was coined by myself and John Matthews in *The Western Way* (1985) to denote one who travels shamanically between the worlds.

Bibliography

Some books listed below are academically technical. I have indicated the more accessible titles with an asterisk. Some of those without an asterisk are currently out of print.

Abram, David, *The Spell of the Sensuous*, New York, Pantheon Books, 1992

*Achterberg, Jeanne, *Woman as Healer*, London, Rider, 1990

– 'The Wounded Healer', in *The Shaman's Path*, ed. G. Doore, Boston, Shamabhala, 1988

Ahlbäck, Tore & Bergman, Jan, eds., *The Saami Shaman Drum*, Abö, Finland, The Donner Institute for Research in Religious and Cultural History, 1991

*Amado, J., *The War of the Spirits*, New York, Bantam Books, 1993

*Arrien, Angeles, *The Four Fold Way*, San Francisco, Harper Collins, 1993

Backman, Louise & Hultkrantz, Ake, *Studies in Lapp Shamanism*, Stockholm, Almqvist & Wikseil International, 1984

*Bausch, William J., *Storytelling: Imagination and Faith Mystic*, Twenty-Three Publications, 1984

*Berry, Thomas, *The Dream of the Earth*, San Francisco, Sierra Club, 1988

*Carr-Gomm, Philip & Worthington, Bill, *The Druid Animal Oracle*, Simon & Schuster, 1994

*Chatwin, Bruce, *The Songlines*, Jonathan Cape, 1987

*Chögyam, Ngakpa, *Journey into Vastness*, Shaftesbury, Element, 1988

Colorado, Dr Pamela, in interview with Jane Carroll, 'A Meeting Between Brothers', *Beshara Magazine*, no. 13, Summer 1991.

Daniélou, Alain, *The Gods of India: Hindu Polytheism*, New York, Inner Traditions Inc., 1985

* – *Shiva and Dionysus*, New York, Inner Traditions Inc., 1984

*De Chardin, Teilhard, *Hymn to the Universe*, Collins, 1975

*Deren, Maya, *The Voodoo Gods*, St Albans, Paladin, 1975

*Ereira, Alan, *The Heart of the World*, Jonathan Cape, 1990

*Estés, Clarissa Pinkola, *Women Who Run With Wolves*, New York, Ballantine Books, 1992

*Fix, Wm. R., *Star Maps*, London, Octopus Books, 1979

*Galembo, Phyllis, *Voudou: Visions and Voices of Haiti*, Berkeley, CA., Ten Speed Press, 1998

*Gallagher, Winifred, *The Power of Place*, New York, Poseidon Press, 1993

*Ginzberg, Carlo, *Ecstasies: Deciphering the Witches' Sabbath*, London, Hutchinson Radius, 1990

*Goodman, Felicitas, *Where the Spirits*

Ride the Wind, Bloomington, Indiana
University Press, 1990

*Gould, Stephen Jay, ed., *The Book of
Life*, Ebury, 1993

*Guss, David M., *The Language of the
Birds*, San Francisco, North Point
Press, 1985

*Hardy, Thomas, *The Mayor of
Casterbridge*, London, Macmillan,
1974

Harner, Michael, *Twenty Thousand Years
of Experiementation with Mid-body
Healing: the Discoveries of the Shamans*
(taped talk), Foundation for Shamanic
Studies, 1992

* – *The Way of the Shaman*, New York,
Harper & Row, 1980

*Heize, Ruth-Inge, *Shamans of the 20th
Century*, New York, Irvington
Publishers Inc., 1991

Hoppal, Mihály & Pentikainen, Juha,
eds., *Uralic Mythology & Folklore*,
Budapest, Ethnographic Institute of
the Ungarian Acadmey of Sciences,
1989

Hoppal, Mihály & Von Sadovsky, Otto,
eds., *Shamanism, Past and Present* (two
vols), Fullerton, Istor Books, 1989

*Hultkrantz, Ake, *Shamanic Healing and
Ritual Drama: Health & Medicine in
Native North American Religious
Traditions*, New York, Crossroad,
1992

*Hutton, Ronald, *The Shamans of
Siberia*, Glastonbury, Isle of Avalon
Press, 1993

Huxley, Aldous, *Heaven and Hell*,
London, Flamingo, 1994

*Ingerman, Sandra, *Medicine for the
Earth: How to Transform Personal and
Environmental Toxins*, New York,
Three Rivers Press, 2000

* – *Soul Retrieval: Mending the
Fragmented Self*, San Francisco, Harper

Collins, 1991

*Jonas, Gerald, *Dancing: The Power of
Dance Around the World*, BBC Books,
1993

*Kalweit, Holger, *Shamans, Healers and
Medicine Men*, Boston, Shamabhala,
1992

Kaplan, Aryeh, *Meditation and the Bible*,
New York, Samuel Weiser, 1978

*Kelly, Karen, *I See With Different Eyes*,
privately printed, Cambridge, 1993

*Launert, Edmund, *Edible and Medicinal
Plants of Britain and Northern Europe*,
Country Life Books, 1981

Lindsay, Jack, *The Origins of Alchemy in
Graeco-Roman Egypt*, Frederick
Muller, 1970

*Lonsdale, Steven, *Animals and the
Origins of Dance*, Thames & Hudson,
1981

*Lovelock, James, *The Ages of Gaia: A
Biography of Our Living Earth*, Oxford,
Oxford University Press, 1988

McAll, Dr Kenneth, *Healing the Family
Tree*, Sheldon Press, 1984

*Macy, Joanna, *World as Lover, World as
Self*, Rider, 1993

*Matthews, Caitlín, *The Ancestral Bequest
in Irish Spirit*, ed. Patricia Monaghan,
Dublin, Wolfhound Press, 2001

* – *The Blessing Seed*, Bristol, Barefoot
Books, 1998

* – *The Celtic Book of the Dead* (ill.
Danuta Meyer), London,
Connections Book Publishing, 2000

* – *Celtic Devotional*, New Alresford,
Godsfield Press, 1996

* – *The Celtic Spirit*, New York, Harper
San Francisco, 1999

* – *Celtic Wisdom Sticks*, London,
Connections Book Publishing, 2001

* – *King Arthur and the Goddess of the
Land*, Rochester VT., Inner
Traditions, 2002

* – *Mabon and the Guardians of Celtic Britain*, Rochester VT., Inner Traditions, 2002

* – 'The Rosicrucian Vault as Vessel of Transformation', in *At the Table of the Grail*, ed. John Matthews, London, Watkins Publishing, 2002

* – *Sophia, Goddess of Wisdom*, Wheaton IL., Quest Books, 2000

*Matthews, Caitlín & John, *The Arthurian Tarot* (ill. Miranda Gray), London, Thorsons, 1990

* – *The Encyclopedia of Celtic Myth and Legend*, London, Rider, 2003

* – *The Encyclopedia of Celtic Wisdom: A Celtic Shaman's Sourcebook*, London, Rider, 2001

* – *The Western Way*, Arkana, 1994

*Matthews, John, *The Celtic Shaman*, Shaftesbury, Element, 1992

– *The Celtic Shaman's Pack* (ill. Chesca Potter), Shaftesbury, Element, 1994

* – *Celtic Totem Animals*, Glastonbury, Gothic Image, 2002

* – *Taliesin: The Last Celtic Shaman*, Rochester VT., Inner Traditions, 2002

Mayne, William, *Earthfasts*, Hamish Hamilton, 1966.

*Meier, C.A., *Healing Dream and Ritual: Ancient Incubation, Modern Psychotherapy*, Einsiedeln, Switzerland, Daimon Verlag, 1989

Merkur, Daniel, *Powers Which We Do Not Know: The Gods and Spirits of the Inuit*, Moscow, Idaho, University of Idaho Press, 1991

*Nachman, Rabbi, *Outpouring of the Soul*, Jerusalem, Breslov Research Institute

*Naess, Arne, *Ecology, Community and Lifestyle*, Cambridge, Cambridge University Press, 1989

*Newham, Paul, *The Singing Cure: An Introduction to Voice Movement Therapy*, Rider, 1993

Oida, Yoshi, 'Means of Expression' *Beshara Magazine*, no. 13, Summer 1991

*Palmer, Martin, *Genesis or Nemesis: Belief, Meaning & Ecology*, Dryad Press Ltd., 1988

*Powys, John Cowper, *A Philosophy of Solitude*, Village Press, 1974

Rasmussen, Knud, *The Intellectual Culture of the Iglulik Eskimos*, Copenhagen, Glydendalske Boghandel, 1929

*Rinpoche, Sogyal, *The Tibetan Book of Living and Dying*, Rider, 1992

*Ripinsky-Naxon, Michael, *The Nature of Shamanism*, Albany, State University of New York Press, 1993

*Rodenburg, Patsy, *The Right to Speak: Working with the Voice*, Methuen, 1992

Seed, John, editorial of *Creation Spirituality Magazine*, vol IX, 2, March 1993

*Seed, John, Macy, Joanna, et. al., *Thinking Like a Mountain: Towards a Council of All Beings*, New Society Publishers, 1988

Sheldrake, Rupert, *The Presence of the Past*, Collins, 1988

Siikala, Anna-Leena, *The Rite Technique of the Siberian Shaman*, Helsinki, Academia Scientiarum Fennica, 1987

*Silko, Leslie, *Marmion Ceremony*, New York, Penguin, 1977

Skafte, R., 'Following the Woman-Faced Deer', *Shaman's Drum*, Summer 1988

*Stewart, R.J. *Earth Light*, Shaftsbury, Element, 1992

*– *Power Within the Land*, Shaftsbury, Element, 1992

*Suzuki, David & Knutdson, Peter,

Wisdom of the Elders: Honouring Sacred Native Visions of Nature, New York, Bantam Books, 1992

*Tompkins, Peter & Bird, Christopher, *The Secret Life of Plants*, Arakana, 1991

*Tompkins, Peter & Bird, Christopher, *Secrets of the Soil*, Arkana, 1992

The Upanishads, trans. Juan Mascaró, Harmondsworth, Penguin, 1965

*Vega, Marta Moreno, *The Altar of My Soul: The Living Traditions of Santeria*, New York, One World, 2000

*Villoldo, A. & S. Krippner, *Healing States*, New York, Simon & Schuster, 1986

*Wombwell, Felicity, *The Goddess Changes*, Mandala, 1991

*Ywahoo, Dhyani, *Voices of Our Ancestors*, Boston, Shambhala, 1987

Resources

Shamanic Training Organizations

No book is a substitute for learning from a good shamanic teacher, not can it give you the wider experience of sharing knowledge with a training group. Readers are strongly recommended to find and study with a reputable teacher or organization. Most of the organizations below can supply information about a shamanic practitioner in your region. When writing to the groups or individuals below, please enclose a stamped addressed envelope (SAE), if writing within the same country, or an envelope and two international reply paid coupons (available at post offices), if writing from overseas.

FOUNDATION FOR INSPIRATIONAL & ORACULAR STUDIES (FÍOS)
BCM Hallowquest, London WC1N 3XX
www.hallowquest.org.uk
FÍOS was founded by Caitlín and John Matthews and Felicity Wombwell to encourage respect for and the practice of the sacred and oracular arts. FÍOS has a programme of courses on Celtic and non-cultural shamanism leading to practitioner training, as well as open courses on other topics. It hosts annual masterclasses, given by leading artists and exponents of the sacred arts from all over the world. Membership of FÍOS brings discounts on courses and a quarterly newsletter. For details of subscriptions and courses, please enclose a medium-sized SAE (within Britain) or an addressed envelope with 4 international reply paid coupons or 5 US dollar bills (outside Britain).

FOUNDATION FOR SHAMANIC STUDIES (FSS)
PO Box 1939, Mill Valley, CA 94942, USA
Telephone 415 380 8282; *Fax* 415 380 8416
email info@shamanicstudies.com • www.shamanism.org
This is a worldwide organization with centres currently in USA, Europe, Australia and New Zealand. Membership brings a semi-annual magazine and calendar listings of FSS courses. FSS faculty teach basic and advanced courses in core (non-cultural) shamanism. Completion of a basic course is obligatory before attempting advanced work. The teaching quality is generally high, as are the course fees. The foundation also has available a register of shamanic counsellors who offer healing and soul-retrieval in USA.

SCANDINAVIAN CENTRE FOR SHAMANIC STUDIES
Artillerivej 63, Lejl 140, DK-2300, Copenhagen, Denmark
Telephone +45 32 54 28 08
www.shamanism.dk
SCSS has a rich programme of events throughout Europe. Jonathan Horwitz
teaches non-cultural, core shamanism all over Europe, while Annette Host teaches
Scandinavian shamanic methods as well as shamanic applications to women's lives.
For details of their courses in Britain, write to Kathy Fried, 29 Chambers Lane,
Willesden, London NW10 2RJ (*Telephone* 0208 459 3028).

Shamanic Help & Practioner Support

CIRCLE OF THE SACRED EARTH
21 Aaron St., Melrose, MA 02176, USA
Telephone 781 665 6032
www.circleofthesacredearth.org
Founded in 1990 by Roy Bauer, D.D. C.S.C. as a church of animism, this supports and
provides a community forum for shamanic practitioners, while encouraging the practice
of direct spiritual revelation among its members. Membership is open to those who
believe in Spirit and the sacred nature of the earth. It also appoints ministers who are
active in most states of the USA and in other countries across the world to provide
ceremonies and shamanic healing and counselling.

CORE SHAMANIC PRACTITIONERS CIRCLE
29 Hill Cottages, Rosedale,
North Yorkshire YO18 8RG
Telephone 01751 417795
email crowan@madasafish.com. • www. practitionerscircle.org.uk
This support group is a professional organization for practitioners working within
core (non-cultural) shamanism. Membership is available for those practitioners who
are well trained and willing to abide by a code of ethics. The Circle provides a list of
teachers and practitioners in the UK.

Drumming Circles

A list of UK drumming circles which help support shamanic students is available in
Sacred Hoop Magazine (for contact details see opposite).

THE HORSE'S MOUTH
Caitlín's shamanic practice in Oxford, England, the Horse's Mouth, occasionally has
vacancies on Shamanic Spirit Consultation courses, whereby clients learn to journey
and find answers, help and healing from their own spirits. Caitlín also sees those who
need shamanic help, vocational or ancestral soul-midwifery and healing. She keeps a
list of fellow shamanic practitioners in different parts of Britain. For details send a
medium-sized SAE (within UK) to Caitlín at BCM Hallowquest, London WC1N 3XX.

SHAMANIC CIRCLES
www.shamaniccircles.org
This is a non-profit organization dedicated to fostering global shamanic community.
It helps individuals, supports shamanic drumming circles and builds community
bridges to create a living network of practitioners worldwide.

Sourcing Tapes & CDs
Sound-source tapes and CDs are available from:
Caitlín Matthews, BCM Hallowquest, London WC1N 3XX
www.hallowquest.org.uk
Please send SAE (within UK) or 4 international reply paid coupons (available at post
offices) to enquire for details, prices and full tape list or see website.

FOUNDATION FOR SHAMANIC STUDIES
PO Box 1939, Mill Valley, CA 94942, USA
Telephone 415 380 8282; *Fax* 415 380 8416
www.shamanism.org

TORBEN WENDELIN
Trommevaerkstedet, Lyngevej 176, 3450 Alleroed, Denmark
Telephone +45 48 17 77 72
email torben.wendeline@vip.cybercity.dk

Shamanic Equipment & Other Services
CREEPING TOAD
email creepingtoad@binternernet.com • www.creepingtoad.org.uk
Gordon MacLellan is a shaman working with environmental art, education and
performance in tne community. His company, Creeping Toad, explores the relationships
between people, places and wildlife; it also helps reconnect people to the world
around them, both as individuals and as communites. Creeping Toad works with
such groups to create celebrations of the places where people live, work and play.

SACRED HOOP MAGAZINE
Heddfan, Drefach Felindre, Newcastle Emlyn, Carmarthenshire, Wales SA44 5UH
Telephone 01834 860 320; *Fax* 0870 054 8946
email nick@sacredhoop.org
Nick Wood supplies journeying CDs and tapes. Contact him for details of courses
and artefacts available.

SCAVENGERS
Telephone 07760 148316
email scavenger_products@hotmail.com
Based in Dorset, these are makers of fine shamanic tools and occult artefacts. All their
products are handmade by them in the UK. Most materials are scavenged from the land

as gifts from Spirit. Ritual is a very important part in their crafting process. They are inspired by and work closely with otherworldly helpers. All items produced are very different and individual, with their own innate energies and talents. Contact Jane Gubb to commission artefacts and to receive personal healing work or news of workshops.

TORBEN WENDELIN
Trommevaerkstedet, Lyngevej 176, 3450 Alleroed, Denmark
Telephone +45 48 17 77 72
email torben.wendeline@vip.cybercity.dk • www.trommevaerkstedet.dk
Superb drum maker of tuneable bodhráns and other drums with goat, sheep, calf, reindeer or Remo Fiberskyn2 heads. His website is in both Danish and English.

Magazines

HALLOWQUEST NEWSLETTER
BCM Hallowquest, London WC1N 3XX
www.hallowquest.org.uk
This quarterly newsletter brings information on forthcoming events, courses, books by Caitlín and John Matthews. Subscription at time of writing: £8 (within Europe) US$25/£16 (outside Europe). Available online.

SACRED HOOP MAGAZINE
Heddfan, Drefach Felindre, Newcastle Emlyn, Carmarthenshire, Wales SA44 5UH
Telephone 01834 860 320; *Fax* 0870 054 8946
email editor@sacredhoop.org • www.sacredhoop.org
This British-based journal is dedicated to the full spectrum of world shamanism and the spiritual teachings of indigenous people. It reflects the integration between old and new ways. It has many feature articles, contact lists for drumming groups and many adverts for shamanic courses and services. Annual subscription at time of writing: £14 (in UK), £19 (outside UK). See website for back issues and features.

SHAMAN'S DRUM
P.O. Box 270, Williams, OR 97544, USA
www.shamansdrum.net
A journal of experiential shamanism and spiritual healing. This quarterly, glossy magazine is devoted to cross-cultural shamanism. It features long, usually academic, articles on contemporary and traditional shamanism; it is highly illustrated and carries many advertisements for shamanic goods and courses.

SPIRIT TALK
www.shamaniccircles.org/spirittalk
This grassroots online newsletter, edited by Karen Kelly, is written by and for practitioners of core shamanism. Recent issues have dealt with areas such as healing, working with the land, shamanism and psychotherapy and more. The emphasis is on personal experience and practical support in developing a shamanic practice.

Index

Acknowledgements

AUTHOR'S ACKNOWLEDGEMENTS

My greatest thanks go to the spirits who have accompanied me on my life journey: they are my teachers. To John Matthews, my husband, for lovingly maintaining the tree of tradition and to our son, Emrys, for all his insights and delights. To Felicity Wombwell, R.J.Stewart and Jane Gubb for the inspiration of their pathways. Special thanks go to Jonathan Horwitz, a shamanic teacher of great skill and wisdom. Thanks to all the Passionate Priestesses for healing laughter and deep soul-nurture. Finally, great thanks to all students and clients who have shared their journeys with me for the purposes of this book: journey extracts are verbatim, but personal details have been changed. Finally, gratitude to all at Eddison-Sadd and Connections for restoring this revised edition to print.

EDDISON•SADD EDITIONS

EDITORIAL DIRECTOR: Ian Jackson
PROJECT EDITOR: Jo Weeks
PROOFREADER: James Ryan
INDEXER: Margaret Cornell
ART DIRECTOR: Elaine Partington
MAC DESIGNER: Malcolm Smythe
ILLUSTRATIONS: Anthea Helliwell
PRODUCTION: Karyn Claridge, Charles James